Exodus

THE JOURNEY TO FREEDOM

CHRISTINE AND BERNARD KEELS

Study Guide by
Loretta Williams, Joe Agne, and J. Ann Craig

EXODUS: THE JOURNEY TO FREEDOM
STUDY GUIDE for EXODUS: THE JOURNEY TO FREEDOM

A publication of the Women's Division
General Board of Global Ministries
The United Methodist Church
475 Riverside Drive
New York, NY 10115

Cover and interior book design by Hal Sadler.

Cover illustration by Melanie Reim.

Printed in the United States of America.

Please address critiques or comments to the Executive Secretary for Spiritual and Theological Development, General Board of Global Ministries, The United Methodist Church, 475 Riverside Drive, Room 1502, New York, NY 10115.

ISBN 1-890569-58-5

Contents

A. Knowledge Pursuit.   B. White Privilege.   C. Being an Anti-Racist
White Person.   D. Racism: How It Operates.   E. From a Monocultural
to a Multicultural World View.   F. African American History Quiz.
G. Should a Color-Blind Society Be the Goal?   H. Answers to African
American History Quiz.   I. Rosa Parks.   J. Answers to Women's Leadership Quiz.
K. Oral History from Virginia Durr.   L. Basic Seder Instructions.
M. Spirituals and Gospel Music.

Preface

Exodus, Race, and Spiritual Growth

Welcome to the Spiritual Growth Study on *Exodus: The Journey to Freedom*. Christine Keels and the Rev. Bernard Keels have provided a deep river of content to draw us through the historical journey of African American Methodists in the United States. For these modern-day successors of the ancient Hebrews whom Moses led out of slavery in Egypt, there is a river between their desert wandering and the promised land; it is the river Jordan, and those traveling to the promised land have to go through it.

Exodus can be read as an ancient history of the Hebrews, showing the power of our God, whom we worship in church each Sunday. This is important. But the United States has its own Exodus story to tell, and we have not crossed over Jordan yet. Many generations have passed since our Civil War, and many have forgotten the story of how freedom was won for an enslaved people in this country. There is no annual commemoration like that of the Jewish Passover. No bread is broken, no wine is spilled, and no story is told about why "this night is different from all other nights" in remembrance of the African American freedom story. There is no solemn celebration to remind the people of the present about the lash and chains suffered by their forebears and about their ancestors' brave resistance and long journey toward freedom.

This more recent freedom saga is complex. The story of Black Americans cannot be told without the story of White Americans. The stories of Native Americans, Spanish descendants, and a multitude of immigrants—the Germans, Irish, Italians, Chinese, Japanese, Koreans, and a host of other transplanted people, some willing, some coerced—are entwined with the story of a nation founded on the genocide of the peoples native to the land and on the slave labor of the Africans.

This brief book does not cover the entire history of Africans in America but focuses on a current need to understand how African American Methodists have dealt with racism in the Methodist family. Several historically Black denominations were formed in reaction to and because of racism. Many Black Methodists stayed in the Methodist Episcopal Church of the North, hoping and struggling for a redeemed church; but their fate in the successor Methodist Church was to be segregated for three decades (1939-1968) into a nationwide "Central Jurisdiction." With the creation of The United Methodist Church in 1968, thanks to the efforts of Blacks and antiracist Whites in both The Methodist Church and the Evangelical United Brethren (EUB) Church—originally an ethnic German denomination—the Central Jurisdiction was disbanded.

Today, many will say that they are tired of talking about race and that we should simply do a Bible study on the Book of Exodus without bringing in all of these "political" agendas. But the story of Exodus is a story of nations and peoples that has a message for the United States and The United Methodist Church—a country and a denomination that still suffer the consequences of centuries of slavery. Exodus is a story of peoples who rose to power and fell from power, of peoples who rose to great faith and descended to idolatry.

Long before any of us reading this study were born, many White forebears faced a spiritual crossroads and, like the pharaohs of ancient Egypt, took the low path leading to the heresy of slavery and the idolatry of skin color. Yet, throughout the ensuing eras, there were some Whites who stood in solidarity with Blacks, claiming their common heritage of being made in the image of God and not in the image of an idolatrous White "race."

The spiritual reality of the church's being the body of Christ calls for such questions as these: What does the body look like? Is it racially defined? Is it gender defined? If it is strictly a spiritual body, with no race or gender, then why are our churches so defined by these social categories? These are spiritual issues with social impact. Our actions loudly proclaim what we believe about being created in the image of God.

Today we step into the ongoing conversation about reuniting the historic Black Methodist denominations—the African Methodist Episcopal (AME) Church, the African Methodist Episcopal Zion (AMEZ) Church, and the Christian Methodist Episcopal (CME) Church—with The United Methodist Church (UMC). The conversation reveals the need for all members of the Methodist family to know more about the histories of the respective denominations in order to understand why our churches are so overwhelmingly segregated, even to this day.

Christine and Bernard Keels point out that, in the Service of Reconciliation at the 2000 General Conference of The United Methodist Church, only elected delegates were seated on the main floor of the hall, while guests and observers were seated in an old-fashioned balcony encircling the hall. While a few key officials of the AME, AMEZ, and CME denominations were on stage, by default all the other guests of those denominations were seated in the balcony. This brought back memories of the days when Black Methodist members were relegated to separate entrances and to the balconies, while Whites sat downstairs and used main entrances.

Black United Methodist elected delegates on the floor were forced to decide what course of action to take when they witnessed their Black sisters and brothers in the balcony—as well as when they realized that, among all the African American constituencies, *they* would not be mentioned. Their centuries of work to counter racism from *within* mainstream Methodism would not be recognized as part of the history leading up to reunion. United Methodism was treated as though it were a wholly White denomination in need of repentance. Ironically, some White delegates hugged Black delegates who kept their heads bowed in prayer while Whites confessed their sins. Few Whites realized that the sins were continuing at that very moment.

When the church proceeds in such ignorance of its past that it repeats the errors of its ancestors, it becomes like those in the parable of the judgment of the nations in Matthew 25:31-46, when those judged say in amazement, "Lord, when did we see you hungry, thirsty, naked, sick, or in prison?" They honestly didn't know. Today, many of us would honestly ask, "Lord when did we discriminate against you because of your race?" The response is clear: "Just as you did it to one of the least of these who are members of my family, you did it to me."

The answer is all around us. It echoes every time members of the dominant culture ask a minority person to remind them if they do something racist. Every time people of color are stopped because someone thinks they don't belong in a neighborhood, or believes they look like "terrorists," or assumes that they are members of the hotel staff rather than guests, the idolatry of racism is repeated.

This book is not a comprehensive history of the historic Black Methodist denominations nor of the Black church within United Methodism. It simply takes its place among the multitude of voices raised against the claim, "We just didn't know." Jesus made it clear: ignorance is not an excuse.

There is so much to do and so many issues to address. Each racial or ethnic group has a history to bring to the story. Many who read this study will be among those who have made the spiritual commitment to a lifetime of resisting the idolatry of racism in all forms. To them, some information will seem old hat. Other people will find virtually all of the information new and sometimes shocking. Most of us, of whatever race, will fall somewhere in between.

As you study this book in a group or by yourself, think of yourself as being among the Hebrew people escaping slavery, wandering through the desert. Remember that your survival depends on the strong supporting the weak and the weak being as strong as they can. Know yourself. Be willing to lead or be willing to follow, but do your best not to be among the grumblers who think God has abandoned them in the desert.

At other points, think of yourself as an Egyptian; but strive to be like the daughter of Pharaoh and her maids, who acted surprised to find a baby in a floating basket and did not report the Hebrew girl who had the audacity to speak to them, volunteering to find a wet nurse.

We can strive to be part of something much larger than our individual efforts. We can look back on the history of United Methodist Women who resisted racism. We can look around for leaders today and know that we have all been called. We can look to the future, when our children and our children's children will have a life of justice, peace, and celebration rather than fear, prejudice, and violence. We are looking for the promised land, where God's will is done on earth. We know that if we do not do God's will, we will continue to wander.

Remember that, just as in the desert the Israelites were never alone, we are never alone. We have the company of the God who led with fire at night and by a cloud of knowing during the day. Remember that the Egyptians had multiple opportunities to repent. Some gave the Hebrews provisions for the journey.

Through it all, we have the company of the dying and rising Christ, who brings the power of love and forgiveness to every moment of life. We also have the company of one another—the very body of Christ alive in the world today. Be prepared to wade in the water of Jordan because there is a promise of new life on the other side.

J. Ann Craig
Executive Secretary for
Spiritual and Theological Development

Note: What's in a title? The title for this spiritual growth study has been a point of discussion. *Exodus* was fine, but should the subtitle be *An African American Methodist Journey? An American Methodist Journey? A Methodist Journey?* The question is, whose journey is it? If we say "African American," it can be understood to be affirming of a people who have been long-suffering on the road to freedom. But does it adequately include the story of White people who used slavery to build this country and who segregated worship, and does it include even those Whites who resisted slavery? If we say "An American Journey," Latin Americans detect a U.S. assumption that subsumes the rest of the Americas. If we say "A Methodist Journey," is it enough? In the end, after much discussion and a review of the original recommendation approved by the elected Women's Division directors, the title is *Exodus: The Journey to Freedom.* Two watershed stories of escape from slavery are woven together. One is thousands of years old, the other is hundreds. Whose story is the story of freedom? Is it yours?

LET MY PEOPLE GO

> *Then the Lord said to Moses, "Go to Pharaoh, and say to him, 'Thus says the Lord, the God of the Hebrews: Let my people go, so that they may worship me. For if you refuse to let them go and still hold them, the hand of the Lord will strike with a deadly pestilence...."'*
>
> *(Exodus 9:1-3a)*

Exodus is the story of an enslaved people brought out of oppression by Moses, the messenger of God. This story came to life anew in the Americas, as African slaves heard of the Hebrew people's liberation from slavery and realized that even the slave master's God was a God of freedom.

John Wesley condemned slavery as "an execrable villainy"[1] and fought long and hard to make it illegal in England. Following Wesley's example, many Methodists in the United States strongly opposed slavery. However, many other U.S. Methodists began to make excuses for slavery. In 1845, the Methodist Episcopal Church (MEC) split into Northern and Southern branches over the issue. But despite the abolitionist stance of the MEC in the North, the racist attitudes of Whites had long made it impossible for Methodists of African descent to worship with Whites on an equal basis. In 1787 and 1796, splits had occurred in Philadelphia and New York, marked by the exodus of Blacks from predominantly White churches and the formation of the African Methodist Episcopal Church (AME) and the African Methodist Episcopal Zion Church (AMEZ). In the South after the Civil War, a group of Black Methodists who were newly freed from slavery petitioned the 1866 General Conference of the Methodist Episcopal Church, South (MECS) for their orderly dismissal and founded the Colored (now Christian) Methodist Episcopal Church (CME) in 1870. [2]

Today, Methodists are at another crossroads related to race relations. Conversations are under way regarding the possibility of reunion between the historic Black Methodist denominations and The United Methodist Church. The complexities of such conversations are enormous. While many free Blacks and former slaves chose self-determination in the historic Black denominations, some members and congregations of African descent continued with the Methodist Episcopal Church down through the decades. When the Methodist Episcopal Church and the Methodist Episcopal Church, South, reunited in 1939, Blacks were segregated into a "Central Jurisdiction," which endured until the formation of The United Methodist Church in 1968 and which was not completely disbanded until 1973. Racial divides in churches, schools, communities, political structures, and economic institutions still perpetuate the legacy of slavery in the United States and in The United Methodist Church.

Even the Bible was used as a rationale for justifying slavery. The "curse of Ham" myth, based on Genesis 9:18-27, dates back thousands of years to the days when the Hebrew Scriptures were first written. For hundreds of years, slave traders cited the story of Noah's curse on his son Ham and grandson Canaan to back up their claim that it was the fate of Africans to be enslaved. The myth of Ham still surfaces among White supremacists, being cited as a biblical foundation for their bigotry.

The other biblical narrative that has influenced race relations in the United States is the Exodus account of the Hebrew people's escape from slavery in Egypt, which preceded their 40-year journey through the wilderness to the Promised Land. Of course, there is no lack of irony and contradiction in the comparison of Hebrew and African slaves, because it was another promised land that Europeans sought as they journeyed to and occupied the Americas. There, they assumed that the indigenous peoples of the land were, in effect, Canaanites, pagans, and "savages" and that, consequently, genocide was acceptable. Millions of Native Americans were also killed in more indirect ways: through diseases introduced by the European colonists and by poverty, addiction, and confinement.

But an exodus from bondage like that of the ancient Hebrews was the hope of every African slave in the United States. Though in slave states, teaching a slave to read and write was against the law, the Africans heard the biblical story of the Hebrew exodus told aloud. For them, the cotton fields became a theological forum and the songs sung there, a means of interpreting the Bible's message of freedom and salvation for their own day. "Go Down, Moses!"[3] was their cry for freedom. Black women's sufferings—especially from rape and from the selling of their children, snatched from their arms—were hummed as they bent over cotton plants or ironing boards and as they washed White children's dirty diapers: "Nobody knows the trouble I see, nobody knows but Jesus...."[4]

Today, Christians are still in the desert in search of a promised land of freedom, justice, and mercy for all. Each generation moves on, and God sustains us with manna from the sky and water from the rock. But we must not settle for the desert. We must continue our forward progress. "We're marching to Zion, beautiful, beautiful Zion; we're marching upward to Zion, the beautiful city of God."[5]

This is not a march for one racial group or another but for all of us. The farther we march, the better we come to understand how complex the stories of race and oppression are and the more our eyes are opened to the needs of the whole family of God.

This study is focused on the journey of African American Methodists because of the current discussion between historic Black Methodist denominations and predominantly White United Methodists. But prejudice, racism, and cultural imperialism affect many peoples in the world and within The United Methodist Church. Work remains to be done in making this a denomination and church with a truly open table.

In the meantime, many will say, "I am tired of talking about racism." Oppressed peoples who have seen minimal change over the years may want to retreat to the relative safety of family and community. Whites in the dominant culture may feel that racism has largely been resolved because they see members of diverse races in leadership positions and do not experience racism on a daily basis. But none of us has yet reached the promised land; so we ask you to journey on with us as we look at the Exodus as an African American Methodist journey.

Our exegetical strategy will be to weave the stories of the Hebrews' escape together with the stories of the Africans' liberation from slavery in the United States, including also the ongoing struggle against racism. Our hermeneutical tool will be African American spirituals. When the pain gets to be too much, we will burst forth in a song of liberation from slavery. A spiritual is a song for all races.

In the text of the book, at times the voice of ancient history will predominate, and at other times the voice of more recent history will be the stronger. Each story will inform the other. Finally, we must remember this: It is to freedom that Christ calls us. We can strive for nothing less.

The Hebrew Enslavement in Egypt

The thirty-seventh chapter of the Book of Genesis tells how Joseph, the eleventh of Jacob's twelve sons and the elder son of Jacob and Rachel, was sold by his older brothers to Midianite merchants because the brothers were jealous of their father's preference for him. Subsequently, Joseph was sold in Egypt to one of the officials of the Egyptian Pharaoh, or king, and he began a new life as a slave. Several circumstances in Joseph's life brought him to the direct attention of Pharaoh. First, though he refused the unwanted attentions of his master's wife, she falsely accused him and caused him to be put into prison. There, he correctly interpreted two other prisoners' dreams, one of whom later recommended him to Pharaoh as a dream interpreter. Finally, Joseph's explanation of Pharaoh's strange symbolic dream included a plan to prepare Egypt to withstand a coming famine by storing up grain during prosperous times. As a result, Pharaoh placed Joseph in charge of Egypt's food production.

When the years of famine came to the land of Canaan, Jacob (whom God had renamed Israel) sent his 10 older sons to Egypt to buy grain from the Egyptians. Now lord of all Egypt, Joseph tested his older brothers, demanding first that his younger brother Benjamin be brought to him. Finally, after further testing, he told them who he was and urged them to bring his father and his whole family to Egypt to settle in the land of Goshen. Returning home to Canaan, Joseph's brothers had to admit to their father Jacob that they had sold Joseph and that he had not died in the wilderness, as they had claimed. So Jacob traveled to Egypt to bless Joseph and to prepare all twelve of his sons for his own death and for their future.

Years later, after Joseph had lived 110 years, he said to his brothers:

> "I am about to die; but God will surely come to you, and bring you up out
> of this land to the land that he swore to Abraham, to Isaac, and to Jacob."
> (Genesis 50:24)

After Joseph, the Hebrews in Egypt, who were called Israelites (descendants of Jacob), did not have anyone they could call their leader. A new king came to power who did not know Joseph and did not respect the covenant made with Joseph's people by the former Pharaoh. Instead, the new Pharaoh was intimidated by the large number of Hebrew people living in Egypt.

> He said to his people, "Look, the Israelite people are more numerous and
> more powerful than we. Come, let us deal shrewdly with them, or they
> will increase and, in the event of war, join our enemies and fight against
> us and escape from the land." (Exodus 1:9-10)

So the king assigned taskmasters over the Hebrews to press them into forced labor and bondage. Yet the more the Hebrews were oppressed, the more they multiplied; so the Egyptian king began to dread their existence. Pharaoh increased their workload and employed still more oppressive tactics. He ordered the Hebrew midwives to destroy the male Hebrew babies as they were born. But the midwives eluded the order by telling the king that the Hebrew women gave birth quickly, before they arrived to deliver the babies. Then Pharaoh issued a new command, ordering that every boy born to the Hebrews be thrown into the Nile River.

God Grooms Moses for Leadership

This order was in force when Moses was born to Hebrew parents who were descended from Jacob's son Levi. First Moses' mother hid him. Then, when he was three months old, his mother and his sister Miriam followed the letter of the law by putting him into the Nile. But they frustrated the intent of the law and saved him by preparing a waterproof basket to hold him and placing the basket in the reeds by the riverbank where Pharaoh's daughter came to bathe. In this basket, Moses was spotted by the Egyptian princess, who adopted him as her son and hired Moses' own mother to nurse him until the child grew up. Then he went to live at the royal court of Pharaoh as an Egyptian.

God heard his people cry out for freedom and chose Moses to lead them. Moses did not start out as a leader, though. As a young man, when he saw an Egyptian beating a Hebrew who was kin to him, he killed the Egyptian, hid the body, and fled from Egypt to the land of Midian. There, he married the priest Jethro's daughter Zipporah, and for years he was content tending Jethro's flocks. But God had chosen Moses, and God called him through the miracle of the bush that burned but was not consumed by fire (Exodus 3:2-4:17). God's call gave Moses many things to fear: not only God's presence in the burning bush but the task of confronting Pharaoh and the work of leading a people.

God reminded Moses that only God can supply our every need and follow us through our fearful ordeals. God prepared Moses to deal with Pharaoh's injustice, treachery, and disbelief and provided Moses' brother, Aaron, to assist him. In Exodus 4, Moses is shown the power that God gives those who are chosen to lead.

Reluctantly, Moses returned to Egypt to face his most difficult challenge. He might have remembered that he had already faced three major challenges and survived. He had survived floating in a basket on the river, his first conflict with an Egyptian (Exodus 2:11-12), and living in a foreign land. God was already in partnership with Moses, grooming him to be a leader.

In Exodus 5:1-2, Moses and Aaron approach Pharaoh for the first time with a demand from the God of Abraham, Isaac, and Jacob: "Thus says the Lord, the God of Israel, 'Let my people go, so that they may celebrate a festival to me in the wilderness.'" The powerful Pharaoh must have thought that Moses was drunk with wine, sick from the sun, or tempting death by willful disobedience. Worse, perhaps Pharaoh and his entire court found Moses' petition to be amusing. Moses had lived in Pharaoh's court as royalty. Perhaps this Pharaoh, now an adversary, had once been considered a brother. Perhaps the memory of Moses as a murderer, one accused of a crime against an Egyptian, surfaced in the conversations of the Egyptians about this man standing before them. Moses also appeared to be a peasant, a farmer, a tender of flocks who was daring to demand that the great Pharaoh release from their work obligations the slaves that Moses called God's people.

Moses must have felt doubt as he stood before one who was powerful enough to end his life with the simple lifting of a finger. He may have trembled while wondering how his staff, even when empowered by God, could frighten such a great ruler. Yet Moses and Aaron mustered every ounce of courage in their confrontation with Pharaoh. God had prepared Moses for an encounter with disbelief and rejection (Exodus 4).

Indeed, in Exodus 5:2, Pharaoh makes a mockery of this Hebrew God who would dare to order him to release the captives. In response, Moses and Aaron explain God's demand and warn Pharaoh of the consequences of a refusal:

"The God of the Hebrews has revealed himself to us; let us go a three days' journey into the wilderness to sacrifice to the Lord our God, or he will fall upon us with pestilence or sword." (Exodus 5:3)

In this verse, Moses identified both the captives and their oppressors as being subjected to God's demands and punishments. But Pharaoh decided to punish God's people for daring to enter his courts with such foolishness. He ordered his Hebrew overseers to stop providing the slave workers with straw with which to make their daily quota of bricks. Instead, they would have to hunt for their own straw, yet produce as many bricks as before. So the Hebrews suffered even more because of Moses' stand for freedom. In this way, Pharaoh caused a schism among God's chosen people. In Exodus 5:21, the Hebrew supervisors confronted Moses, complaining that he had made things worse for the people. Their feeling was that the Hebrews would suffer less if Moses stopped provoking Pharaoh's wrath.

Again, in Exodus 6, God promises deliverance. In a profound declaration to Moses in Exodus 6:1. God states that he will use Pharaoh to drive his people out of Egypt to the freedom that he promised. Moses is reminded by God that God has been with him and his people since the beginning of time. God tells Moses not to be deterred by the schemes of Pharaoh. God enlightens Moses by warning him that the oppressor has hardened his heart and increased the suffering of God's people (a scheme) to cause divisiveness among the leadership (a schism) in order to weaken Moses' power and authority. Then God fortifies Moses and instructs him to remind his people of God's covenant with Abraham, Isaac, and Jacob.

In Exodus 6:9, Moses reports to the people that God is still in charge and that, while weeping may endure for now, Canaan (the Promised Land) is coming. But Moses wasn't prepared for the broken spirit of his fellow Hebrews and blamed himself for not being clear in presentation or worthy of their respect. In Exodus 6:14-28, God reminds Moses of his lineage and of the history of courage his people possessed, but Moses still feels that he lacks the quality of a leader. God again fortifies Moses, in Exodus 7:1-2, by reminding him that Aaron will be his spokesperson. When God calls someone into leadership, God provides the instruments needed to get the job done.

It was time for the first performance, and God used Aaron and Moses' staff to demonstrate his miracles. The staff became a snake, but Pharaoh's sorcerers also had staffs that were transformed by magic. Nevertheless, the staff of God consumed Pharaoh's snakes. Pharaoh was not moved by what appeared to have been simple magic, but he was soon to learn that the Hebrews would become a nightmare for Egypt. For every subsequent refusal by Pharaoh to heed God's demand to "let my people go" (Exodus 7-12), there was a miracle to counteract Pharaoh's earthly powers. Each miracle was designed to show God's supreme power and Moses' authority, and each was planned to strengthen Moses' faith.

Pharaoh's arrogance and thirst for power led to schemes, schisms, and nine plagues.

The Nine Plagues of Egypt

1. *The Plague of Blood.* The water of the Nile turned into blood, killed the fish, and made the river stink.
2. *The Plague of Frogs.* Frogs came up from the waters of Egypt, covered the land, and invaded the houses.
3. *The Plague of Gnats.* The dust turned into gnats, and the gnats covered both humans and animals.
4. *The Plague of Flies.* Dense swarms of flies poured into Pharaoh's palace and into the houses of the Egyptians; but the land of Goshen, where the Hebrews lived, was spared.
5. *The Plague of Disease.* Disease killed the livestock of the Egyptians, but no animal belonging to the Hebrews died.
6. *The Plague of Boils.* Handfuls of soot tossed into the air became dust over the whole land of Egypt and caused festering boils on humans and animals throughout the land.
7. *The Plague of Hail.* A fierce hailstorm struck down humans, animals, and plants in the Egyptian fields; but no hail fell in the land of Goshen.
8. *The Plague of Locusts.* Swarms of locusts covered the ground, devouring any growing plant left by the hailstorm.
9. *The Plague of Darkness.* Total darkness covered Egypt for three days, so that no Egyptian could see anyone else or move about; but the Hebrews had light in the land of Goshen.

The Tenth Plague: Death of the Firstborn

Every firstborn son of the Egyptians, including Pharaoh's firstborn, and all the firstborn offspring of the animals were killed. But the Hebrews were given God's instructions for the Passover, and the blood they put on the doorposts and lintel of each house caused the plague to pass them by.

When Israel was in Egypt's land, let my people go;
oppressed so hard they could not stand, let my people go.
Go down, Moses, way down in Egypt's land;
tell old Pharaoh to let my people go![6]

("Go Down, Moses," *The United Methodist Hymnal,* 448, v.1;
see also *Songs of Zion,* "Negro Spirituals," 112, v.1.)

Each time a plague struck, Pharaoh scoffed or bargained for relief. Each time, he schemed to go back on his promises. Each time, he offered less than the freedom God required. Each time, another plague followed Pharaoh's treachery.

The Hebrews presumably experienced the plagues of blood, frogs, gnats, boils, and locusts but were spared the plagues of flies, diseased livestock, hail, darkness, and death of the firstborn. One might ask why God would have the Hebrews experience the plagues of bloody water, frogs, gnats, boils, and locusts. God was getting the attention and the obedience of the Hebrew people. God needed the Hebrews to respect Moses as their leader. Further, God wanted the Hebrews ready to move when the time came, free of any loyalty to Egyptian people, places, or things.

God's plan was for the Hebrews to be healthy and whole for travel and to take their livestock with them. God wanted to make a distinction by showing love and loyalty toward the Hebrew people and by reserving anger and disappointment for the Egyptians. Just think of how loyal the Hebrews must have felt to God in the days of darkness when they were the only ones who could see, while the Egyptians were paralyzed—deprived of light for three days. During the plagues, Moses became the heroic leader and truth-teller for God's chosen people, the Hebrews.

The Hebrews Become God's People

Through their suffering of oppression and their resistance to slavery, the Hebrews were shaped into a people of God. Without the burning of chaff, they might have identified with the Egyptians—longing for their privileges, at best; at worst, longing to enslave others.

Slavery forged identity and theology. In the ancient world, the God you served was central to your group identity. Although descendants of Joseph were numerous among Egyptian slaves, Egyptians conquered many peoples, and prisoners of war were enslaved as a matter of course. The slave population would have been diverse indeed. Some peoples would have brought their gods with them into slavery. Others would have adopted their master's gods. Moses himself would have been expected to worship the Egyptian sun god when he lived in the Pharaoh's court. But out of the diverse mix of peoples who came or were brought to Egypt from various lands emerged a galvanized people united by the experience of suffering and by their covenant with the God of creation and freedom—the God of Moses.

Moses' Mission Strategies

Early on, Moses realized the limits of his ability to confront power structures. He first pleaded with God to let this heavy burden pass and later told God that he needed help. God sent help in the form of miracles and in the voice of Aaron, who was offered by God as Moses' more fluent spokesperson. Leaders always need fortifying and God strategically planned for fortifying Moses and later Aaron.

Moses demonstrated a number of key mission strategies and skills. For example, he examined his calling from God and assessed his abilities and needs. He prayed for wisdom, direction, and skills that would enhance his mission journey. He asked for God's help in providing other strengths that he felt could aid God's mission. Moses used the following great mission strategies to confront Pharaoh's power structure. These were his imperatives:

- Respond to God's call.
- Examine God's calling and assess the missionary's need and risk.
- Develop an action plan.
- Use direct confrontation with a prepared platform statement.
- Demonstrate symbolic gestures of God's power and strength.
- Educate the people.
- Build community around the movement.
- Prepare the people to accept change.
- Plan for a response to resistance.
- Pray for wisdom, strength, direction, and resources.
- Prepare resources for action and relocation.
- Develop a supportive community.

Power Structures in America

God has labored in the Americas to raise up new liberators, as slavery and racially divided societies became the building blocks for vast national wealth. While we do not have legalized slavery today in the United States, the residue of past centuries is still with us. Markers like poverty, prison populations, and salary rates trace a line directly back to beliefs in Anglo-Saxon superiority. While Moses dealt with the power structures of his day, we must know the roots and outlines of our own contemporary structures.

White Europeans came to America in search of personal freedom, opportunity, and a new and better life. Many sought freedom from religious or political oppression. Others came from debtors' prisons to get a fresh start. Some of the poor signed limited-term indentures in exchange for their passage to the New World. The more privileged colonists came as "landed gentry," with land grants from members of the European nobility; they set the rules for the control of land and wealth. The landed gentry realized that cheap labor was needed to exploit the potential profits from cotton and tobacco, which were raised on small farms and large plantations in the South.

At first, Native Americans were forced to perform the arduous work of clearing fields, cultivating the soil, planting, tending the crops, and bringing in the harvest; but they resisted these tasks. The Native Americans succumbed to the diseases that were brought to America by the Europeans, and there was a conflict in beliefs, values, and ways of life. Enslaved Native Americans frequently ran away, since they knew their way in the wilderness, and their spirits could not easily be broken. The first Africans to come to the English colony in Jamestown, Virginia, arrived in 1619 as indentured servants. They, like White indentured servants, were contracted to work for a given period of time, after which they were guaranteed freedom—a chance for a new start when the contract ended.

A few [Africans]—like Anthony Johnson, who became a prominent landholder on Virginia's eastern shore—prospered after their indenture had ended. The seventeenth century, however, saw the evolution of the American slave system, which severely limited the chances of many Africans to follow Johnson's example.[7]

As time passed, the planters who raised cash crops like cotton and tobacco on large Southern plantations found that it was cheaper for them to acquire laborers through the African slave trade. Blacks were seized along the coasts of western Africa and brought forcibly to America. It was only the sons and daughters of Africa who were thus captured, crammed into the belly of ships, sold in slave markets, and forced by any means necessary to do unpaid labor for former Europeans now living in the English colonies of America.

Profit-seeking slave traders and plantation owners rationalized their actions in enslaving Africans. They assumed that these black-skinned people—snatched away from their tribes and communities, dehumanized in the airless, overcrowded slave ships, and separated from their friends and families on the New World's shores—would have no choice but to concede their freedom and yield obedience to their new slave masters. Having lost their homelands and families, the slaves were even stripped of their identities by being renamed by their masters. The crafty plan of mixing tribes and developing slave populations that could not communicate with one another in the same African language was intended to destroy personal contact and humble those in bondage. Initially, slave traders focused on capturing African men, but women were soon seen as useful breeding instruments for male slaves. The women often suffered from forced sexual contact with slave traders or new owners and grieved deeply when they were separated from their children. By the eighteenth century, most Africans working in the Southern colonies—in the fields, in the master's house, and at trades on the plantation—were slaves.

Contrary to popular belief, African slaves also rebelled, ran away, or died from disease, mistreatment, or arduous labor. Some married Mexicans or Native Americans. Some fought with Native Americans against the "great White conquest." Many refused to use the names given to them by Europeans but retained their African names as a form of resistance and a means of maintaining their African heritage. To resist the control of "the master," slaves found ways of communicating with Africans who spoke different tribal languages. Thus slaves became multilingual, learning the various African tongues as well as the European language spoken by their master, which might be English, French, Spanish, Portuguese, or Dutch. Slaves also found ways of communicating through the rhythms of their handmade flutes and drums. Music became the avenue for expressing pain, frustration, or joy and a means of crying out for freedom.

Africans did not take well to bondage. They resonated to the story of Moses leading the Hebrews to the Promised Land. They could relate personally to the story of the crucifixion of Christ and the promise of a heavenly reward after death. In fact, slaves believed in a theology of liberation long before James Cone wrote about it in his noted book, *Black Theology and Black Power.*[8] Slaves developed a pedagogy of the oppressed through singing and preaching long before "liberation theology" became a popular term for explaining social movements in Latin America. African slaves worked and sang and survived as best they could. In this respect, they were similar to the Hebrews who waited for a Moses to lead the way to freedom. God has sent many people like Moses to lead the way.

Slavery and the U. S. Constitution

Not all White Americans believed in slavery. In fact, the Constitution, which went into effect in 1788, allowed Congress to ban the importation of slaves into the states beginning in 1808 (Article I, Section 9), which was done. However, the founders of the United States owned slaves. Even as Thomas Jefferson was writing the Declaration of Independence, declaring "that all men are created equal" and naming life, liberty, and the pursuit of happiness as unalienable rights, he had slaves working on his estate—as did George Washington when he took the oath of office as the first President. Later, after Washington, D. C., became the nation's capital and the seat of U. S. political power, it was home to both abolitionists and racists, slaves and free Africans.

In 1800, when the First Congress convened and Washington became the federal government's official seat, 3,244 slaves and 783 free blacks accounted for 29 percent of the District of Columbia's 14,000 inhabitants. [9]

In fact, Congressional leaders brought with them their "property"—slaves—to care for their needs. Living in such an urban society often allowed for attendant "slaves" to have more freedom and dignity than would exist on an estate or a plantation. Since the capital had to be built from the ground up as a new city, laborers and skilled craft workers were needed. Benjamin Banneker—a free Black and a self-taught land surveyor, as well as a mathematician, scientist, and astronomer—was the first Black to receive a Presidential appointment. He was hired to help lay out the borders of the District of Columbia, and when Congress fired the French architect, Pierre L'Enfant, Banneker continued L'Enfant's work.[10]

Some members of Congress hired out their slaves to build Washington. Eventually, authorities looked the other way as slaves acquired separate housing from their owners. This mobility often occurred with the consent of the slave owner. Such partial freedom was a risky business, because the slaves were still owned by a master. With mobility came the vulnerability of being captured by a slave trader or of being surrendered by the authorities to a local auction block as a form of control and restraint. Codes were developed to control slaves, including curfews and restrictions against gambling, drinking in public, and carrying a firearm. Despite protests, restrictions remained; but other doors opened, such as federal service jobs. Thomas Jefferson benefited from such a plan:

> The federal government also opened a few service jobs to free blacks. Beginning with Thomas Jefferson's presidency, a substantial number of black servants attended the chief executive and most other officeholders. The White House domestic staff included several blacks, as did staffs of most other government buildings. In addition, a few blacks secured jobs as government messengers.[11]

Black slaves fought side by side with their masters during the American Revolution, yet they did not win the same freedoms. One of the first three casualties of the Revolution in the Boston Massacre was a Black man named Crispus Attucks.[12]

After the war, abolitionists looked forward with great expectation to the freeing of slaves as part of the new nation's Constitution. But at the Constitutional Convention in Philadelphia in 1787, the abolitionists were disappointed. Though the importation of slaves was prohibited after 20 years, effective in 1808, freeing slaves and ending the practice of slavery was not on the minds of policymakers. In fact, in a compromise reached in Article I, Section 2, regarding representation and taxation based on population, the Constitution counted only three of every five slaves. Thus each Black slave was counted as only three-fifths of a White American. Lawmakers also satisfied slave owners by adding Article IV, Section 2:

No person held to service or labor [a slave] in one State, under the laws thereof, escaping into another, shall, in consequence of any law or regulation therein, be discharged from such service or labor, but shall be delivered up on claim of the party to whom such service or labor may be due [the slave master].[13]

The nation's founders considered slaves as property. Slavery was a controversial subject that they believed would compromise the development of the U. S. Constitution. Consider Thomas Jefferson's views, as expressed below:

"As a property," said Jefferson, who had yet to set free the hundred-odd slaves he held at his Monticello estate, "they [slaves] are lawfully vested and cannot be taken away."

Though committed to the gradual ending of slavery, Jefferson was not at all inclined to "retain and incorporate the blacks into the state." To do so, he considered the "height of folly." He regarded amalgamation as both revolting and socially impossible."[14]

Yet later Jefferson was impressed by an almanac sent to him by Benjamin Banneker, who had written and published it after completing his surveying work in Washington, D. C. Banneker included a letter calling for the abolition of slavery and "saying he hoped [his almanac] would prove that any 'narrow prejudices' about Blacks...were false." Impressed, Jefferson sent the almanac to the Royal Academy of Sciences in Paris as an illustration of the abilities of Blacks.[15]

Freedom has a legacy of struggles and contradictions, schemes and schisms. In the writing of the U. S. Constitution, the nation's founders struggled over how to make whole the lives of all human beings while satisfying the thirst for profit and the greed of the slave owners. In the end, the Constitution guaranteed all White male property owners full human rights. Everyone else had to live through a whole series of schemes before even approaching the full promise of a freedom that had been hard won in the American Revolution.

The Passover of the Israelites

"Thus saith the Lord," bold Moses said, "let my people go;
if not, I'll smite your firstborn dead, let my people go."
Go down, Moses, way down in Egypt's land;
tell old Pharaoh to let my people go![16]
("Go Down, Moses," *The United Methodist Hymnal,* 448, v. 2;
see also *Songs of Zion.* "Negro Spirituals," 112, v. 2)

Struggles, schemes, and schisms were shaping the ancient revolution in Egypt. The Hebrews had seen the wonders of God and knew that they were chosen for a special deliverance, though the actual plan to deliver the Hebrews had still not been revealed. In Exodus 12, God begins to reveal the plan through Moses, his chosen messenger, and the people began to prepare for the journey. Moses helps the Hebrews to understand that before the journey begins they must enter into a covenant—an agreement—with God. In Exodus 12:2, God instructs the Hebrews that "This month... shall be the first month of the year for you." This is the beginning of a new life for God's people.

God knows that slavery, like racial prejudice, is taught. To unlearn the patterns of subservience and defeatism, rituals of freedom must be practiced. Changing the mindset of the Hebrews from an acceptance of slavery to a state of becoming free beings under God's grace was an important part of liberation. God's plan of action included a new rite of passage in the flight from bondage to freedom: the feast of the Passover.

God gives Moses and Aaron detailed instructions for the observance of the Passover feast, including the selection and preparation of the Passover lamb, the way it is to be eaten, and the use of its blood as a sign.

> Your lamb shall be without blemish, a year-old male....This is how you shall eat it: your loins girded, your sandals on your feet, and your staff in your hand; and you shall eat it hurriedly. It is the passover of the Lord. (Exodus 12:5a, 11)

This ritual, the predecessor of the Christian Communion service, began as a rite that marked the movement from slavery to freedom. The food prepared the people for flight. The blood marked each Hebrew household for God's rule rather than Egypt's. The meat was to be eaten with unleavened bread and bitter herbs. By morning. any meat that remained was to be consumed by fire.

This Passover feast provided a significant role for women, for they prepared, led, and maintained God's Passover plan of action. The Passover required the selection of an unblemished lamb for each household on the tenth day of the month. The lamb was to be preserved until the fourteenth day and then slaughtered in the evening. Blood from the lamb was to be smeared on the two doorposts and the lintel of each Hebrew home.

> The blood shall be a sign for you on the houses where you live: when I see the blood, I will pass over you, and no plague shall destroy you when I strike the land of Egypt. (Exodus 12:13)

By the time the Passover instructions were written down, the rite had become a well-established part of the people's rituals. You can hear the tone of priestly instruction and remembrance as you read.

Although the Passover events were marked by a sense of haste, overnight preparation, and readiness for departure, the bread rites that were to be perpetuated in the future took seven additional days of observance, from the fourteenth until the twenty-first day. Unleavened bread at Passover was the symbol of God's promise for the future and the people's commitment to remember how God delivered them. That first Passover, God placed in the Hebrews' minds the idea that they must condition themselves to separate from the Egyptians in order to be freed from bondage.

In Exodus 12:15-20, they are instructed to remove leaven from their homes on the first day of Passover to avoid the temptation of adding leaven to the bread. On the first and seventh days of Passover, they are to participate in a solemn assembly. Those two days were set aside for rest and a time for prayer. Other than preparing food to eat, no one was to perform any work. The Hebrews were given specific instructions that anyone who violated this covenant was to be removed from the congregation.

It is important to examine the symbols that God used to build a covenant. The lamb was symbolic of the vulnerability that the Hebrews experienced in Egypt. It also foreshadowed the coming of a Jewish savior whose life would be sacrificed for all. Blood was the fluid of life. The lamb provided the blood that was a symbol of God's people and a visual signature for the covenant. The bread was to be prepared in haste—unleavened because there was no time to wait for it to rise. Instead, God's people were to eat hurriedly, dressed and ready to take immediate action.

God promised that the Hebrews would be fed for the journey, rested for the journey, spiritually prepared for the journey, and freed for the journey. The people had begun to taste victory and the people wanted the promised freedom. God wanted freedom for them, obedience from them, and a commitment from them to remember the bond between God and God's people.

Escape by Night

O, 'twas a dark and dismal night, let my people go;
When Moses led the Israelites, let my people go.
Go down, Moses, way down in Egypt's land;
tell old Pharaoh to let my people go.[17]
("Go Down, Moses," *Songs of Zion*, "Negro Spirituals," 112, v. 5)

All was ready. After the death of all the firstborn children of the Egyptians, Pharaoh called Moses and Aaron and commanded them:

> "Rise up, go away from my people, both you and the Israelites! Go, worship the Lord, as you said. Take your flocks and your herds, as you said, and be gone." (Exodus 12:31b-32a)

So the Hebrews left hurriedly after midnight. They fled from the city of Rameses to Succoth, led by God along a roundabout route through the wilderness toward the Red Sea. Many generations had been born in the 430 years since Joseph's family arrived in Egypt, and they had been raised under the rule of Pharaoh. But it was now time to leave the security of bondage and the familiar places and to venture out into the unknown with a new leader.

The Hebrew children had not had a leader since Joseph. Furthermore, Moses had reached adulthood not in their community but in Pharaoh's court. He had fled from the area as a murderer, married into a foreign family, and returned performing miracles, claiming to speak for God. The thought of going away with this distant relative—who performed miracles and who spoke of a God who would deliver them—was bewildering.

Moses had actually told old Pharaoh to let God's people go, and it was actually happening. We can imagine that the Hebrews must have moved quickly, tying pottery and baskets to the animals, tightening their children's sandals, securing and putting away the provisions for the trip, praying that they were not dreaming. They encouraged and assured each other that whatever they faced in the wilderness could not be any worse than what they were experiencing in bondage. The reality must have hit home that they could not turn back to Pharaoh. Death was behind them and life or death lay ahead.

God was right; the time to flee was in the night while the Egyptians wept over the loss of their firstborn children. The time to flee was now while the Hebrews were well fed, rested, and spiritually prepared for the journey. The time to flee was now, with Moses walking among them and leading them out of bondage. The time to flee was now, because they had made a covenant with God for the future of their children. The time to flee was now, because their God's power had been proved and their own task was to march to freedom.

Even though Exodus (chapters 12 and 13) gives the impression that the Hebrews quietly listened and followed Moses' lead, we know that the nature of people is to doubt, to complain, to find fault, and to struggle with leadership when the stakes are high.

We can imagine Moses moving among the pack animals, the children, and the cloaked adults, reminding them of the stories of God's protection for their ancestors. The courage of their ancestors and the pain of their own bondage were driving forces as they prepared for peril and probable death—either at the hands of the Egyptians or in the hostile desert.

Of course there may have been complaints about Moses emerging from their surging fears: "Who does he think he is?"; "Where is he taking us?"; "This man is mad!" But Moses, the crafty leader, had already given power to the elders in the Passover preparation; responsibility and authority to the women in organizing the provisions and the families; and the dream of a future without bondage to the children. Moses would not turn around.

Harriet Tubman, the "Black Moses"

Slavery for Black people in the United States was just as oppressive as that the Israelites suffered. And God did not leave the American slaves without their Moses. Her name was Harriet Tubman. She was dubbed "Moses" by freed slaves who were liberated through one of her 19 forays into slave country in the 1850s. Born a slave in Maryland around 1820, she escaped to the North in 1849 by means of a secret, strategically organized network of escape routes, safe havens, and law-defying sympathizers known as the Underground Railroad. But her own freedom was not enough. Though many rewards were offered for her capture, dead or alive, Harriet Tubman dared to keep coming back to the South, again and again, to lead more of her people to freedom. No one ever caught her. In all, she helped more than 300 slaves escape from bondage, and she never lost a "passenger."

Travel along the Underground Railroad was generally by foot. The passengers crossed fields, forests, lakes, and rivers, hiding and sleeping in barns, wagons, storehouses, and other secret places provided by sympathizers along the way. As a "conductor" for escaping slaves, Harriet Tubman was often referred to as the "Black Moses" because she boldly led her people to freedom. She also used some of the same tactics that the original Moses employed. Ms. Tubman prayed to God for wisdom and courage, developed crafty plans that tricked the slave owners, and gave her people the courage to cross unknown regions and bodies of water to reach new lands. It is recorded that:

She [Harriet Tubman] escaped from slavery and brought to freedom her sister, her two children, and her aged mother and father. A frail woman, she suffered from dizzy spells. She could not read or write, but she showed great ingenuity in managing escapes of slaves. After her own escape to the North, she said: "I looked at my hands to see if I was the same person now I was free. There was such a glory over everything! The sun come like gold through the trees and over the fields and I felt like I was in heaven."...[She] is said to have gone South nineteen times to bring out more than three hundred slaves. She raised money for her Underground Railroad trips by working as a domestic. She usually began her journeys out of the South on Saturday nights, so that she and the fleeing slaves could get a good head start before Monday. Impatient with cowardice, she carried a gun and threatened to kill any slave who wanted to turn back. She also carried drugs to put to sleep any babies who cried and endangered the group. So incensed did slaveowners become at her work that rewards adding up to $40,000 were offered for her capture.[18]

Between 1830 and 1860, the Underground Railroad helped thousands of slaves escape. During the decade when Harriet Tubman was a conductor, her organizing skills came to be feared and respected by her adversaries. The Underground Railroad reportedly reached from Missouri, Kentucky, North Carolina, Virginia, and Maryland to Pennsylvania, New Jersey, and ultimately Canada. Routes might follow the Ohio River or the

Atlantic Coast and might involve crossing one of the Great Lakes. Some trips were relatively short, for example, from Maryland to Delaware; but in those times the forests, lakes, and rivers; the wild animals; the bounty hunters; and the vicious bloodhounds used to track the scent of slaves were major obstacles to overcome.

As with the Hebrews, there were slaves who believed in the movement and slaves who were afraid. Ms. Tubman and her organized group of women and men had to know their purpose and trust in God. Like the Egyptians who gave the Hebrews goods for their journey (Exodus 12:35-36), there were White people and free Blacks who helped the fugitive slaves along the way. They marked their houses, put lanterns out in the night or docked boats at the riverbank, and gave the traveling slaves sustenance for the journey and peace along the way. Like the Hebrews, the fleeing slaves had to leave quickly, gathering whatever they could take on their backs, preparing food that would not perish, and eating and drinking whatever God provided from the land, waters, and sky. They too were in search of a promised land.

Those freed slaves who traveled to the Midwest met up with family members or White sponsors. Many journeyed on to Canada, where there was freedom and greater opportunity for them to live as free people. In the United States, there was always a chance of being returned to captivity. Slave owners placed an enormous price on the head of runaways.

During the daytime, the slaves rested and hid under porches or in barns, wagons, fields, or even boxes and barrels. At night, the darkness served as a cloak, just as it had when the Hebrews escaped after midnight. Whites who believed in their hearts that slavery was wrong took a big risk by providing funds, food, clothing, shelter, and identity papers for the fugitives and by making a public protest against what was the social norm. In order to appear free, slaves needed sufficient amounts of cash to seem independent of an owner, so as not to draw suspicion.

Besides resources, former slaves needed healing and reorienting. In the homes of Christian "White folks" they found the space to begin a transition—letting go of the past and letting God lead the way. The courage of these "White folks" who helped Harriet Tubman at stations of the

Underground Railroad is another piece of American history that is often untold.

Harriet Tubman, the "Black Moses," used her gifts from God to free her people, with the help of the angels of mercy, White abolitionists and free Blacks. Ms. Tubman, a member of the African Methodist Episcopal Zion Church, made history as she joined the struggle of women in the United States to be recognized as leaders of the nation. The spirituals that gave wings to her flight and that of her passengers must have been hummed in the midnight hours and sung boldly on Sunday mornings: "Nobody Knows the Trouble I See"; "Steal Away to Jesus"; "I'll Fly Away"; and "Swing Low, Sweet Chariot."[19]

Egypt's Hardened Hearts

> When the king of Egypt was told that the people had fled, the minds of Pharaoh and his officials were changed toward the people, and they said, "What have we done, letting Israel leave our service?" (Exodus 14:5)

Even after all the plagues and the loss of all their firstborn males, Pharaoh and the Egyptians could not conquer their own sense of superiority and entitlement to face the fact of defeat. Pharaoh began to reconsider his plight. We can imagine that, as it got closer to daybreak, the Egyptians must have begun the process of drying their eyes and realizing that they had lost more than their firstborn sons. Egyptian heads of household and government leaders must have asked, "But what will happen now that our slaves are gone?" Pharaoh must have been jarred to reality with their pleas of "We must stop the Hebrews!" The Egyptians must have been confronted with a series of questions:

- Who will plant and harvest our crops?
- Who will nurse our babies?
- Who will prepare the meals and clean our homes and palaces?
- Who will carry the straw and make the brick?
- Who will shepherd our flocks?

- Whom will we blame for our problems?
- Whom will we blame for our losses? Ourselves?

Pharaoh saw that freeing the slaves would bring economic disaster to Egypt; so he sent for his chariots, war weapons, and soldiers to attack and stop the Hebrews. Pharaoh composed himself and decided that his people had suffered too long. So we can imagine that Pharaoh girded himself for battle and walked into the courtyard to proclaim to his troops: "We must fight. We will fight. We will bring the Hebrews back to Egypt in chains, and their afflictions will be far greater than ever imagined. The blood of our firstborn children will be avenged with the blood of the Hebrew children!" Can't you just hear the crowd roar with anticipation?

> The Egyptians pursued them, all Pharaoh's horses and chariots, his
> chariot drivers and his army; they overtook them camped by the sea
> by Pi-hahiroth, in front of Baal-zephon. (Exodus 14:9)

Pharaoh thought that his midnight hour of loss was over, but instead we see Pharaoh's final scheme and God's ultimate victory. The relentlessness of the Egyptians' greed, lust for power, and racism led them to challenge God but resulted in God's display of power over such evils.

Shackled by a Heavy Burden

> Is not this the fast that I choose: to loose the bonds of injustice, to undo
> the thongs of the yoke, to let the oppressed go free, and to break every
> yoke? (Isaiah 58:6)

The cries for freedom from slavery sing through the millennia. The prophets confronted and condemned such oppression. John Wesley heard Moses and the prophets and rose to the task in his day. Social arrogance, the institution of slavery, impoverishment of widows and orphans, and inhuman prisons were affronts to God in Wesley's eyes. He set the bar high for early Methodist leaders. Barely a week before his death in 1791, John

Wesley made a final passionate statement on slavery. He wrote a letter to William Wilberforce, a member of Parliament who was fighting a stiff battle to abolish the slave trade in England. His encouraging words to Brother Wilberforce stated anew his view that the heinous estate of slavery was an evil that the human race could no longer endure:

Dear Sir,

Unless the divine power has raised you up to be as *Athanasius contra mundum,* I see not how you can go through your glorious enterprise in opposing that execrable villainy which is the scandal of religion, of England, and of human nature. Unless God has raised you up for this very thing, you will be worn out by the opposition of men and devils. But if God be for you, who can be against you? Are all of them together stronger than God? O be not weary of well doing! Go on, in the name of God and in the power of his might, till even American slavery (the vilest that ever saw the sun) shall vanish away before it.

Reading this morning a tract written by a poor African, I was particularly struck by that circumstance that a man who has a black skin, being wronged or outraged by a white man, can have no redress; it being "law" in all our colonies that the oath of a black against a white goes for nothing. What villainy is this?

That he who has guided you from your youth up may continue to strengthen you in this and all things, is the prayer of, dear sir,

Your affectionate servant.[20]

White Methodism and the Color Line

One could imagine the tremendous pain and disappointment John Wesley must have felt at the cruel treatment of African Methodists by their White brothers and sisters. White Christians had become increasingly selective in their reading of the Holy Bible. They neglected the story of Exodus. The Pharaoh who enslaved God's people in Egypt had been replaced by American slave masters, some of whom called themselves "Methodist." About one-fourth of Southern Whites owned slaves or were members of slave-holding families, and more than half of the 4 million slaves in the slave states were owned by about 45,000 wealthy planters. However, "these planters controlled the economy and government of the Southern States. Even the many Southerners who did not own slaves accepted the planters' view that the South's economy would collapse without slavery."[21]

White Methodists in the New World did not find loving their neighbor to be easy. From the first introduction of Methodism to the North American continent, colonialists struggled with John Wesley's revolutionary application of the Gospel to social concerns. Wesley was quite explicit in denouncing slavery. From the early circuit riders to the Methodist Episcopal General Conferences of the nineteenth century, slavery was the watershed issue for the denomination.

Many White Methodists in North America chose slavery over freedom and thus put Methodism in shackles. They called Wesley domineering, while they rationalized slavery with scripture. Slavery was seen by many White church leaders as an economic necessity for nation building, while the Wesleyan concept of Kingdom building was rejected.

The schisms that developed over the issue of slavery within the Methodist Episcopal Church emerged long before the General Conference of 1844. So when that Conference was convened, one writer could already describe the split:

> We have not attempted to conceal the fact that some portions of our Connection have been greatly agitated on the question of slavery, and that the conflict of parties has, in this instance, as in most others, driven the antagonists to opposite extremes; that we must expect to find in the General Conference two contrary ultraisms represented.[22]

Promoters of slavery pointed to texts which command slaves to be obedient to masters (Ephesians 6:5, Colossians 3:22, Titus 2:9, and 1 Peter 2:18). The abolitionist voices within Methodism argued that one human being should not hold ownership over another. They turned to the Exodus story, the story of creation, Jesus' love for all people, and the rejection of slavery by Paul in Galatians 3:28. African Methodists worshiped in the church to hear Christ's liberating call. As the message became more widely proclaimed, the institution of slavery could not stand up under the rallying cry of "Let my people go!"

American Methodists and the Color Line

> O, infinite amiableness! When shall I love thee without bounds? without coldness or interruption, which, alas! so often seize me here below? Let me never suffer any creature to be Thy rival, or to share my heart with Thee; let me have no other God, no other love, but only Thee. Whoever loves, desires to please the beloved object; and according to the degree of love is the greatness of desire; make me, O God diligent and earnest in pleasing Thee; let me cheerfully discharge the most painful and costly duties; and forsake friends, riches, ease, and life itself, rather than disobey Thee.
>
> —The Right Rev. Richard Allen [23]

Africans comprised a sizeable portion of the growth in early American Methodism. It didn't take long for African Methodists to recognize the widening schism between the American Methodist movement and the intent of John Wesley. Rather than submit to second-class status in the Methodist Episcopal Church, Africans began to withdraw from the church and form their own congregations. Richard Allen and Absalom Jones led the group of Black Methodists who withdrew from the segregated St. George's Methodist Episcopal Church in Philadelphia in 1787, with Allen later forming the AME Church. Another protest group withdrew from the John Street Methodist Episcopal Church in New York City in 1796 to form the AME Zion Church.[24] Throughout the early 1800s, the Methodist Episcopal Church would be confronted with its deep compromises with evil over the issue of slavery. Indeed, the subject of slavery at the General Conference of 1844 caused the Methodist Episcopal Church to split, with the new Methodist Episcopal Church, South, separating from the Methodist Episcopal Church in the North.

As far back as the spring 1780 Conference in Baltimore, Francis

Asbury had warned that slavery was contrary to divine and human justice. But slave holders slowly began to chip away at Asbury's and John Wesley's warnings against the evils of slave ownership. In 1785, the rules that prohibited slave owners from holding ministerial office in the Methodist Episcopal Church were suspended. The deep-seated belief in inequality held not only by slave holders but also by many other Whites infiltrated the church so that, by 1844, Bishop Joshua Soule felt free to express racist assumptions in a public address to the General Conference:

> We may preach the gospel of Christ to them, unite them in the communion of his Church, and introduce them to a participation of the blessings of her fellowship, and thus be instruments of their preparation for the riches of the inheritance of the saints in glory. This, as ministers of Christ, is our work, and should be our glory and joy. This, by the grace of God helping us, we can do; but to raise them to equal rights and privileges is not within our power. Let us not labor in vain nor spend our strength for naught.[25]

The defiant message in Bishop Soule's address to the 1844 General Conference provides a window into the minds of many White Methodists at that time and, more importantly, reveals the place in which they saw African American members of the church. Specifically, Methodist slave holders and many other Whites believed that slaves were of inferior biological status and thus could be held as "property." Slaves were to be denied education and all other freedoms because of their supposed inferiority—and because of the unspoken fear of insurrections.

God's Word Used for Evil

White Methodist slave owners and others justified their actions and practices by citing the Word of God. They felt free to worship at the altar on Sunday when they were buying and selling men, women, and children daily. Some people were ushered into God's sanctuary, while others were ushered into suffering through beatings, rapes, forced labor, family division, and theft of their heritage. Many Whites prayed for their own children while preying on the children of Black parents.

The "curse of Ham" became the fatalistic rationale for many Whites who believed God was punishing Africans for an ancient misstep:

> The sons of Noah who went out of the ark were Shem, Ham, and Japheth. Ham was the father of Canaan. These three were the sons of Noah; and from these the whole earth was peopled. Noah, a man of the soil, was the first to plant a vineyard. He drank some of the wine and became drunk, and he lay uncovered in his tent. And Ham, the father of Canaan, saw the nakedness of his father, and told his two brothers outside. Then Shem and Japheth took a garment, laid it on both their shoulders, and walked backward and covered the nakedness of their father; their faces were turned away, and they did not see their father's nakedness. When Noah awoke from his wine and knew what his youngest son had done to him, he said, "Cursed be Canaan; lowest of slaves shall he be to his brothers." He also said, "Blessed by the Lord my God be Shem; and let Canaan be his slave. May God make space for Japheth, and let him live in the tents of Shem; and let Canaan be his slave." (Genesis 9:18-27)

We find in this scripture that Noah awakens and is embarrassed that his sons found him in a naked and drunken stupor. But rather than admit to his shortcomings, Noah punished the first to report his condition.

Personal Note From Christine Keels

When I read this scripture as a Black child growing up in America, I tried and tried to understand why African Americans would be cursed because a son saw his father sinning and reported to his brothers, who then covered up the father's sin. Ham didn't attack Moses sexually or violently and he didn't gossip about his condition or sell tickets to a peep show. It's a big leap to go from Ham's dilemma to the enslavement of a part of God's people. It was Noah, not God, who called down punishment on Ham and his descendants.

Cain Hope Felder, in his book, *Troubling Biblical Waters,* refers to:

> ...the so-called curse of Ham (Gen. 9:18-27), which rabbis of the early Talmudic periods and the Church Fathers at times used to denigrate Black people. Later Europeans adopted the so-called curse of Ham as a justification for slavery and stereotypical aspersions about Blacks.[26]

Felder goes on to state:

> In error, Ham leaves his father uncovered (an act of great shamelessness and parental disrespect in Hebrew tradition) while he goes to report Noah's condition to Shem and Japheth, his brothers (v.22). Ham's two brothers display proper respect by discreetly covering their father (v.23). When Noah awakens (v. 24), the problems begin. Noah pronounces a curse—*not* on Ham, but on Ham's son Canaan....Noah also blesses Shem and Japheth, presumably as a reward for their sense of respect.[27]

Although, throughout time, humankind has tried to rewrite the scripture to indicate that Ham committed a sin toward his father and was therefore punished, instead Ham was guilty only of violating a social norm by not showing proper respect for his father. Felder also comments on the issue of color:

> Similarly, the Babylonian Talmud (sixth century A.D.) states that "the descendants of Ham are cursed by being Black and are sinful, with a degenerate progeny." The idea that the blackness of Africans was due to a curse, and thus reinforced and sanctioned enslaving Blacks, persisted into the seventeenth century.[28]

Slave owners also used Numbers 12 as an attempted justification for slavery. This is the story of Miriam's and Aaron's refusal to accept Moses' wife, a Cushite woman (presumably a Black woman from Ethiopia, though in Exodus 2, Zipporah is identified as a Midianite from the Arabian Peninsula). So the notion that Blacks were part of a cursed generation, that they married into Moses' family and were not a true part of the Hebrew people, and that they were slaves to be treated as the master desired were false ideas traced to tenuous biblical roots and altered to suit the occasion. "Slaves, obey your masters!" (see Ephesians 6:5) became the catch phrase for the ethic stemming from Ham's wickedness. Many Whites believed that it would take White America to save Black people from damnation. Slavery was seen as a means for teaching Blacks how to work and care for family and as a means for introducing them to Christianity. In the name of the Christian cross, misery was bestowed upon a people.

This theology was woven into the tapestry of racialized ministries, as Southern Methodists created major evangelizing programs on the slave plantations. By saving souls, they salved their consciences. Despite this, the deeper message of freedom and the condemnation of slavery by prominent early Methodists, such as Wesley, Coke, and Asbury, brought hundreds and then thousands of slaves to Christ in the Methodist family. Many Black converts took up the cause of evangelization and brought thousands more to the faith.

Initially, slave owners allowed slaves to conduct camp meetings led by slaves who were unsupervised. Eventually, however, slave owners became fearful of such gatherings. They then insisted that their slaves worship with them and that they be seated in the balcony, gallery, rear, or other restricted area of the church or churchyard. In some cases, personal or beloved servants, though still slaves, were allowed to sit with their White families, particularly to care for children. For African slaves, the formalized White worship style may have been restrictive, unemotional, and not at all appropriate to their struggles as slaves. In fact, sermons were often used to justify their bondage and to reinforce slavery. Africans listening to the misinterpretation of the Letter of Paul to the Ephesians (see Ephesians 6:5-6) may have felt that God did not speak to *them*. The Book of Exodus surely was not presented as a story of freedom for slaves brought from Africa. Listening to ceremonies that did not include their salvation and freedom must have caused slaves to sing, "Were you there when they crucified my Lord?" When members of the clergy refused to baptize African babies because of the color of their skin and the bondage of their parents, the slaves must have moaned: "Oh! sometimes it causes me to tremble, tremble, tremble. Were you there when they crucified my Lord?"[29]

In the North, although there were many free Blacks counted among the Methodists, full participation by Black people in the Methodist Episcopal Church was blocked at every turn. Although slavery was condemned, nevertheless a basic belief in the inferiority of people of African descent was rampant among Northern Whites.

Free Blacks and freed slaves were beginning to outnumber Whites in some Methodist Episcopal churches in the North. And they were demanding more freedom than Whites had expected. White society was about to change, and even Whites who were abolitionists were not ready for such drastic changes. Freedom was knocking at the door of the church but the door was quickly slammed. Sometimes Northern White Methodists provided places of worship for Blacks with sufficient strings attached to enable the Whites to still count former slaves in their membership and to maintain control over the development of African Methodism and properties. But sometimes the new Black churches achieved true autonomy. For example, in Washington, D. C.:

> Mt. Zion Negro Church in Georgetown was founded in 1814 with the support and under the guardianship of the Washington Foundry Methodist Church's white congregation. In 1820 several black members withdrew from the largely white Methodist congregation at the Ebenezer Church, on Fourth Street near Virginia Avenue, to form the first autonomous, formally organized, black congregation....In addition to conducting religious services, they established their own Sabbath school. Shortly thereafter, the congregation purchased a building at the foot of Capitol Hill to house what became the Israel Bethel Colored Methodist Episcopal Church.[30]

However slow its progress, change was inevitable, and change was coming.

The Hebrews' Paralyzing Fear

> O Moses, the cloud shall cleave the way, let my people go;
> a fire by night, a shade by day, let my people go.
> Go down, Moses, way down in Egypt's land;
> tell old Pharaoh to let my people go![31]
> ("Go Down, Moses," *The United Methodist Hymnal,* 448, v. 8;
> see also *Songs of Zion,* "Negro Spirituals," 112, v. 12.)

Escape from slavery involves much more than just walking away from captivity. For the Hebrews, traveling in strange territory on what seemed to be a roundabout route must have been frightening. The Hebrews were guided as they traveled by a pillar of fire by night and a pillar of cloud by day. God's angel hovered over them in the cloud and fire, providing guidance, protection, and reassurance (see Exodus 14:19-20).

> The most direct route to Palestine was along the coast. But this would have thrown Israel [the Hebrews] into immediate conflict with powerful enemies. They needed time to learn to trust God. So God led them by a roundabout route, paralleling the Red Sea for about 100 miles southward down the Sinai Peninsula. Their journey brought them to the shore of a great body of water, in Hebrew called *yam suph.* This means, literally, "sea of reeds," and is probably best identified as the Bitter Lakes....It was at this point, trapped against the waters and a dry wilderness, that [the Hebrews] realized the Egyptians were pursuing them.[32]

The people had left everything they had ever known, and they were frightened. But the children of God marched on because Moses provided encouragement and God provided the angel of protection. Still, the battle was not yet over. Pharaoh and his army were fast approaching.

> As Pharaoh drew near, the Israelites looked back, and there were the Egyptians advancing on them. In great fear the Israelites cried out to the Lord. They said to Moses, "Was it because there were no graves in Egypt

that you have taken us away to die in the wilderness? What have you done to us, bringing us out of Egypt? Is this not the very thing we told you in Egypt, 'Let us alone and let us serve the Egyptians'? For it would have been better for us to serve the Egyptians than to die in the wilderness." (Exodus 14:10-12)

At this point, the Hebrews were losing control. They had forgotten about the pains of slavery and about the victory given them by God in the plagues, the Passover, and the pillars of cloud and fire. How quickly we forget "from whence cometh our help." The Hebrews' memories of Abraham, Isaac, Jacob, and Joseph became distant legends in the midst of their present paralyzing fear.

The Egyptians must have appeared to the Hebrews as a phenomenal force. It is so often the case that when evil raises its ugly head, the effect is overwhelming. There must have been many taunting remarks, such as "We've got you now!"; "Let's see what your God is going to do now!"; "We are going to lift high the name of Pharaoh and bring victory to Egypt by striking down *your* firstborn and returning you to bondage."

Pharaoh must have had his own pillar of fire and cloud of triumph. The dust from the rapidly moving chariot wheels and the rumbling sound resounding from the earth must have made Pharaoh appear awesome. The fire of the torches on the chariots reflected in the eyes of the soldiers must have been chilling and threatening. But there was no angel of mercy guiding this war party. Greed, anger, grief, power, and vengeance motivated this war march through the desert.

Pharaoh thought his plan was perfect. While the Hebrews had their backs to the Red Sea, he would perform the ultimate in surprise attacks, which would cause him to be portrayed in history as a great Egyptian ruler. He probably told his scribe: "Get out your scroll and record this day when the great Pharaoh brought the Hebrews to their knees in the desert and returned them to Egypt in chains, rebuking the God of Abraham."

Oh, but what a mighty God we serve. For the God of Abraham said to Moses, in effect: "Go forward and I will be with you always, even unto what appears to be the end of the earth."

At the Morning Watch

> Come, Moses, you will not get lost, let my people go;
> stretch out your rod and come across, let my people go.
> Go down, Moses, way down in Egypt's land;
> tell old Pharaoh to let my people go![33]
> ("Go Down, Moses," *The United Methodist Hymnal,* 448, v. 5;
> see also *Songs of Zion,* "Negro Spirituals," 112, v. 8.)

Pharaoh's pillars of fire and clouds of confusion were human-made and did not have the mystery and power of the Holy Spirit. God moved his angel of mercy and placed the pillar of cloud between the Hebrews and the Egyptian army. Throughout the night, the cloud kept the Egyptians from approaching (Exodus 14:19-20). Think about a cloudy, misty night in which the dust of Pharaoh's army mingled with the cloud cover to lower visibility and cause confusion. Meanwhile, the light on the other side provided vision and hope for the Hebrews, who needed such reinforcement. There is always a torchlight to freedom.

God placed power in the hands of Moses. As Moses stretched out his hand over the sea, an east wind came up to divide the Red Sea and create a dry path for the Hebrews to follow. All night they crossed over, a wall of water on either side of them. The divided waters, the torchlight of God, two faithful leaders—Moses and Aaron—and the dry path through the sea must have been breathtaking sights. But the enemy was in hot pursuit.

> At the morning watch the Lord in the pillar of fire and cloud looked down upon the Egyptian army, and threw the Egyptian army into panic. He clogged their chariot wheels so that they turned with difficulty. The Egyptians said, "Let us flee from the Israelites, for the Lord is fighting for them against Egypt." (Exodus 14:24-25)

What a powerful image: God taking the last watch of the night—the morning watch—and confounding the Egyptian army to protect the fleeing Hebrews.[34] Pharaoh's forces were confused and couldn't explain what was happening to them. They got lost in the fog, the wheels of their chariots were clogged, their commanders were dazed and had no power. Can't you just imagine their look of defeat when they realized that there were no slaves to summon to push the mired chariots because the slaves were on the other side of the dark cloud? The Egyptian soldiers began to flee as they realized "the Lord is fighting for them against Egypt."

Then God instructed Moses to stretch out his hand over the sea and close the curtain. All of Pharaoh's Egyptian army drowned in the Red Sea pursuing the God of the Hebrews and God's people. Pharaoh's struggle to hold on to Egypt's slaves, like the struggle of the Confederacy in the U. S. Civil War, had been destined for failure.

Endnotes

1. Albert Outler, ed., *John Wesley and Slavery* (New York: Oxford University Press, 1964), pp. 85-86.

2. *The World Book Encyclopedia* (Chicago: World Book, Inc., 1987), vol. 1, "African Methodist Episcopal Church" and "African Methodist Episcopal Zion Church," pp. 126-127. See also Grant S. Shockley, "Editor's Introduction," *Heritage and Hope: The African American Presence in United Methodism* (Nashville: Abingdon Press, 1991), p. 17.

3. "Go Down, Moses," *The United Methodist Hymnal* (Nashville: The United Methodist Publishing House, 1989), no. 448. See also *Songs of Zion* (Nashville: Abingdon Press, 1981), "Negro Spirituals," no. 112.

4. "Nobody Knows the Trouble I See," *United Methodist Hymnal,* no. 520; *Songs of Zion,* no. 170.

5. "Marching to Zion," *United Methodist Hymnal,* no. 733; *Songs of Zion,* no. 3.

6. "Go Down, Moses," op. cit., v. 1.

7. James Oliver Horton, "The Genesis of Washington's African American Community" in Francine Curro Cary, ed., *Urban Odyssey: A Multicultural History of Washington, D. C.* (Washington: Smithsonian Institution Press, 1996), p. 20.

8. James H. Cone, *Black Theology and Black Power* (New York: The Seabury Press, 1969).

9. James O. Horton, op. cit., p. 22.

10. Bernard A. Weisberger, *From Sea to Shining Sea: A History of the United States,* 3 ed. (New York: Webster Division, McGraw-Hill Book Company, 1976), p. 211. See also *The World Book Encyclopedia,* op. cit., vol. 2, p. 67.

11. James O. Horton, op. cit, p. 31.

12. *The World Book Encyclopedia,* op. cit., vol. 1, p. 850. For more information about Africans in the American Revolution, see the following websites:
http://americanrevolution.org/blk.html
http://www.pbs.org/wgbh/aia/part2/2p24.html.

13. William Kottmeyer & Thomas F. Eagleton, *Our Constitution and What It Means,* 6 ed. (New York: School Division, McGraw-Hill Book Co., 1987), p. 34.

14. *Ebony Pictorial History of Black America, Vol. 1, African Past to the Civil War* (Chicago: Johnson Publishing Co., Inc., 1971), p. 87.

15. Weisberger, op. cit., pp. 211-212. See also *The World Book Encyclopedia,* op. cit., vol. 2, pp. 67-68.

16. "Go Down, Moses," *The United Methodist Hymnal,* no. 448, v. 2; *Songs of Zion,* no. 112, v. 2.

17. "Go Down, Moses," *Songs of Zion,* no. 112, v. 5.

18. *Ebony Pictorial History of Black America,* op. cit., p. 232.

19. See *The United Methodist Hymnal,* nos. 520, 703, 704 and *Songs of Zion,* nos. 170, 134, 183, 104.

20. Outler, op. cit., pp. 85-86. Wesley's Latin quotation, *Athanasius contra mundum,* means "Athanasius against the world." St. Athanasius was a third-century Greek patriarch and defender of Christian orthodoxy.

21. *The World Book Encyclopedia,* op. cit., vol. 17, "Slavery," p. 416.

22. Quoted in James S. Thomas, *Methodism's Racial Dilemma: The Story of the Central Jurisdiction* (Nashville: Abingdon Press, 1992), p. 19.

23. Richard Allen, *The Life Experience and Gospel Labors of the Rt. Rev. Richard Allen* (Philadelphia, 1793; reprinted New York/Nashville: Abingdon Press, 1960), p. 46.

24. See note 2, above.

25. *Journal of the General Conference of the Methodist Episcopal Church,* 1844, p. 165, quoted in James S. Thomas, op. cit., p. 25.

26. Cain Hope Felder, *Troubling Biblical Waters: Race, Class, and Family* (Maryknoll, New York: Orbis Books, 1989, p. 38.

27. Ibid., p. 39.

28. Ibid, p. 40.

29. "Were You There?" *The United Methodist Hymnal,* no. 288; *Songs of Zion,* no. 126.

30. James O. Horton, op. cit., p. 32.

31. "Go Down, Moses," *The United Methodist Hymnal,* no. 448, v. 8; *Songs of Zion,* no. 112, v. 12.

32. Larry Richards, *Freedom Road: Studies in Exodus, Leviticus, Numbers, and Deuteronomy*, Bible Alive Series (Elgin, IL: David C. Cook Publishing Co., 1976), p. 49.

33. "Go Down, Moses," *The United Methodist Hymnal,* no. 448, v. 5; *Songs of Zion,* no. 112, v. 8.

34. See Exodus 13:21-14:25. God in the pillar of cloud and fire is referred to both as "the Lord" and as "the angel of God."

STANDING ON THE PROMISES OF GOD

> [The Hebrews] saw the great work that the Lord did against the Egyptians. So the people feared the Lord and believed in the Lord and in his servant Moses.
>
> *(Exodus 14:31)*

For a job well done, Moses and Aaron deserved letters of commendation, a testimonial banquet, medals of honor, or a well-financed retirement. They completed the task of getting the Hebrews out of Egypt safely. To accomplish this task, they were challenged to demonstrate enormous strength and courage. Both leaders possessed notable skills that are worthy of duplication in mission service today. Among their many strengths, they drew upon their ability to teach, organize, serve, lead, record history, and provide vision for a people who had been enslaved.

Moses continually used the journey as a series of teachable moments—times to instruct the Hebrews and the Egyptians about the God of Abraham, Isaac, and Jacob. Moses also taught the Hebrews what was needed to prepare for freedom and what was required for the journey.

- Lesson #1 - Moses helped the Hebrews develop a covenant relationship with God.
- Lesson #2 - Moses taught the Hebrews how to prepare for the Passover and the journey.
- Lesson #3 - Moses taught lessons on faith, endurance, and a forward vision.

Along with teaching, Moses had to design the Hebrews' travel plans strategically. With directions from God, he had to make sure that there were provisions to meet any complications. The vision that Moses carried for the Hebrews included both short-term planning and long-term dreams. Moses envisioned his people free from bondage, free from sin, and in covenant with God in a land they could call home and pass on to their children. His vision statement for the Hebrews included faithfulness, courage, and obedience in relationship and harmony with God. To fulfill this vision, he had to prepare the Hebrews for a day when all people would be free and for a coming Savior who would bring this freedom of the spirit.

> O let us all from bondage flee, let my people go;
> and let us all in Christ be free, let my people go.
> Go down, Moses, way down in Egypt's land;
> tell old Pharaoh to let my people go![1]
> ("Go Down, Moses," *The United Methodist Hymnal,* 448, v. 10;
> see also *Songs of Zion,* "Negro Spirituals," 112, v. 17)

Moses and Aaron had to be efficient organizers. They had to teach and to instill vision and hope, while at the same time organizing people, property, and livestock. More importantly, they had to stay in touch with God, following God's blueprint for liberation. It was an awesome task to instruct, gather the resources, plan the activity, set the plan into motion, hold people accountable, perform the prescribed rituals, watch for enemy attack, watch the time, and listen to God. Moses and Aaron had to instruct the elders and the women on the Passover procedures, which included gathering the right resources and preparing the unleavened bread. The two leaders had to hold the people accountable for the Passover plans and make sure only those who met all requirements joined the journey. They also had to watch for the right time of night to flee, watch for Pharaoh to avoid sudden attack, and watch for God's signs and miracles as pointers along the path.

Though Moses and Aaron were ordinary people, they were called on to perform extraordinary tasks. God's performance plan was not easy, the incentive awards weren't always appealing, and the desired outcomes were not readily achieved; but the reward for a satisfactory performance was freedom from bondage and a new identity—not as Egypt's slaves but as God's people. As leaders, teachers, visionaries, and organizers, Moses and Aaron accepted the challenge and performed the tasks at hand, for they had faith that the Hebrews would soon be free:

> We need not always weep and mourn, let my people go;
> and wear those slavery chains forlorn, let my people go.
> Go down, Moses, way down in Egypt's land;
> tell old Pharaoh to let my people go![2]
> ("Go Down, Moses," *The United Methodist Hymnal,* 448, v. 4;
> see also *Songs of Zion,* "Negro Spirituals," 112, v. 18)

Moses and Aaron were also the historians, helping the people maintain the memory of the journey and the events brought about by God's liberating power. Just as Pharaoh's scribes must have been prepared to write the story of Pharaoh's victory, Moses and Aaron recorded God's victory over the Egyptians—through the plagues and through the desert and through the Red Sea. Having the tasks of supervising the sacred rites and making sure that the Hebrews preserved their history, Moses carried with him the bones of Joseph, keeping the promise made to Joseph 400 years earlier by the Hebrews' ancestors (Exodus 13:19).

Songs of Celebration

When the waters of the Red Sea closed over Pharaoh's army, the waters farther from shore remained parted so that the Hebrews could complete their passage to the other side.

> Then the Lord said to Moses, "Stretch out your hand over the sea, so that the water may come back upon the Egyptians, upon their chariots and chariot drivers." So Moses stretched out his hand over the sea, and at dawn the sea returned to its normal depth. As the Egyptians fled before it, the Lord tossed the Egyptians into the sea. The waters returned and cov-

ered the chariots and the chariot drivers, the entire army of Pharaoh that had followed them into the sea; not one of them remained. But the Israelites walked on dry ground through the sea, the waters forming a wall for them on their right and on their left. (Exodus 14:26-29)

Once the Hebrews were free of the threat of pursuit, they could fully experience and savor the victory. Thus there was great jubilation when they stood on dry land, with the Red Sea providing a divide between them and Egypt.

When they had reached the other shore, let my people go;
they sang a song of triumph o'er, let my people go.
Go down, Moses, way down in Egypt's land;
tell old Pharaoh to let my people go![3]
("Go Down, Moses," *The United Methodist Hymnal,* 448, v. 7;
see also *Songs of Zion,* "Negro Spirituals," 112, v. 10)

As the African slaves in America sang the history of their bondage and the dream of their liberation in spirituals, so their predecessors, the former Hebrew slaves in Egypt, also turned to song and dance to record their history and to proclaim God's triumph over their oppressors. You can hear the song of Moses and the Israelites in Exodus 15:1-18, especially verses 1-15. The first stanza is also the song of Miriam and the women, dancing with tambourines in Exodus 15:20-21. Portions of this song of praise and triumph also appear in *The United Methodist Hymnal* as the "Canticle of Moses and Miriam."[4]

"I will sing to the Lord, for he has triumphed gloriously;
horse and rider he has thrown into the sea.
The Lord is my strength and my might,
and he has become my salvation;
this is my God, and I will praise him,
my father's God, and I will exalt him.
The Lord is a warrior; the Lord is his name.

"Pharaoh's chariots and his army
he cast into the sea;
his picked officers were sunk in the Red Sea.
The floods covered them;
they went down into the depths like a stone.
Your right hand, O Lord, glorious in power—
your right hand, O Lord, shattered the enemy.
In the greatness of your majesty
you overthrew your adversaries;
you sent out your fury, it
consumed them like stubble.
At the blast of your nostrils the waters piled up,
the floods stood up in a heap;
the deeps congealed in the heart of the sea.
The enemy said, 'I will pursue, I will overtake,
I will divide the spoil, my desire
shall have its fill of them.
I will draw my sword, my hand shall destroy them.'
You blew with your wind, the sea covered them;
they sank like lead in the mighty waters.

"Who is like you, O Lord, among the gods?
Who is like you, majestic in holiness,
awesome in splendor, doing wonders?
You stretched out your right hand,
the earth swallowed them.

"In your steadfast love you led the people
whom you redeemed;
you guided them by your strength
to your holy abode." (Exodus 15:1-13)

What a celebration the Hebrews had, with Moses and the men singing;

with Miriam and the women singing and dancing; and with everyone feasting on unleavened bread and unalloyed joy. The children must have danced too and must have prayed and thanked God for bringing them safely across the sea.

When the people follow God's will, there is progress. Where there is progress, there is deliverance and celebration. Where there is celebration, there is spiritual harmony. But in reality, the long journey to freedom had only just begun.

The U. S. Civil War

For African Americans, both slave and free, the Civil War was a war against slavery. For generations, slaves gathered in remote wooded areas of plantations, free blacks congregated in grand churches of northern cities, and small groups of slave and free, meeting in homes, had sung of suffering in bondage, longing for a Moses to lead the people, and anticipating the year of jubilee. Many African Americans, of course, had not waited for the year of jubilee to bring them freedom, but had struck out on their own, seeking a sometimes precarious freedom in the North or in the relative anonymity of the city.[5]

Violence is a sad solution to oppression. But acquiescence to systematic violence is even sadder. Abolitionists in the United States could not have foreseen the level of carnage that the Civil War would produce, but slavery itself was fraught with violence. The history of massive deaths in the Middle Passage—the forcible transporting of captive Africans to the Americas, crammed into the holds of ships under cruel, inhuman, and often unsurvivable conditions—and the systematic violence needed to enforce slavery were common knowledge. The violence of slavery could not go on.

The Civil War began in April 1861 after years of national controversy over the issue of slavery; after secession from the Union by seven Southern states, which formed the Confederate States of America (the Confederacy) in 1860; and after Confederate troops fired on and then captured Fort Sumter in South Carolina, a U.S. fort. Around 620,000 soldiers, both White and Black, lost their lives during the Civil War—almost as many Americans as were killed in all other U.S. wars combined, from the American Revolution through Vietnam.[6]

While the Civil War heralded the end of slavery, it was not overwhelmingly a war fought over slavery. Initially, war rhetoric focused on the reunification of the country. However, everyone knew that at issue was a web of slavery, property, and commerce. In fact, President Abraham Lincoln's efforts were slow to address slavery. Lincoln sought to find a compromise between freeing slaves and satisfying the owners of slave "property." Members of the U. S. Congress passed a law in 1862 that allowed for a commission to receive petitions from slave owners, listing the financial worth of their slaves and possible compensation of up to $300 per slave. Petitions were filed (including some filed by slaves themselves) and the law resulted in 161 slaves receiving their freedom.

Earlier, abolitionists had chosen the seat of government, Washington, D. C., to initiate a model for eliminating slavery in America. In 1830, former slaves and White abolitionists sent hundreds of petitions to Congress to abolish the selling of slaves and slavery itself in Washington. Heavy debate occurred in both the House of Representatives and the Senate, and two decades went by before a series of bills passed that were called the Compromise of 1850. As part of the compromise, Congress outlawed the buying and selling of slaves in Washington, D.C. Though the keeping of slaves in Washington was allowed to continue, this act opened the door to freedom in the federal jurisdiction.[7]

Removing the selling block from the nation's capital created another problem. For escaping slaves, Washington became a southern extension of the Mason-Dixon Line that separated Maryland and Pennsylvania, dividing the slave states from the free. Although the selling of slaves had been abolished in Washington, the federal law related to the return of escaped slaves was still in force.

Anxious to retain the loyalty of border states like Maryland, the Lincoln administration devised a temporary legalistic solution: slaves escaping from states at war with the Union would be considered "contraband of war," or captured property, and placed under the jurisdiction of the U.S. Army. Fugitive slaves from loyal states, however, were to be returned to their masters.[8]

Abolitionists had mixed feelings about the Civil War. Some welcomed a war that would finally resolve the issue of slavery. Others were concerned that the South might win or the North might compromise over slavery. In the words of a Black abolitionist, John S. Rock:

Now it seems to me that a blind man can see that the present war is an effort to nationalize, perpetuate, and extend slavery in this country. In short, slavery is the cause of the war: I might say, is the war itself. Had it not been for slavery, we would have had no war! Through two hundred and forty years of indescribable tortures, slavery has wrung out of the blood, bones, and muscles of the Negro hundreds of millions of dollars, and helped much to make the nation rich. At the same time it has developed a volcano which has burst forth....[9]

John Rock's pro-Union rally speech summarizes clearly the struggle in which the United States was engaged. Slavery in the South was part of a way of life that was supported by a political platform which led men to war. For some abolitionists in the North and the South, opposition to slavery was grounded in a moral argument that was worth fighting for on ethical grounds. However, the whole argument over slavery was shaded by the fact that slavery provided economic momentum for the entire nation.

The Civil War was also a struggle between the industrial North and the agrarian South. The North favored a high tariff on manufactured goods imported from Europe. The South feared that such a tariff would endanger its trade with Europe and raise the price of its imports. When the war began, the North expected a quick victory, while the South was prepared to fight to the bitter end in defense of its way of life.

When President Lincoln realized that the North needed help in winning the war, he issued the Emancipation Proclamation on January 1, 1863. He had two primary reasons for doing so:

His main concern, at first, was the military significance of the Proclamation. He knew it would greatly undermine the South's military strength by turning loose about four million slaves. The Proclamation would also strengthen the Union Army, which would gain additional manpower and put it to work—not just behind cooking stoves, but behind shooting irons. Lincoln also believed that the Proclamation would win diplomatic support from England, and that this achievement would help the North's military effort by eliminating the possibility that the British would break the North's blockade on Southern ports. Both the North and the South had been competing for British support.[10]

The Emancipation Proclamation applied only to slaves living in the Confederacy—in rebel states that were not then under Lincoln's control. Thus the Union did not have the authority to enforce it unless the Confederate slaves escaped. The order did not apply to Union states or to Union-controlled areas in the South. But because former slaves and escaping slaves believed that the Proclamation would eventually end slavery everywhere, they flocked to join the Union Army.

Just as they fought against slavery before and during the war, after the war abolitionists such as the Black activist, orator, author, and editor Frederick Douglass and his White counterpart, William Lloyd Garrison, continued to fight for the rights of former slaves. Such abolitionists continued to lobby for federal guarantees that slavery would remain a closed issue. They also strongly believed that only with the power of the vote, political representation, education, land ownership, and employment equal to Whites would former slaves ever be completely free.

On January 31, 1865, Congress passed a law that developed the Thirteenth Amendment to the Constitution, which abolished slavery in the United States. With the end of the war in April 1865, there were several victories. Abolitionists experienced a victory over the end of slavery. Northern industrialists saw potential profit as they surveyed the war damage in the South. And, most importantly, African slaves were freed at last!

Reconstruction

From 1870 to 1914 few of the more than four million slaves released from legal slavery in the 1860s left the South. Many hoped that the land their unpaid labor had made productive for generations would one day be theirs. But that was not to be. Instead, freed people found themselves engulfed by the South's age-old social liabilities and economic backwardness. By 1900, they faced a new wave of violent intimidation: unremitting restrictions on their traditional means of survival—including sharecropping and tenant farming—and Jim Crow legislation that denied them political and civil rights.[11]

The end of the war accelerated changes that had begun before the war and that, in part, precipitated it. While the South clung to an agrarian way of life, American society in other regions was becoming more urban and industrialized. The South's lack of industrialization was instrumental in its loss of the war. The Reconstruction period after the war brought new ways of doing things and new living patterns. The old South, supported largely by tobacco and cotton, no longer had the slave labor force to produce substantial profit. Also, given the massive destruction caused by the war and by battles over land rights, life in the South was hard for all Southerners—particularly for former slaves.

Reconstruction was the period from 1865 to 1877 when the former Confederate states were under U. S. government control and were forced to modify their political and social institutions to gain readmission to the Union. President Lincoln's plan for Reconstruction—the bringing of the 11 Confederate states back into the Union—was moderate and charitable toward the former rebels. After his assassination, however, Republican radicals in Congress—who favored a punitive approach toward former Confederate soldiers and supporters—prevailed and imposed harsh military rule. Though their motives were mixed, these Republicans were successful in passing the Fourteenth and Fifteenth Amendments, giving Blacks full citizenship and Black men the right to vote.[12]

In June 1867, after Congress passed a bill extending the right to vote to former male slaves, many Whites protested by boycotting the polls. But in Washington, D. C., such resistance backfired when the voters turned out to be predominantly Black—newly freed slaves. To prevent such occurrences in the future, Northern Whites began to develop systematic forms of racism, such as the realignment of voting jurisdictions, educational requirements for voting, schedules that kept Blacks at work during hours when the polls were open, and physical threats.

While the North was becoming a paradise for immigrants from Europe, the South was left as a ruined and devastated land. Besides the destruction of many homes and the loss of family members, Whites in the South had lost their ruling social and economic status, along with their political power—including their right to vote. Much of their resentment and bitterness was focused on White carpetbaggers from the North and White Republican Southerners, whom they called scalawags—both of which prospered during Reconstruction at their expense. But many White Southerners, especially those who were most racist, also blamed the former slaves for their defeat and persecuted them in ways that evaded federal law, sometimes with the support of local law enforcement. For example, the terrorist Ku Klux Klan was formed shortly after the Civil War ended.

To protect themselves, many former slaves sought refuge in the church. A small number migrated to the North for work and a better life. Those White Southerners who wanted to see equal opportunity for former slaves tried cautiously to help the newly freed Blacks without incurring the wrath of their White neighbors. More often, though, White resentment over Reconstruction prevailed.

As soon as the war was over, the U.S. government set up the Freedmen's Bureau (1865-1872) to prepare Southern Blacks for a life of liberty. In 1863, White abolitionist William Lloyd Garrison had introduced the concept of a Bureau of Freedmen whose purpose would be to advocate for and oversee a transition from slavery to freedom. After the war, volunteer teachers came from the North like missionaries to teach Blacks in Freedmen's schools. Besides extending public education, opening hospitals and medical centers, and providing food relief to Blacks and Whites alike, the Freedmen's

Bureau worked to restore the economy by helping plantations, farms, and other businesses resume operations and by drawing up one-year paid-labor contracts for former slaves. Even so, in its political activities, its missionary outreach, and its extension and protection of Black civil rights, as advocated by abolitionist visionaries, the Freedmen's Bureau was deeply resented and rubbed more salt into White Southerners' wounds.

After the Reconstruction era ended in 1877, Southern Whites instituted a system of Jim Crow laws that prevented Blacks from voting and owning land and that deprived them of other rights of full citizenship. Night riders of the Ku Klux Klan burned houses and lynched Black men who resisted. Thus White power was reasserted through terrorism as well as through the Jim Crow laws. These were laws and practices that White power elites constructed to maintain the subordination of Blacks, who were beginning to strive for economic security. The term *Jim Crow* is synonymous with segregation—that system of White dominance that emerged quickly as the South reacted to the ending of the Civil War and the emancipation of those who had been enslaved. The name *Jim Crow* comes from the minstrel show tradition, in which a White man would blacken his face and arms with burnt cork, dress in shabby clothes, and pretend to be an uneducated, happy-go-lucky, lazy Negro. Jim Crow was a stereotypical caricature of the supposed inferiority that Whites saw in those of African descent.

In the North, conditions for Blacks were not a great deal better than in the South. Former slaves, who were often uneducated and skilled only in farmwork, were not ready for a machine-driven world. Colored people had to take whatever jobs they could find, which often meant menial work as domestics in the homes of Northern Whites or heavy labor building railroads, digging in coal mines, or carrying out public-works projects. Factory jobs and office jobs were reserved for the White male work force, while menial work and heavy labor were considered suitable for people of color and recent immigrants, such as the Irish, Italians, and Chinese.

African Americans again established or located churches and other institutions that would reinforce them in their struggle to survive under difficult circumstances. Social clubs and other gathering points became rallying places where colored people could support one another and find a sense of release from the oppression of overt and covert forms of racism. These new institutional forms of racism included redlining,[13] school segregation, separate colored accommodations, and legal means of racial profiling. The Thirteenth Amendment had ended slavery in the United States, but U.S. laws, customs, attitudes, and power structures supported White supremacy in new guises.

Standing for Freedom: The African Methodist Episcopal (AME) Church

American Methodists, whether in the North or South, mirrored the culture around them. In the North, long before the Civil War, abolition of slavery might have been the watchword, but White control of society was the practice. As early as 1787, the need to "be made whole" compelled some African Methodists to turn away from the humiliation and degradation they experienced within the Methodist Episcopal Church. The authority exerted by White Methodists over African slave converts gave birth to the AME Church. Its founder, Richard Allen, was born a slave in Philadelphia to parents in bondage to a slave owner name Benjamin Chew. Along with his mother, father, and three siblings, Allen was sold to an estate near Dover, Delaware. His introduction to Methodist class meetings shows the importance and impact Methodism had upon African slave converts:

> I was upwards of twenty years of age, during which time I was awakened and brought to see myself, poor, wretched and undone, and without the mercy of God must be lost. Shortly after, I obtained mercy through the blood of Christ, and was constrained to exhort my old companions to seek the Lord....I was constrained to go from house to house, exhorting my old companions, and telling to all around what a dear Saviour I had found. I joined the Methodist Society and met in class at Benjamin Wells's, in the forest, Delaware state. John Gray was the class leader. I met in his class for several years.[14]

For Allen and many fellow African slaves, Christian conversion and reception into Methodist Societies meant an escape from the spiritual, and sometimes even physical, bondage of slavery. Following his conversion, Allen purchased his freedom from his slave owner, Stokeley Sturgis, in 1783. Happy in his newly purchased freedom, he and other Africans attended St. George's Methodist Episcopal Church in Philadelphia.

St. George's Church set the stage for Deacon Allen to exercise his calling. Africans were allowed to continue worshiping in the church after the freedom bell rang. After all, Philadelphia's Methodists were known abolitionists and openly advocated the freeing of slaves. But when power, status, and longstanding customs came into question, discrimination became the order of the day.

Africans thirsted for fellowship and a supportive community. It had been the Gospel they heard and the spirituals they sang that had motivated them and maintained their strength throughout their years of bondage. The social-justice ministries of John Wesley were particularly inviting to a people looking for equality, justice, advocacy, and comfort. However, contradictions between preaching and practice flourished in the church. Richard Allen and other freed Africans soon learned that they could worship and pay tithes, but leadership, decision making, and even seating arrangements were still matters for White people to control. In spite of such obstacles, the African membership at St. George's grew to the point where worshipers (primarily Africans) stood in the aisle during services. Seating arrangements allowed for the presence of Africans in the church without inconveniencing the White members.

As membership soared, St. George's Methodist Episcopal Church began a building campaign. African members joyfully gave of their time and tithes to build a balcony to accommodate the need for expansion. However, even with expansion, seating arrangements were discriminatory, and Africans continued to speak of a separate facility. Some Whites viewed the increased numbers of African members as a blessing, but others either saw the increase as a nuisance or feared the idea of a separate house of worship for Blacks.

Tension mounted. On a particular Sunday in November 1787, during prayer, the African Methodists took seats in the balcony above those where they had sat below. While they were on their knees praying, Allen recalled:

> ...I heard considerable scuffling and low talking. I raised my head up and saw one of the trustees, H__M__, having hold of the Rev. Absalom Jones, pulling him up off his knees, and saying, "You must get up—you must not kneel here." Mr. Jones replied, "Wait until the prayer is over." Mr. H__ M__ said "No, you must get up now, or I will call for aid and force you away." Mr. Jones said, "Wait until prayer is over, and I will get up and trouble you no more." With that he beckoned to one of the other trustees, Mr. L__ S__, to come to his assistance. He came, and went to William White to pull him up. By this time prayer was over, and we all went out of the church in a body, and they were no more plagued with us in the church. This raised a great excitement and inquiry among the citizens, in so much that I believe they were ashamed of their conduct.[15]

The cadre of African Methodists whom Richard Allen and Absalom Jones led out of the worship service left the Methodist Episcopal Church because of its racist practices and the African members' refusal to be in bondage again.

After Richard Allen faced the Pharaohs of his time in Philadelphia, he began to organize and lead free Africans beyond a slave mentality. He wanted to take them on a spiritual journey from Egypt to a new promised land. Allen began this process by leading prayer meetings in his home.

After he developed a following, Allen approached the Methodist Episcopal Church about a separate congregation. The African congregation wanted to focus on the needs and concerns of African people. The Methodist Episcopal Church, while restricting Black participation, denied Blacks permission to form a separate church of their own. So Allen, along with another noted leader, Absalom Jones, developed an alternate proposal and organized a nonsectarian benevolent group called the Free African Society. The Society grew and received a legal Article of Association. Allen, like Moses, saw injustice and became a leader in a movement that had widespread consequences. He was called beyond his early longing—

for freed slaves to have a place where they could form a supportive community—to the founding of an entire denomination.

The prayer group allowed a space and format for African Methodists to continue worshiping and a nucleus with which to strategize as they planned for freedom. Secondly, Jones and Allen had the advantage of supportive White friends who provided meaningful advice. The Quakers, in particular, were instrumental in assisting Jones and Allen in reorganizing the prayer group to meet the needs of a congregation.

Unfortunately, the Quakers' advice also became controlling and somewhat overwhelming for a newly developing movement. The Quakers sought to proselytize the African Methodist group and to impose the Quaker values and worship style, to which Allen adamantly objected. Allen felt that, if the African Methodists assumed the Quakers' methods, they would only be switching masters while, at the same time, losing their Methodist tradition.

Because of this disagreement, in 1789, Richard Allen departed from the Free African Society. After Allen's departure, the group was fractured, with some choosing to follow Jones and become Episcopalians and with those remaining Methodist following Allen. Additionally, a number of noted philanthropists supported the Free African Society in formulating a code of ethics and disciplines that were similar to their own lifestyle, while seeking to assimilate Africans into their own White culture. St. George's Methodist Episcopal Church was unimpressed with the Free African Society's plans to build a church and thus develop a separate congregation. The White Methodists were also unimpressed with Allen's affiliation with the Quakers and the rich White philanthropists. They did not see the Quaker religion as acceptable for the former slaves and did not value the advice given by White people from the community who appeared to be meddling in Methodist Church affairs.

The irony is that White Methodists should have been able to understand Allen's demand for full participation and freedom. John Wesley condemned slavery and pressed hard to set the captives free. As often happened, society's evils were creeping into the church and choking the gospel of freedom.

First Allen and his followers had expected full participation in their Methodist Episcopal church. When that failed, they sought independence from the St. George's Church and permission to form a church of their own—again without success. The White Methodists had refused to "let my people go." With an arrogance similar to Pharaoh's, White Methodists believed they could control God's plan for the church and its people.

Richard Allen believed in the doctrines of the Methodist Episcopal Church and had no intention of being anything other than a Methodist. However, he was not willing to be consumed by White power structures. African Methodists confronted White power structures with the following mission strategies:

• prayer and seeking God's direction
• direct confrontation
• development of alternative plans and options (prayer groups and the Free Society)
• development of a supportive community
• legal protection of religious freedom (the Article of Association)

Finally, St. George's Methodist Episcopal Church sponsored an African congregation by providing a separate worship space. Zoar Methodist Episcopal Church was established as a worship place for St. George's Africans. But it was too little too late and was just one more example of resistance to African autonomy. It only complicated the racial divide because strings were attached to allow White control of the African church.

African Methodists were not to have any control over the property or to make any decisions, and there would not be an African preacher ordained for their leadership. The Zoar Church was a scheme used to create a schism among Allen's followers. St. George's Church hoped that by providing space and limited resources they would lure Allen's followers back to St. George's paternal controls. The cry to "let my people go" was being subverted rather than answered. Although Allen admired Zoar's image of independence, like Moses he could not settle for a crooked path to freedom. Richard Allen was called by God to deliver a message to a people who refused to let the people of God be free.

The Formation of the African Methodist Episcopal Zion (AMEZ) Church

During the century before the Civil War, slaves were told that the farther north they traveled, the farther they would remove themselves from slavery, and that was true. But the practice of White supremacy and its attendant racism was still waiting for them around every corner. In New York City, former slaves and free Black members of the Methodist Episcopal Church found themselves isolated and unequal in what was supposed to be Zion, the promised land.

It is ironic that the word *Zion* can mean the Hebrew people, their home-land, a religious community devoted to God, the city of God, or any utopia; for the African Methodist Episcopal Zion Church emerged from splits in the religious community. The White members of the John Street Methodist Episcopal Church were having a fight. Former slaves who were members of the church were coerced into choosing sides in the argument. The former slaves decided to support the side that provided for them the most benefits. Samuel Stillwell enticed the former slaves with more freedom. They were told that their loyalty would produce the freedom to manage their own affairs and to ordain their own elders.

When the dust settled, no freedoms materialized. There was no manna on the ground. The African Methodists in New York needed a break-through, for the people of dark complexion were not happy. When their moment came, it was not as dramatic as the AME's or as calculated as the CME's, but it was just as monumental. In 1796, they appealed to Bishop Francis Asbury for a separate worship space, and the space was granted as an "African Chapel" called Zion.

The AME Zion Church was founded in New York City in October 1796, when about 30 African Methodists withdrew from the John Street Church. The organization of the AMEZ was a direct result of the dissatis-faction of African Methodists with the prejudicial and racist treatment they experienced in the Methodist Episcopal Church. The AMEZ founders, like the founders of the AME and like Moses, knew that they had to separate their people from the confusion of Egypt's land in order for them to prosper and worship their God in freedom. A century later, J. W. Hood, an AMEZ bishop, described the state of the church at the time of separation:

> [The Negro] was wanted in the Church for the support he gave it, for the numbers he enabled sectarians to claim in exhibiting their strength, and, with the minority, who were truly pious, he was wanted there for the good of his soul. For these and other reasons he was not kept entirely out of the Church. But in the Church he was hampered and regulated. His privileges were proscribed and limited; every possible effort was made to impress him with a sense of inferiority. Preachers were selected who delighted in discoursing to him upon such texts as *"Servants obey your masters,"* and who were adepts at impressing the Negro with his inferiority in the most ingenious and least offensive way.[16]

By 1821, the members of the AMEZ were known as the "Zionites." and their church had become the second largest African Methodist denomination. James Varick, the first AMEZ bishop, is known for leading his people to independence through organizing against those who sought to deny them freedom of worship. Like Moses, the AMEZ leaders focused on the goal of freedom. They did not allow themselves to be compromised by the White leaders who patronized them, many of whom had helped to secure freedom for their families.

It should be noted that the formation of the AMEZ Church was not an action taken to repudiate Wesleyan doctrinal standards but a well-considered response to the humiliations and restrictions imposed by the White power structure within the framework of the Methodist Episcopal Church. When describing the enabling action that prompted the formation of the AMEZ Church, William J. Walls writes:

> The fathers [of the AMEZ Church] agreed that they had no fault to find with the doctrines, form of government, and evangelistic and soul-saving emphases of Methodism, but they could not endure the constant humilia-

tion and restriction imposed by the people into whose hands Methodism had fallen. The founders were opposed to slavery and inhumane treatment of slaves, so that they could logically remain Methodists because of the spirit of the originators....[17]

The Christian Methodist Episcopal Church (CME)

John Wesley's antislavery stance was nowhere to be seen in the post Civil War South. After the abolition of slavery, the White Southern Methodists and the freed Methodist slaves had little in common other than the elements of their religion and their sense of being Southerners.

Sixteen years before the Civil War, the Methodist Episcopal Church, South, had split from the Northern church. It would be almost a century before the Northern and Southern churches would reunite. After the Civil War, as former slaves began to leave the MEC, South, often taking church property with them, White members of the Southern church encouraged and helped to set up a separate, but controlled, Black denomination.

It will be remembered that in the wake of Union Army advancement into the South during the Civil War, preachers and missionaries of the Northern churches began receiving former slave members of the M. E. Church, South, into their churches by the thousands. With many of those members came the houses of worship they were using—properties that legally belonged to the Methodist Episcopal Church, South. Possession of such properties came by different means: Often entire congregations, or a large contingent thereof, "voted" to join the A.M.E., A.M.E. Zion, Presbyterian, or whatever denomination was most prominent or popular in a given area.[18]

White Northern Methodist missionaries, even while continuing to control African members in the North, were claiming land in the South for missions to help former slaves. The threat of land claims by Northern churches and the desire to separate Blacks from Whites propelled the Methodist Episcopal Church, South, to set up the Colored Methodist Episcopal Church in 1870.

The General Conference authorized the bishops to begin a process of disenfranchisement for its former slaves. The process was described as a free, friendly, and favorable separation. And, despite its shortcomings, former slaves had no desire to take on the White MEC, South. In reality, after the devastation and destruction of the Civil War, the White church was not as powerful as it previously appeared. In any case, former slaves journeyed to freedom in their own church in the South. Although it may not have been like the plunder of Egypt, former slaves took from the White Southerners what the Lord placed in their hearts to give.

Some might say that their approach in dealing with the White power structure was not as flamboyant as Richard Allen's or as vigilant as James Varick's. Nevertheless, it provided what the people needed: a separate conference in which they could begin building the community of God. One of the CME Church's notable leaders, Lucius H. Holsey, stepped into leadership at a time when a misstep could be a last step:

> Gifted with natural leadership qualities and a forceful personality, [Lucius H. Holsey] quickly advanced to the office of bishop in 1873. During the next two decades he fought long and hard to strengthen the Colored Methodists, but tried to steer clear of entanglements in Reconstruction and post-Reconstruction politics. "As ministers of the gospel," he wrote, "we make no stump-speeches and fight no battles of the politicians."[19]

The continuing Egyptian bondage of the Christian Methodist Episcopal (CME) Church was similar in nature to but different in chronology from other African Methodist traditions. In the Southern church, separate and unequal worship was one way imposed by White power elites to reorder Southern society. The Methodist Episcopal Church, South, was to provide separate space and facilities where the former slaves could worship and to ordain Black men to the ministry to serve these congregations. In the words of Lucius Holsey, who was originally from the MEC, South, written in 1882:

> In 1870, we were "set up" as a distinct and independent branch of the great Methodist family by and under the authority of the Methodist Episcopal Church, South. I understand we were "set up" and not "set off."[20]

Referring to the CME as "the youngest branch of American Methodism," Holsey noted that "as far back as 1866, its organization was contemplated and desired by both classes of those who composed the membership of the Methodist Episcopal Church, South."[21] But clearly, the former slave members of the MEC, South, were "set up" in facilities and locations to segregate them from the White members. "Set off" would mean that they were being abandoned, discarded, and deserted. They were being allowed to take the Methodist tradition with them (if one can be given Methodism) but were no longer to participate jointly in worship with Whites and were not to share in decision making or ownership of Methodist property (other than what was given to them or that they worked to purchase). They were also denied burial in White Methodist cemeteries—segregation being continued even after death.

Personal Note From Christine Keels
I grew up in Memphis, Tennessee, and spent an enormous amount of time visiting relatives in Potts Camp, Mississippi. My relatives are Baptists, and when we drove to their church, we passed the ME Church and its cemetery. I remember, as a child, wondering why we had to climb the hill behind the old Baptist Church to bury my relatives when there was a nice, well-kept cemetery near the road and on flat land. I must have asked this question, for painted in my memories are the words: "Colored people are not buried in the White Methodist cemeteries."

Eventually, besides setting up the CME Church, Southern Whites also encouraged former slaves to join the AME Church. Both strategies institutionalized racism in the church through segregation. Despite every roadblock, CME churches developed under the fine leadership of former slaves, who encouraged their people to pull themselves up by their bootstraps and said: "Let's have church. Let's praise God for our freedom. It may not be the way we thought it would be, but, Lord, it's been a mighty good day."

The 1870 plan of the Methodist Episcopal Church, South, for the separation of colored Methodists included three key elements:

- separate colored pastoral charges
- the creation of an order of ministry that provided for colored ministers' being properly licensed and ordained by the mother church
- a separate conference structure

Like Moses—and like Richard Allen, Absalom Jones, James Varick, and the unsung women and men of the African Methodist churches—the leaders of the CME Church knew that it was time to move on and to worship their God in a church of their own.

The Bonds of Slavery and Covenant of Freedom

Freedom is at the heart of God's covenant. This covenant can best be understood as an organic, living relationship between the God of freedom and the people who follow God. It connects the social, religious, and societal institutions of a people and calls for a faithful and effective response to the state in which the people find themselves. The covenant between God and God's people is central to the implementation of the faith that leads enslaved people of any era to their freedom from bondage and suffering.

The flight to freedom of the Hebrews and that of the African Methodists, though separated by millennia, are bound together by the commonality of covenant. The primary factor contributing to the African Methodists' embracing of Exodus was their identification with the condition of the enslaved Hebrews in the scriptural account. The noted historian Franklin E. Frazier, in his thought-provoking study, *The Negro Church in America,* gives insight into the role of religion among African slaves:

Then there were other factors in the situation that caused the slaves to respond to the forms of religious expression provided by the Baptists and Methodists. As we have indicated, the slaves who had been torn from their homeland and kinsmen and friends and whose cultural heritage was lost, were isolated and broken men, so to speak. In the emotionalism of the camp meetings and revivals some social solidarity, even if temporary, was achieved, and they were drawn into a union with their fellow men. Later, common religious beliefs and practices and traditions tended to provide a new basis of social cohesion in an alien environment....Not only did religion draw the Negroes into a union with their fellow men, it tended to break down barriers that isolated them morally from their white masters....[22]

The sense of social solidarity derived from their religious response allowed African Methodists the understanding and faithfulness sufficient to adapt Hebrew and Christian stories to their own experience. They refashioned the Hebrew tradition through the zealousness of Methodist preaching that spoke to the core of their victimization and suffering. Of particular comfort to the Africans within the Methodist Church were the powerful sermons preached around God's covenant with Abraham and promise of deliverance:

Then the Lord said to Abram, "Know this for certain, that your offspring shall be aliens in a land that is not theirs, and shall be slaves there, and they shall be oppressed for four hundred years; but I will bring judgment on the nation that they serve, and afterward they shall come out with great possessions."...On that day the Lord made a covenant with Abram, saying, "To your descendants I give this land, from the river of Egypt to the great river, the river Euphrates...." (Genesis 15, 13-14, 18)

The story of Abraham, as preached in the passionate style of men like Richard Allen and Absalom Jones, struck a chord of hope in the minds and hearts of Black Methodists. Blacks exhibited a strong belief that their strength came from God's covenant. They believed their prayers would be answered in God's promise to Abraham: "I am your shield; your reward shall be very great" (Genesis 15:1b). As life in God brought strength and hope to Abraham, so it would also strengthen and empower African Methodists so long as they lived faithful lives in covenant with God.

During slavery and after it was ended, the constant burden borne by Blacks, who were forced to live as second-class believers within the life of the Methodist Episcopal Church, called forth from them the oft-repeated rallying cry: "Let my people go!" For Black Methodists, past and present, God is the strength that undergirds their existence and the very hope and promise for a brighter future for their children. Like Abraham, members of the AME, AMEZ, and CME churches discovered that when they trusted in God the most, they were the strongest in their belief that God would honor the promise of covenant with a people living in a strange land.

Abraham and his African Methodist counterparts trusted the voice of God that called them out in order to send them forward. They discovered that deliverance comes from God, not from good works or from a process of the law. God's covenant of freedom did not begin with the story of Moses but went back to Abraham and even to God's creation of the world, which God declared to be good. That freedom traced a path through the desert to the Promised Land, from exile to return, and even through the story of God, whose very self was free to come to earth as Jesus Christ and free to die on the cross for the salvation of each person's freedom. Today, in the spiritual, "Oh, Freedom," we can lift up our voices and sing about the covenant: "Oh, freedom! Oh, freedom! Oh, freedom all over me when I am free! And before I'd be a slave, I'll be buried in my grave, and go home to my Lord and be free."[23] ("Oh, Freedom," *Songs of Zion,* "Negro Spirituals," 102)

Endnotes

1. "Go Down, Moses," *The United Methodist Hymnal,* op. cit., no. 448, v. 10; *Songs of Zion,* op. cit., no. 112, v. 17.

2. "Go Down Moses," *The United Methodist Hymnal,* no. 448, v. 4; *Songs of Zion,* no. 112, v. 18.

3. "Go Down, Moses," *The United Methodist Hymnal,* no. 448, v. 7; *Songs of Zion,* no. 112, v. 10

4. Portions of this song also appear in *The United Methodist Hymnal*, no. 135, as the "Canticle of Moses and Miriam."

5. Lois E. Horton, "The Days of Jubilee: Black Migration During the Civil War and Reconstruction," in Francine Curro Cary, ed., *Urban Odyssey,* op. cit., p. 65. In the Hebrew scriptures (see Leviticus 25:8-17), the year of jubilee was to be observed every fiftieth year, during which slaves were to be set free and debts forgiven.

6. *The World Book Encyclopedia,* op. cit., vol. 4, "Civil War: Results," p. 492.

7. Weisberger, op. cit., "Compromise of 1850," pp. 327-329; *The World Book Encyclopedia,* vol. 4, p. 739.

8. Lois E. Horton, op. cit., p. 66.

9. *Ebony Pictorial History of Black America,* op. cit., p. 246.

10. Ibid., p. 272.

11. Elizabeth Clark-Lewis, "'For a Real Better Life': Voices of African American Women Migrants, 1900-1930," in Francine Curro Cary, ed., *Urban Odyssey,* op. cit., p. 97.

12. Weisberger, op. cit., pp. 360-375; *The World Book Encyclopedia,* op. cit., vol. 16, "Reconstruction," pp. 168-172.

13. *Redlining* is the refusal of financial services, such as home mortgages or home insurance, to people living in minority neighborhoods because of stereotypes labeling these people as poor financial risks.

14. Richard Allen, op. cit., pp. 15-16.

15. Ibid., pp. 25-26.

16. Bishop J. W. Hood, *One Hundred Years of the African Methodist Episcopal Zion Church* (New York: African Methodist Episcopal Zion Book Concern, 1895), p. 3.

17. William J. Walls, *The African Methodist Episcopal Zion Church: Reality of the Black Church* (Charlotte, NC: A.M.E. Zion Publishing House, 1974), p. 45.

18. Othal Hawthorne Lakey, *The History of the CME Church (Revised)* (Memphis: The CME Publishing House, 1996), p. 138.

19. Milton C. Sernett, ed., *Afro-American Religious History: A Documentary Witness* (Durham: Duke University Press, 1985), p. 234.

20. Lakey, op. cit., p. 131.

21. Lucius H. Holsey, "The Colored Methodist Episcopal Church," in Sernett, ed., op. cit., p. 234.

22. Franklin E. Frazier, *The Negro Church in America* (New York: Schocken Books, 1963), pp. 8-9.

23. *Songs of Zion,* no. 102.

MIDWIVES OF JUSTICE

Never doubt that a small group of thoughtful, committed citizens can change the world.

—*Margaret Mead[1]*

In every generation, there are those who tell women how powerless we are and how whatever we have accomplished has been because men "allowed" us to do it. Nevertheless, in every generation, women come into their own despite the special obstacles of their particular time and place. Of course, there are women (as there are men) who weigh the consequences of resisting social injustice, and sometimes a woman must proceed with utmost care for her own survival and that of her children or other loved ones. Even so, many find a window of opportunity through which they glimpse a vision, find their voice, embrace their destiny—and stand up at just the right moment, in just the right place. We encounter these women in the story of the Exodus and in many other parts of the Bible. We meet them throughout history, active in the resistance to slavery and racism. We also find them sitting next to us in church today. And sometimes we find a woman like this in ourselves.

Midwives of Strategic Subversion

In chapter one of the Book of Exodus, the Egyptian Pharaoh, concerned over the number of Hebrews in his land, instructed the Hebrew midwives to kill all the male newborns of the Hebrew women at the moment of their birth.

> The king of Egypt said to the Hebrew midwives, one of whom was named Shiphrah and the other Puah, "When you act as midwives to the Hebrew

women, and see them on the birthstool, if it is a boy, kill him; but if it is a girl, she shall live." (Exodus 1:15-16)

The two Hebrew midwives, Shiphrah and Puah, strategically subverted the king's edict by allowing all of the male babies to be born. These strong women of faith disobeyed Pharaoh and risked their own safety by ignoring his order. But the midwives were ingenious in their strategy for saving the lives of God's people. When they were summoned to Pharaoh's court, charged with failing to follow a royal decree, they cleverly made use of the dominant culture's stereotyped beliefs about Hebrews. "...The Hebrew women are not like the Egyptian women," they said, "for they are vigorous and give birth before the midwife comes to them" (Exodus 1:19). These two women of courage, Shiphrah and Puah, laid the foundation for the Hebrew people to survive—and, in fact, thrive—under difficult circumstances.

Pharaoh continued with his schemes by next giving an order to all his people. "Every boy that is born to the Hebrews you shall throw into the Nile," he said, "but you shall let every girl live" (Exodus 1:22). The women of God would have to develop another strategic plan to subvert the evil of the times.

Biblical Women's Survival Plan

The actions of Shiphrah and Puah laid the groundwork for the plan of Moses' mother and his sister, Miriam. After hiding the baby Moses for three months, they decided to follow the letter of the law, while creating a strong likelihood that Moses would be saved from certain death. First, they would "throw" Moses into the Nile—but in a well-prepared and water-proofed basket. Moses' mother carefully placed the basket that held her baby in a strategic spot—among the reeds on the riverbank near the place where women from the palace came to bathe. Doubtless she knew that Moses could be saved only if an Egyptian family rescued and adopted him. In fact, Moses' mother and her daughter may well have been audacious enough to target the women of Pharaoh's court as the most desirable rescuers, counting on the assumption that the baby Moses would win their hearts. This conspiracy of women to save a child grew and crossed both race and class lines.

> The daughter of Pharaoh came down to bathe at the river, while her attendants walked beside the river. She saw the basket among the reeds and sent her maid to bring it. When she opened it, she saw the child. He was crying, and she took pity on him. "This must be one of the Hebrews' children," she said. Then his sister said to Pharaoh's daughter, "Shall I go and get you a nurse from the Hebrew women to nurse the child for you?" Pharaoh's daughter said to her, "Yes." So the girl went and called the child's mother. Pharaoh's daughter said to her, "Take this child and nurse it for me, and I will give you your wages." So the woman took the child and nursed it. When the child grew up, she brought him to Pharaoh's daughter, and she took him as her son. She named him Moses, "because," she said, "I drew him out of the water." (Exodus 2:5-10)

Perhaps the princess had wondered out loud about finding a surrogate mother to nurse the infant. We can almost hear her speculating in a raised voice to make sure anyone nearby would hear. Or perhaps Miriam, appearing at just the right moment with her helpful suggestion, prompted the princess's affirmative reply. Whoever spoke first, the woman and the girl conspired together without voicing the treason in which both were participating. Instead, they agreed on a win-win solution that benefited both. So Miriam took her baby brother Moses back to his terribly anxious, then greatly relieved and extremely thankful mother. And so it was that Moses' own mother nursed him until it was time for him to assume his place in Pharaoh's court as a royal child.

But what about the courage of the attendants of the princess, who also deceived Pharaoh and did not follow his command? Because of the king's edict, the princess's attendants could easily have become the scapegoats if anything had gone wrong. It took courage to rescue the basket containing the Hebrew baby. It took courage and a commitment to justice and faith for the princess of Egypt to bring a Hebrew child into the royal palace. The attendants risked their lives while participating in this strategic subversion.

Pharaoh might have forgiven his daughter, who may have been barren, but his wrath could easily have fallen on those who served her.

The princess identified with the suffering of the Hebrew women and honored the God of the Hebrews with her actions. The princess further honored the birthright of her adopted child by allowing him to be suckled by his mother and to be exposed to his Hebrew culture.

> The Hebrew mother nursed him. The point is that Moses was a real Israelite. In ancient Hebrew as in current Arabic thinking, ethnic solidarity is established by the suckling of the infant. Israelites took equal pride in the notion that the child was nursed by his Hebrew mother and that he was adopted by a princess of Egypt. As a deliverer he must belong to Israel as well as to Egypt; and the bond with Israel is more profound.[2]

Moses experienced Hebrew life and culture in his early, formative years and was able to compare that culture to the rich and privileged way of life he later encountered in the palace. His earlier experiences allowed Moses to identify with the suffering of the Hebrews, while understanding that not all Egyptians participated in the evil of enslavement. Later, while he was passing as an Egyptian in the palace, Moses experienced love from his Egyptian mother and her attendants. Perhaps Pharaoh knew that the princess had not given birth and that this was probably a Hebrew child. If so, Moses may have been accepted by the Pharaoh because of his love for his daughter and his belief that, if the child was raised as an Egyptian, his future would be certain. Who could resist Egyptian privilege?

Shiphrah, Puah, Moses' mother, Miriam, and Pharaoh's daughter all took dangerous risks in order to save children. In the end, they saved the future of the entire Hebrew people. Shiphrah and Puah played on popular stereotypes; Miriam and her mother followed the rules but found the loopholes; and the Egyptian princess and her attendants used their relatively privileged positions to place themselves above the law, while pretending ignorance of their infractions. In each case, oppressive laws were subverted, and Pharaoh, despite all his power, did not have the final word. Through the women's resistance, God placed a Hebrew with a mission in the midst of Pharaoh's court.

Each of the five women named at the beginning of the Exodus story—the two midwives, the mother, the sister, and the princess—experienced a type of burning bush in her life and accepted the calling. Today, women face the repressive powers of the world and still walk away with the victory when God calls them to the task. Like Moses, we have rarely felt ourselves to be the best equipped for the job; but, despite this, we have faced the fire and journeyed through the wilderness to seek God's justice and freedom.

American Women Confront Racism

Racism is a formidable opponent—a chameleon, changing outwardly in its forms but resistant to change in its essence. Once established deep within the mind and the emotions, it is extremely hard to eradicate. It leads the mind along the crooked path of prejudice, which has always had the purpose of misleading God's people, bringing us to the belief that inequalities in status are fixed and immutable and that sin and suffering are simple realities that everyone has to accept.

Despite this, throughout history, many have resisted racism's subtle and insidious brainwashing. Though their story is not often told, there were White women before and during the Civil War who spoke out against slavery and utilized diverse techniques of resistance. White female abolitionists reminded their husbands of the Word of God, nurtured the antislavery movement, and spoke out publicly, often risking their own reputations and well-being.

White women in the North participated in the Union cause during the Civil War. Besides sending their sons off to fight, some provided refuge to Union soldiers, while others secretly carried important messages, documents, and manifests, and a few even risked their lives as spies. In both the North and the South, White women volunteered in the army camps–cooking, doing the washing, nursing the injured, and helping to bury the dead. It was at this time of dire need that Clara Barton seized her window of opportunity and stood up at just the right moment. Following the example of the British nursing pioneer Florence Nightingale in the Crimean War in Europe, Ms. Barton set up a system of battlefield nursing that saved the lives of countless Union soldiers. After the war ended, Clara Barton went on to found the American Red Cross.

Many Southern White women supported the institution of slavery. The small minority who belonged to wealthy slave-owning families benefited from the privileged lifestyle that such families enjoyed at the expense of their human "property." Wealthy women were well-indoctrinated into the systematic oppression of captive African laborers. But many or most Southern women in the nonslaveholding majority had also been carefully taught to support the institution of slavery. Since, for White Southerners, the "War Between the States" was waged in defense of the Southern way of life—which included and, in many respects, rested upon the enslavement of Blacks—Southern families at all economic levels sent their sons to the slaughter.

On the other hand, before the war, Southern White women sometimes educated Black slaves, breaking local laws and violating social custom. Some of them could clearly see the evils and injustices of slavery. They wanted to make changes in both private practices and public policies that made racism an integral part of their region's way of life. These women shared their convictions and concerns with other women, risking banishment from the social structure of their communities if they happened to catch an unsympathetic ear. The bolder ones assisted the Underground Railroad and encouraged their churches and other community groups to get involved in order to effect social change.

Before and after the Civil War, Black and White women of faith in both North and South were instrumental in the struggle to heal spiritual wounds and to root out racist beliefs, attitudes, and practices. These sisters in spirit took strong stands against injustice. They challenged those around them to reconcile with the God of freedom and with all of humankind.

Harriet Beecher Stowe: The Power of the Pen

Harriet Beecher Stowe (1811-1896) was the daughter of Lyman Beecher, a

New England Protestant theologian, and the sister of Catherine Beecher, a reformist educator, and Henry Ward Beecher, a Protestant minister, editor, and abolitionist leader. She chose to raise her own voice for the abolitionist cause not through speeches, sermons, or editorials but through a novel, *Uncle Tom's Cabin: Life Among the Lowly.* It was serialized in an antislavery paper in 1851, published as a bestselling book in 1852, and later translated into at least 23 languages. The book was based on Ms. Stowe's own knowledge and experience gained during travels in the South and during the 18 years that she lived in Cincinnati, Ohio, with only the Ohio River separating her home from a slave-holding community in Kentucky. In Cincinnati, she had first-hand contact with fugitive slaves escaping across the river and journeying north along local routes of the Underground Railroad.[3]

By creating memorable characters—such as Uncle Tom, Little Eva, Topsy, and Eliza—and by bringing the evils of slavery to life in vivid and affecting scenes—such as those involving the cruel slave master, Simon Legree—Ms. Stowe had an overwhelming impact on public opinion, especially in the North and abroad. For the first time, White Americans had a strong fictional picture of the fundamental evil and utter inhumanity of slavery, because they could experience its impact on characters in the book that they had come to know and care about. They now had an unforgettable portrait of the poverty, exploitation, abuse, and suffering visited upon Black slaves in their country. They could no longer live in ignorance of the consequences of slavery or unlearn the moral lessons Ms. Stowe had taught them. Given the widespread controversy that the novel stirred up—the strong emotions that Ms. Stowe aroused in her readers—President Abraham Lincoln greeted her with the comment: "So you're the little woman who wrote the book that made this great war!"[4]

Not only was Harriet Beecher Stowe's novel used as a sociopolitical sword in her own day, when it was a critical weapon in the fight against the sin of slavery and for the human rights of the people held as slaves, it has also influenced later works of art. For example, exactly 100 years after the first episodes of *Uncle Tom's Cabin* appeared, Richard Rodgers and Oscar Hammerstein II used the story to great effect in their American musical *The*

King and I (1951), set in nineteenth-century Siam. It inspired a ballet that is central to the musical, called "The Small House of Uncle Thomas," put on by Siamese slaves of the king. No one who has seen the stage or film version of *The King and I* can forget the frantic singing of the chorus, "Run, Eliza, run from Simon!" as the slave Eliza, fleeing with her baby across the ice of the frozen Ohio River, tries to escape the slave catchers set upon her by Simon Legree. His name is now justly synonymous with "a slave driver or brutal master." But Uncle Tom, whose name has come to mean "a subservient Black person, deferential to Whites," was actually both dignified and brave in the Stowe novel, choosing to die rather than betray other slaves who were trying to escape.

Few popular writers have ever had as great an impact as Harriet Beecher Stowe. As an advocate, agitator, and political instigator, she enraged White Southerners, but she forced White Americans in the North to face what they were allowing to happen. Beyond this, she spurred the abolitionists on to take corrective action so as not to forfeit the future of freedom in the United States.

The Underground Railroad Women

The story of Harriet Tubman's life as a conductor on the Underground Railroad has already been told in chapter one. Still, more might be said about the role of White and Black abolitionist women in the operation of this South-to-North escape route for runaway slaves. Some women provided assistance in the form of money and food. Some lent the runaway slaves their identities to help them along the way. Others spread the word of the passengers' progress through secret grapevines. Women also helped to find safe places where the fleeing slaves could hide, rest, and eat. Some churches and public establishments allowed their basements and storehouses to be used as "stations" in this way. The Quakers were instrumental in raising funds to help maintain the Underground Railroad. Southern Whites who opposed the system of slavery also aided the movement. White women who supported freedom often acted as buffers for the escaping Africans and spearheaded the travel arrangements from one tunnel, river, town, and barn to the next.

Harriet Tubman escaped to the North and then returned to the South, time after time, to guide others to freedom. Some other escaped slaves remained in the South, in hiding, to help others get away. All such selfless Blacks demonstrated enormous courage because they remained at risk of being caught and returned to slavery themselves. Some of them raised money and provided homes for the new fugitives who were seeking liberty. These Blacks, along with the White abolitionists who aided the escapees, did so despite the fact that federal fugitive slave laws not only imperiled the escaping slaves but also threatened those who aided and abetted them. Among them all, Harriet Tubman was one of the greatest heroes and she was aptly compared with Moses for her bold, courageous leadership. Through brave actions and inspiring words, the two Harriets, one Black, one White—Harriet Tubman and Harriet Beecher Stowe—advanced the journey to freedom.

Methodist Women in the Vanguard

> Our predecessor organizations once belonged to a flourishing company of relatively autonomous women's missionary societies. Methodism and United Methodism enjoy some distinctions, but being at the periphery is not usually counted among them!
>
> —Theressa Hoover [5]

Pre-Civil War Methodist women were not sidelined on the periphery of the action but were committed reformers, actively involved in the issues of their time, just as United Methodist Women are today. Like their present-day sisters, these nineteenth-century women were in the vanguard of social movements that were to change the ways in which people lived in the United States. They were part of the guiding force of the Abolitionist Movement, whose object was to end slavery and free American Blacks, and they were movers and shakers in the Suffrage Movement, working tirelessly to win for American women the right to vote.

It would be naïve for us to think that White Methodist women in the

South did not feel for the pains of those who suffered under the conditions of slavery. There are surely countless untold stories of White Southern women who assisted the Underground Railroad and spoke out against their husbands' sexual abuse of female slaves. Many Southern women, including many Methodists, helped empower slaves by teaching them skills and giving them a primary education.

After the Civil War, this educational effort continued and was increased. Some White Methodist women came from the North to the South as teacher-missionaries with the purpose of educating former slaves. There were also White women in the South who assisted in the post-war effort. Both Northern and Southern Methodist women felt they could help heal the wounds of racism through reaching out and teaching the victims, giving them access to the education they had been denied for so long.

However, freedom—and even education—for the former slaves did not mean equality. Racial segregation, with White dominance in all spheres of activity, was the established practice in both North and South. Both White and Black women were denied full citizenship, lacking the right to vote, and both lived in a world dominated by White males in government, church, and society. But still, despite what they had in common, these women remained separated by race. Yet it was Methodist women in the vanguard, on both sides of the racial divide, who made some of the first moves to reach across that chasm and join forces.

Sojourner Truth: Called to Preach

One of the most prominent Black women among the pre- and post-war Methodist activists was Sojourner Truth. Like Harriet Tubman, she was a member of the African Methodist Episcopal Zion Church.

Sojourner Truth was the activist name taken by Isabella Baumfree (1797?-1883), one of the most famous abolitionists of her time. Born into slavery in Ulster County, New York, she was freed in 1828, thanks to the New York State Emancipation Act of 1827. In 1843, when she was about forty-six years old, she experienced a call from God to preach. As part of her call, she took the name Sojourner Truth. A *sojourner* is someone who resides in a place only briefly—a temporary resident, not a permanent one. By her new name, Isabella Baumfree was saying that she was just a temporary resident of this world but that, while she was here, passing through, she would spread the truth—and speak it boldly. Given her quick thinking and ready wit, her eloquence as an orator, her deep, imposing voice, and her strong, unshakable faith, she became the first Black woman to condemn slavery and call for abolition as a public speaker. Her speaking tours took her throughout New England and the Midwest. There, she taught that showing love and concern for other people was the best way to express love for God, and she called openly for the end of slavery.

During the Civil War, Sojourner Truth raised money to buy gifts for the Union soldiers and went into their camps to deliver these presents. She even visited President Abraham Lincoln in the White House in 1864, and she remained in Washington, D. C., to help find homes and jobs for slaves who had escaped and to work for better living conditions for all of Washington's Black residents. After the war, she tried without success to get the U. S. government to set aside some Western lands for Blacks to own as farms.[6]

Women Organize for Mission

Another forward movement for women took place during the three decades following the Civil War. It was then that women in our predecessor denominations—the Methodist Episcopal Church; the Methodist Episcopal Church, South; the Methodist Protestant Church; the Church of the United Brethren in Christ; and the United Evangelical Church—were organizing for mission. Weary of watching the men in the churches make all the decisions, and concerned by the fact that the needs of women and children were not being met by an all-male missionary corps, small groups of women decided to start mission societies of their own. As Theressa Hoover has pointed out:

In general, our predecessors did not claim leadership on the basis of exceptional spiritual gifts, nor were they called to the preaching ministry.

Instead they were inspired to meet the combined evangelical, physical, and social needs of marginal people—especially women and children, who could not be reached by male missionaries abroad and who were ignored by church and society at home.[7]

Both church and society often overlooked the needs of women and children under the misguided belief that their welfare depended on the good offices of male family members. In the United States, men were the sole heads of their households and held legal power over their wives and children. Male power was even more absolute in other parts of the world. Early in the church's missionary efforts, Methodist men traveled abroad to areas such as Africa and India, seeking to evangelize new populations. Traveling in patriarchal societies, they soon found that they were not allowed even to talk to women in many of the countries they visited, much less to give the women medical treatment or to educate them. So the church decided to send married couples to these countries to perform evangelistic work.

Once activist Methodist women decided to organize for mission themselves, they began to raise money to support their efforts. Other Methodist women responded to the activists' cries from the wilderness by funding both foreign mission service and local charity, thus enabling women to prepare for mission duty at home and abroad.

Like Moses, these Methodist women in mission prayed to God for strength and direction, assessed their needs, and didn't allow the known risks to deter them. Mission efforts abroad strengthened the courage of women in the United States who were challenging sexism, racism, and poverty in their own country and communities. Methodist women in mission took action: they built schools, hospitals, community centers, and transitional homes for women and children. More importantly, they changed the role of women in the church, the image of women in society, and the face of Christian mission as they responded personally to Christ's Great Commission. The Abolitionist Movement had shown many women what they could achieve when they worked together. Now God was calling them again to speak out.

Post-Civil War American women brought the model of foreign missionary service to the United States, where they replicated missionary patterns of service. Such service involved health care, education, Bible study, and speaking out against social ills and injustice. The women were also faced with the struggle of maintaining their autonomy within the larger church, which resisted the women's plan to organize their own missionary groups. As Theressa Hoover has observed:

> ...Once the initial fervor of foreign missions had passed, churchmen were uneasy with women's skillful direction of their own corporations, without the slightest need of male supervision. A situation not controlled in a proper gender hierarchy was less untidy than it was threatening.[8]

Male leaders believed that women could not possibly manage even local efforts—much less global ones. As a result, since the men maintained church-wide control, women's organizations in all branches of Methodism had male oversight. Either the men were members themselves or they were represented by the bishops' wives, who spoke for and reported to their husbands. Thus, as Theressa Hoover has noted, the women were denied autonomy:

> In view of churchwomen's talent in their work and joy in their autonomy, it is painful to relate that between 1910 and 1964, male interests and perspectives prevailed. Every quasi-autonomous women's mission organization, including our own [United Methodist Women], was integrated [by gender]. Despite varying degrees of resistance and expressed outrage, the women leaders were in most cases co-opted.[9]

Sojourner Truth would have well understood what these women were up against. Though she vowed, "I must sojourn once to the ballot box before I die," she was not to realize that goal, despite her talent and strength of spirit.[10]

Strategies on the Road to Freedom

In the years before and after the Civil War, American women worked in the Temperance (anti-drinking) Movement and launched the Woman Suffrage

Movement, confronting the power structures that excluded them as women or that jeopardized their families. Women in New Jersey had the right to vote for 20 years, only to see it taken away in 1807. Four decades passed before Elizabeth Cady Stanton and Lucretia Mott called their famous Women's Rights Convention in Seneca Falls, New York, in 1848. But frontier women proved more successful in winning the franchise than their Eastern sisters. The first three states to give women the right to vote were Wyoming in 1890, Colorado in 1893, and Idaho in 1896. By the time the Woman Suffrage Amendment became law in 1920, women could already vote in 15 states, mostly in the West. [11]

The Challenge of Social Change

Female missionaries were also a vital part of the battle against discrimination. They became advocates for change by speaking, writing, and establishing forums where they could meet and share their viewpoints. They strove to be a part of America's new growth in medicine, science, agriculture, journalism, education, and many other career fields that had traditionally been closed to women. Women supported each other financially and spiritually in what was to be the next frontier for their advancement. Their challenge was to bring about social change for women of all colors and nationalities. To reach this goal, they used the following mission tools:

- They prayed for strength, courage, and direction.
- They identified the need and assessed the problem.
- They organized around an issue or purpose.
- They developed methods for raising and managing funds.
- They empowered communities for action.
- They educated others and planted seeds of hope.
- They built facilities that allowed for continuity and community.
- They confronted structural resistance when they encountered it.
- They planned meetings with other groups of women in order to strengthen bonds, develop solidarity, and narrow racial divides by seeking common ground.

White Methodist women raised their awareness by learning that Black and White women shared some common threads of oppression and suffering. Each group was denied equal partnership with men in the United States. Each group was denied the franchise, being forbidden to vote. Each group was devalued and oppressed. Both groups saw their children caught in the stranglehold of a developing economic system that overvalued male leadership and undervalued the role and contributions of women and family.

White women were left out of the plans for the new U. S. power structure, while African women were treated as workhorses, considered fit only for heavy, low-paid labor and for breeding an exploited labor force that kept commerce and racism working hand in glove. In this new power structure, African women worked in the fields as sharecroppers and in privileged White homes as maids and surrogate mothers, providing their employers with domestic labor along with part-time parenting of their children.

White and Black women had individual stories, separate pains and griefs, and different historical contexts. But their common experiences of discrimination beckoned Methodist women of black skin and white skin to meet at the crossroads and find common ground.

Women's Day and Heritage Day

There is a tradition in the African American church that extends beyond denominational lines; it is called "Women's Day." This is a time in the life of the church when congregations reflect on and celebrate the stewardship, leadership, and missionary work of the church's women. Women's Day officially began in 1907 in Washington, D.C. It was founded by Nannie Helen Burroughs, a well-known civic leader. Because she appreciated the work of churchwomen in advancing the life of Christian women and families, Ms. Burroughs began the tradition of recognizing them and celebrating their accomplishments.

Yet, although African American history records 1907 as the inception of the practice, we know that Women's Day actually began several millennia earlier with the Hebrew midwives Shiphrah and Puah. They planned their strategy with great ingenuity and took a stand for women. Then

Moses' mother, his sister Miriam, and Pharaoh's daughter declared Women's Day when they contrived to save the baby Moses' life. It was Women's Day when Miriam sang her song of celebration and led all the Hebrew women in the singing. Let us also proclaim that Women's Day happened when the unnamed Hebrew women who lived in the land of Goshen in Egypt prepared the lamb and the unleavened bread of the Passover feast—and when they held the hands of the children and helped the elderly and infirm as they crossed the Red Sea. Moses might have been the leader and the hero, but the women's involvement in successfully carrying out the plan was pivotal.

After the Civil War, Black women kept the church alive while also keeping their heritage alive. As former slaves migrated to the North in search of a better life, the women found that, as domestic workers, they were not allowed time off to visit family members in the South. Even those few who had the time to travel found it too costly or too unsafe for them to do so. So women in Black churches—including those in the AME, the AMEZ, the CME, and the Methodist Episcopal churches—organized such events as North Carolina Days and South Carolina Days in order to remember their past on the rich soils of Africa and in the Southern United States. At Heritage Days, these newly freed women—who had to work on Sundays, cooking and serving Sunday dinner for White families—carved out time to unite with friends and relatives and to share their memories of the past and hopes for the future. Social clubs developed in these local churches, and fundraisers were held there, geared toward helping these hard-working, often young, Black women save up enough money to go "down home" for a visit.

Women Unite to Fight Lynching

One important cause that Black and White Methodist women had in common was their opposition to lynching. Whether from the North or the South and whether members of the AME, AMEZ, CME, or Methodist Episcopal churches, they began to lift voices of protest.

Once freedom from slavery was won, Methodist churchwomen turned their attention to women's political rights and to the ongoing struggle against racism in the church and in society. It was obvious that the Methodist Episcopal Church, whether in the North or South, was not yet ready to take a firm stand against racism and sexism in the United States. It was equally obvious that the White men who held political power in the South after Reconstruction were not doing nearly enough to end the lynching of Black men. Lynching involved the instant execution, usually by hanging, of men suspected of wrongdoing, without due process of law.

Many White women were numbered among the 40,000 members of the Association of Southern Women for the Prevention of Lynching. Significantly, they began to question the White male claim that lynching was a means of protecting the purity of White women and girls by instantly avenging offenses against them. Instead, the women clearly saw the ugly face of racism behind the men's rush to murderous mob violence and vigilante "justice." The actions and statements of the White women in the Association for the Prevention of Lynching had a powerful effect on perception, making it more difficult for racist mobs to justify their actions by claiming to be acting on the women's behalf.

The women also used public forums and education to advocate for the rights of Black men who were wrongly accused and persecuted. This advocacy required courage, because any White Southerner who publicly defended former slaves who were acting "uppity"—that is, acting as though they were free and equal—was considered subversive.

Also, Southern White women developed educational programs that trained former slaves to be missionaries, deaconesses, and educators. When strings were not attached (as they often were), this type of assistance helped empower former slaves to become independent and self-supporting. The White women also purchased and developed centers in major cities and rural areas where Black people could find help. Centers dedicated to working with former slaves were developed and managed in bureaus concerned with educational institutions, medical work, social work, town and country work, and urban work. These centers of social change and empowerment, such as the Bethlehem Centers, still exist today throughout the United States.

Interracial Dialogues

In 1920, the year women got the vote, middle-class Black women established a number of vital, influential community organizations. Some began to have dialogues with White women about the injustices in U.S. society. Among these women were Mary McLeod Bethune and Lugenia Burns Hope—founders, respectively, of the National Council of Negro Women and the Neighborhood Union in Atlanta.[12] From these efforts came numerous civic organizations committed to improving race relations, including the Commission on Interracial Cooperation. Southern White women who were not willing to serve as an excuse for racism and Black women who wanted a different future for their children came together there and found common bonds. Black women believed that, by working with activist groups of White women in confronting the nation's social ills, their faithful action and committed witness could change history. The women chose as their organizing strategy interracial dialogues and studies on race relationships. Though there was limited commitment on the other side, since some White women could clearly see the evils of lynching but could not perceive any problem with segregation, nevertheless the White women accepted the journey as their social responsibility. It was their work in racial relations, especially in the anti-lynching effort, that turned increasing numbers of Methodist churchwomen into political activists. As Alice Knotts observed:

> Methodist women became aware of issues of power and privilege inherent in racism, especially through their experiences on account of gender. When studying racism, white women recognized parallels with the second-class treatment they received in the name of being proper and appropriate. They began to question and [to] cross traditional social boundaries of gender and race.

> In the 1930s, leaders of the WMC [Women's Missionary Council] advocated changing their mission emphasis from work *for* to work *with* women of color. The WMC's program of interracial work quickly reflect-

ed the objectives of the ten-year program of the revitalized thirty-six member Women's Committee of the CIC [Commission on Interracial Cooperation]. Methodist women developed sustained race relations programs characterized by committee work and local efforts. Of the many race-related activities of Methodist women in the 1930s, the anti-lynching effort proved to be the largest, best supported, and most sustained. It moved churchwomen into political action.[13]

Besides their race-relations programs and interracial dialogues, Methodist women also used the strategy of gathering information on acts of racism and monitoring occurrences. Dorothy Tilly, a noted Methodist woman from Atlanta, was responsible for tracking planned lynchings and for organizing women to protest and confront the lynching parties in an effort to prevent such abuse. A third strategy involved taking political action—demanding that the criminal-justice system try those who committed such crimes and insisting that the vigilante injustice of lynching cease.

Methodist women actively engaged in anti-lynching dialogues. They spoke out against all individuals and institutions that were apathetic and allowed racism to permeate institutional structures. The women created an atmosphere of caring and took those strengths into their Methodist Church and their nation to demand freedom from prejudice and racism. They drew on the teachings of Jesus Christ, Moses, and John Wesley. This groundswell of courage and fortitude created dynamic leaders such as Thelma Stevens, Theressa Hoover, Peggy Billings, Cora Ratliff, and Susie Jones, to name a few of the Methodist women who were beacons of hope lighting the way. Under the auspices of the Women's Division, Methodist women planned and orchestrated this segment of the Methodist Church's exodus from racism.

Initially, White women thought that they would teach Black women how to influence social movements; but they soon realized that they had much to learn themselves and that, even in the midst of the wider effort, they would have to struggle personally with cleansing, healing, and reconciling their own racist belief systems. In fact, White paternalism and maternalism threatened to compromise the movement in the 1940s. White women in the South tried to take on the dual role of being "Miss Jane" in the big house and God's servant in the church as they tried to convince Black women to take the path of least resistance. The path of least resistance meant that Black people would be given some of their constitutional rights, but they would still be segregated in schools, churches, social clubs, public transportation, housing, and other areas.

Privileged White women learned that God challenges the Pharaohs of racism and that God's demand to "let my people go" is not satisfied by a negotiated, compromised, or gradual movement. Black women knew that they had "come this far by faith, leaning on the Lord" and they were not willing to settle for only one part of the package. In fact, Black women weren't willing even to take off the wrapping of the package if the contents were not complete, bringing them full inclusion. Separate and not equal was the bargain the Pharaoh of racism offered God, and God said to Methodist women, Black and White: "Go back to Pharaoh and demand that he 'let my people go!'" God wanted Black women to be free and equal, and God wanted White women to be free from the bonds that separated them from women of color. God wanted all to appreciate the beauty of diversity in the Creation. So, in voices of harmony, White women and Black women called for equal access to public facilities and accommodations, which included churches. Meanwhile, in light of World War II, other Methodist leaders turned their attention to issues of national peace, often overlooking issues of *local* peace and the church's urgent need to be healed from the plague of racism.

The Methodist Federation for Social Action championed the cause of equality and provided yet another platform around which women could organize their efforts. The Federation had opposed the separation of the segregated Central Jurisdiction from the rest of the reunited Methodist Church in 1939. After the separation occurred, socially conscious church leaders turned their attention away from the institutional racism in the church and began to organize within their groups and communities to eradicate racism in the United States. The models they developed later became tools for social change in the church itself. The women in the Federation also worked on legislation to eliminate the terrorist system of lynching in America.

Mary McLeod Bethune: Advisor to Presidents

Mary McLeod Bethune (1875-1955) was deeply committed to education from her earliest childhood. She was born in Mayesville, South Carolina, the seventeenth child of parents who were freed from slavery just 10 years before her birth. At that time, there was no school for her to attend, and she had to wait until age 10 to begin her education at a mission school. Eagerly, she learned to read, and she quickly made up for lost time, going on to graduate from Scotia Seminary in Concord, North Carolina, and from the Moody Bible Institute in faraway Chicago, Illinois, where she was the only Black student.

Returning to the South to teach in various mission schools, Ms. Bethune then moved to Florida, where she opened her own school in 1904 in a rented cottage in Daytona Beach. She began with $1.50 in cash, five students, and unlimited faith. In 1923, her Daytona Normal and Industrial Institute for Girls was merged with the Cookman Institute for Men, and Bethune-Cookman College, a United Methodist institution, was born. Ms. Bethune served as the college president from 1923 to 1942 and again from 1946 to 1947.

During and after her college presidency, four U.S. Presidents—Calvin Coolidge, Herbert Hoover, Franklin D. Roosevelt, and Harry Truman—called Ms. Bethune into government service. In the Roosevelt Administration, she was Special Advisor on Minority Affairs (1935-1944); and, as Director of the Division of Negro Affairs in the National Youth Administration (1936-1944), she became the first Black woman ever to head a U. S. government agency. In this capacity, she created the unofficial "Black Cabinet" of Roosevelt's New Deal. In 1935, the year that she founded the National Council of Negro Women, the National Association for the Advancement of Colored People (NAACP) awarded her the Spingarn Medal, recognizing her as the Black person who had reached the highest level of achievement that year. Not only was Ms. Bethune a vice president of the NAACP but in World War II, she advised the Secretary of War in selecting officer candidates for the Women's Army Auxiliary Corps. And, at the war's end, in 1945, she was a consultant on interracial under-standing for the U. S. State Department at the founding conference of the

United Nations. In 1974, a national memorial was erected to honor her in Washington, D. C. A lifelong Methodist, Mary McLeod Bethune helped to educate and to break barriers for the Black women who followed her.[14]

Undertaking an Exodus From Racism

In addition to her college and government work, Mary McLeod Bethune was a member of the Department of Christian Social Relations in the Women's Division of the Board of Missions. In the course of her career, she joined the Methodist Federation for Social Action, increasing its diversity and bringing a new perspective to its work. Other great organizations, such as the NAACP, worked with the Women's Division to increase the number of people opposing racism and to strengthen the message condemning it. Thus, just as God influenced the minds of the people of Egypt to give the Hebrews the resources they needed for their journey out of slavery, various organizations brought their own gifts and resources together for use in the journey out of racism. And women from all of the various branches of Methodism came together to confront the plague of prejudice that had sickened God's people for so long and to steer the people onward in the path of an exodus.

From Shiphrah and Puah, to abolitionists and anti-lynching advocates, down to today's anti-racial-profiling activists, women spoke out about God's message of freedom, justice, and love.

Endnotes

1. See *The New Beacon Book of Quotations by Women,* Rosalie Maggio, ed. (Boston: Beacon Press, 1996), p. 7, which includes a variant version of this quotation, See also the website: www.mead2001.org/timeline.html. Click FAQ (frequently asked questions) and then click "What is the source of the 'Never doubt...' quote?" It states: "Although the institute has received many inquiries about this famous admonition by Margaret Mead, we have been unable to locate when and where it was first cited, becoming a motto for many organizations and movements....We know, however, that it...reflected a conviction that she expressed often, in different contexts and phrasings."

2. *The Interpreter's Bible* (Nashville: Abingdon Press, 1952), vol. 1, *General Articles on the Bible, General Articles on the Old Testament, The Book of Genesis and The Book of Exodus,* p. 860, note 9.

3. See *The World Book Encyclopedia,* op. cit., vol. 18, "Stowe, Harriet Beecher," p. 723, and vol. 20, "Uncle Tom's Cabin," pp. 12-13. See also *Encyclopaedia Britannica* (Chicago: Encyclopaedia Britannica, Inc., 1961), vol. 21, "Stowe, Harriet Elizabeth Beecher," p. 445.

4. The source of this quotation is Carl Sandburg's *Abraham Lincoln: The War Years* (1936), vol. 2, ch. 19. See Elizabeth Knowles, ed., *The Oxford Dictionary of Quotations,* 5th ed. (Oxford: Oxford University Press, 1999), p. 469.

5. Theressa Hoover, *With Unveiled Face: Centennial Reflections on Women and Men in the Community of the Church* (New York: Women's Division, General Board of Global Ministries, 1983), p. 13.

6. See *The World Book Encyclopedia,* op. cit., vol. 19, "Truth, Sojourner," p. 387. See also Weisberger, op. cit., "Sojourner Truth," p. 323.

7. Theressa Hoover, op. cit., p. 13.

8. Ibid., p. 16.

9. Ibid.

10. Weisberger, op. cit., p. 323.

11. See *The World Book Encyclopedia,* op. cit., vol. 21, "Woman Suffrage," p. 322.

12. For more information about Lugenia Burns Hope and the Neighborhood Union, see

the website: http://www.auctr.edu/arch/nuc.htm.

13. Alice G. Knotts, *Fellowship of Love: Methodist Women Changing American Racial Attitudes, 1920-1968* (Nashville: Abingdon Press, 1996), p. 69.

14. See "Bethune, Mary McLeod" in *The Encyclopedia of Black America,* W. A. Low and Virgil A. Clift, eds. (New York: McGraw-Hill Book Company, 1981), p. 173, and The *New Columbia Encyclopedia,* William H. Harris and Judith S. Levey, eds. (New York: Columbia University Press, 1975), p. 287. See also *The World Book Encyclopedia,* op. cit., vol. 2, p. 215; and *Encyclopaedia Britannica,* op. cit., vol. 3, p. 486.

DESERT PASSAGE

Despite many White Methodists' active engagement in education for former slaves after the Civil War and the continued activism of churchwomen in anti-lynching campaigns, still, between 1939 and 1968, segregation prevailed in American Methodism. When White Methodists in the North and the South reunited in 1939 after decades of discussion about how to deal with Black Methodists, their decision was to segregate them. To understand where The United Methodist Church in the United States is today, it is important to examine the role played by slavery and racial dominance on the part of White Methodists as they formed The Methodist Church in 1939 with a segregated Central Jurisdiction.

By the time the U. S. Constitution was ratified in 1789, 170 years had passed since the first Africans were brought to the Jamestown colony as indentured servants. In the intervening colonial period, the institution of slavery had established its grip on all aspects of American society, culture, and religion. Despite John Wesley's adamant condemnation of slavery, many White Methodists on American soil came to accept it, succumbing to racial propaganda and acquiescing in the economic exploitation at the core of the slave system.

As the Northern and Southern economies diverged, the battle lines were drawn between those who saw slavery as unnatural and immoral and those who regarded it as a financial necessity that could be justified based on their belief that Africans were inferior by nature.

The bishops of the Methodist Episcopal Church (MEC) tried to keep abolitionists at arm's length to avoid angering and isolating the Southern part of the church. But the establishment of a "Committee on Slavery" by the General Conference of 1840 did little to calm the brewing storm. Slavery was splitting the church as well as the nation. Well-meaning church members—North and South—hoped to avoid all-out confrontations by downplaying the problem, but this strategy was woefully inadequate.

The prophetic words of John Wesley, written in the "General Rules" he set down for the Methodist Societies, stated:

...It is therefore expected by all who continue [in these societies] that they should continue to evidence their desire of salvation,

First, By doing no harm, by avoiding evil of every kind, especially that which is most generally practised: such as...

The buying and selling of men, women, and children, with an intention to enslave them.[1] [This was the fourth example in a long list of sins.]

When the Rev. Francis A. Harding and Bishop James O. Andrew of Georgia refused to free slaves they had acquired through marriage, Southern Methodists split the Methodist Episcopal Church and founded the Methodist Episcopal Church, South, (MECS) in 1845. Race created two churches as similar as they were different. It was a duality that would last for almost a century. The division was also played out internationally, as the Northern church founded Methodist missions in southern China and the Southern Methodists planted their missions in northern China. Today, congregations once identified with the North or South often still have theological differences rooted in their old conflict over slavery and in the literalist interpretations of scripture that were used to "justify" it.

Although the Methodist churches of the North and South reunited in 1939, a long, arduous, and ultimately unsatisfactory outcome was preceded by a series of denominational meetings and negotiations. Karen Y. Collier's chapter on "A Union That Divides" in *Heritage and Hope: The African American Presence in United Methodism*[2] provides careful documentation of the painful process and outcome of reunification.

Initially, both regional groups postured, the Northern church accusing the Southern church of having broken away and the Southern church claiming to have been pushed out. In an 1876 meeting in Cape May, New Jersey, representatives from North and South agreed that each church was "a legitimate branch" of the "one Methodist family."[3] For the next decade they debated issues of property, race, and episcopacy. In 1908, both North and South agreed to a federation of the churches without merging property or direct governance. Black members would become part of the independent African Methodist bodies.

Increased involvement of the Methodist Protestant Church (MPC) put all the issues back on the table in pursuit of a more organic union. Commissions from the MEC, MECS, and MPC were delegated to come back with a new federation proposal. They returned in 1910, proposing a connectional system in which quadrennial conferences would deal with local issues (thus keeping the configuration of the three denominations) and a General Conference would deal with connectional concerns. There was a familiar division of representatives between lay and clergy. The glaring omission was that absolutely no reference was made to race. It is not as if the subject had not been discussed.

Separate and Unequal: The Central Jurisdiction

In the so-called "Chattanooga Proposal," presented to the Commission on Union that met in Cincinnati, Ohio, on January 18-20, 1911, it is stated that:

> The colored Methodists would best be served through a union of all the colored Churches and members with the active financial and personal interests of the unified Church....If the union of all colored Churches cannot be secured, try to plan for the union of the Colored Methodist Episcopal Church and the colored membership of the Methodist Episcopal Church. If that is not practicable, make another General Conference District for the colored membership, giving them the additional power to elect their bishops (with authority limited to their own district), and, as a fair offset, their delegates would not have voting power in the General Conference.[4]

The Methodist Protestant Church and the Methodist Episcopal Church, South, affirmed the proposal in principle, but the Methodist Episcopal

Church held back because the proposal diminished the power of General Conference. Yet, the Southern church's idea of affirmation included a huge caveat regarding race. In what became known as the "Oklahoma Declaration," this statement, reflecting the Southern church's stance, was added: "However, we recommend that the colored membership of the various Methodist bodies be formed into an independent organization holding fraternal relations with the reorganized and United Church."[5]

The MPC dropped out of the conversation until 1928, but the Northern and Southern churches continued their negotiations. Increasingly, the conversation began to focus on the issue of race and, in particular, the role of Black bishops in the new denomination. (The Northern church had already established a means for African American bishops to be elected, and two Black bishops were elected in 1920.) The January 1918 meeting in Savannah, Georgia, dealt almost exclusively with race for 13 days. The meeting ended with an uneasy proposal to unify the churches and set up a separate Black church within the united church that would govern itself and elect its own bishops as if it were in a foreign country. It would be "subject to the Constitution of the unified Church."[6]

In true form, another meeting was held with the sole subject of race on the table. The Methodist Episcopal Church wanted a Black jurisdiction of equal stature to the White jurisdiction. The MEC, South, wanted the Black jurisdiction to be equal to an international jurisdiction. Varied proposals for separate but unequal jurisdictions were introduced repeatedly and debated, but nothing was approved during perennial and lengthy gatherings. In 1926, a four-year moratorium on the topic of unification was declared. By 1930, various parties were testing the waters again. In 1934, a Joint Commission was established and held two meetings before the 1939 union.

It was at the 1936 General Conference that the "Plan of Union" was adopted. Six U. S. jurisdictions were established, five of them geographic and one specifically for African American churches. Bishops were now to be elected by their jurisdictions rather than by the General Conference. Karen Collier notes that the plan—which segregated more than 320,000 Black Methodists into the new, nongeographic Central Jurisdiction—was soundly rejected by Black delegates to the General Conference. On a 470 to

83 vote, 36 "no" votes came from Black delegates. Eleven Blacks abstained and none stood during the singing of the hymn, "We're Marching to Zion," after the plan was voted in.[7] Thus it was under the cloud of racism that The Methodist Church (1939-1968) was born.

It is important to note that, at this time in U.S. history, racial segregation was the social norm in the country as a whole and was reinforced by law in the South. Thus the three uniting Methodist denominations were following the same practice as other U. S. institutions rather than leading the church to a higher level of consciousness and behavior. This is not surprising since, in many instances, official board members of the church held similar positions in the secular society. In the final analysis—after endless and exhausting debates, meetings, petitions, and prayer gatherings—there were precious few voices from North or South that raised the troubling question of a segregated structure. A new covenant was needed, for God had to rid the church of its racist sins.

Methodist Women Create a New Covenant

At the 1938 General Conference of the Methodist Episcopal Church, 250 African American leaders met to protest the provisions for segregation and creation of a Central Jurisdiction that were part of the 1939 merger. Thirty-three of the forty-four official African American delegates decided to protest the Plan of Unification.[8]

As a result of the many issues in which Methodist women—both White and Black—were involved, a high level of social consciousness had begun to emerge early in the twentieth century. In 1914, Lily Hammond, a noted woman in mission in the Methodist Episcopal Church, wrote a book called *In Black and White*. In it, she appealed to White women to confront racism in the home, community, and church. Addressing the issue of racism in the minds and lifestyles of White women, Ms. Hammond sought to empower them to seek justice. She challenged her readers to come face to face with their "White privilege"—the ways in which they, as Whites, benefited from racism without even being aware of it. She also urged them to understand how institutional racism prevented Blacks from reaching their full potential.

Methodist women used the power of organizing and networking to get local members of Methodist churches to focus on their message: "A change is going to come." The Women's Division educated local women about the denomination's policies on race in order to create a groundswell of passionate concern. Its members made a strong statement on racial discrimination, indicating that it violated "the Christian beliefs in the fatherhood of God, the brotherhood of man, and the Kingdom of God." In addition to the *Discipline*'s emphasis on race, the organization of Methodist Women issued statements on racism in the church, one of which was entitled "The Christian Church and Race." The women clearly identified racism as being "vile" and "unchristian." Within the women's organization, racism was to be eradicated because it was incompatible with Christian social responsibility. This progressive stance challenged local women to reach beyond themselves and to find new ways of working together interracially within The Methodist Church. Five significant events and actions that were spearheaded by Methodist women in the past half century changed the church and its structures.

Charter for Racial Justice (1950-1966)

First, in 1950, the Women's Division undertook the writing of *The Charter for Racial Justice Policies;* and the Division adopted the policy for its organizational structure in 1952. In 1954, 65 conference presidents of Methodist Women signed the charter as a symbolic commitment on behalf of the women in their conferences to pursue racial justice. In 1962, while commemorating the original charter, the Women's Division revised it. This revision maintained the charter's theological foundation but challenged the church to demonstrate its commitment to justice in its life and ministry.

In 1964, the organization of Methodist Women put before the General Conference the past, the present, and a new plan for the future that God, society, and Methodist Women were demanding of the church. They did so because, while the women were pursuing inclusiveness within the church, the General Conference, which spoke for the church as a whole, continued to be plagued by schism and schemes. As Alice Knotts observed:

> The 1964 General Conference chose an unusual way to deal with the church's racism. Instead of writing in details and protections for integration, the conference instructed the Commission on Union with the EUB to omit from the draft of the constitution any reference to racial structures.[9]

A special session of the Methodist General Conference was called in 1966 to vote on the proposed new constitution for the coming Methodist and EUB merger. At this session, Knotts tells us, delegates clarified the following:

> "...All local Methodist churches *are open* to all persons without discrimination based on race, color, nationality or economic status." The church encouraged full participation of all persons in the life of the church, at least until new categories for discrimination came to light. Annual conferences, likewise, were expected to extend full participation to all persons and eliminate racial discrimination. All institutions and agencies of The Methodist Church were mandated to extend their services and establish employment practices without discrimination.[10]

Methodist women were unrelenting in their efforts and so put forward their *Charter for Racial Justice* during this special session of the General Conference. As a result of their advocacy work, the special session adopted *The Charter for Racial Justice* in 1966.

March on Washington (1963)

The next pivotal movement of the Women's Division was its involvement in the 1963 March on Washington. Members of the Women's Division and other Methodists carried with them a message from The Methodist Church that stated:

Our support of this March comes from our desire: (1) to witness the concern of the American people to the national moral issue of racial injustice and (2) to give support to justice implemented through civil rights legislation. [11]

This public witness, statement, and demonstration served the Women's Division as a catalyst for the presentation of its *Charter for Racial Justice* to the whole church. It pointed out a way to put words of reform into actual practice within the institutional structure. The Charter served to open the eyes of the church to the fact that its institutional practices did not match its public witness.

The Women's Division was built on a strong foundation of activism on behalf of civil rights. So, as the church began to restructure, Methodist Women found that they would need to play a pivotal role and that internally the organization would need to make changes. Its Racial Relations Program under the Christian Social Relations section had brought about many accomplishments and was known for its policy of "speaking out in the public space"—which, of course, included The Methodist Church. Historically, there has always been a correlation between racial injustice and sexism; thus the Women's Division was best suited to lead the church onto an inclusive, unprejudiced path. Having adopted a strong civil rights agenda, the church was looking for ways to complete the desegregation process. Like society, which was learning to adhere to (or circumvent) federal legislation that outlawed discrimination in housing, voting rights, education, employment, and access to public accommodations, the church was also being driven by societal wheels of progress.

Commission on Religion and Race (1968, 1972)

The next major effort of the Women's Division was to support the creation of the Commission on Religion and Race and efforts to strengthen ethnic minority local churches. Many Women's Division leaders, including Thelma Stevens and Peggy Billings, did not agree with The Methodist Church's lukewarm response to the issue of institutional racism within it.

Therefore the Women's Division continued to advocate for actions by the denomination to bring about racial justice. The Division pushed for the development of a commission that would address racial inequities and monitor church progress in eliminating them. Once the commission was in operation, the Division worked with it in orchestrating conferences on race relations to assist United Methodist churches after the 1968 merger.

Empowerment Conferences

In another major action, the Women's Division led empowerment conferences for Black Methodist Women, designed to help them articulate their concerns and their position with reference to the merger with the EUB. The Women's Division joined ecumenical groups such as Project Equality, which dedicated its efforts to fair employment and economic justice. The Division felt strongly that the key to a successful merger was the empowerment of all affected parties—women and men, Black and White. As Peggy Billings wrote:

> We had witnessed this [need for empowerment] firsthand in the workshops on racism held to facilitate the conference merger process. Ethnic group leadership could definitely be lost, and would be lost, if plans were not made to empower minorities more effectively. Empowerment became a major strategy to achieve social change. We had already held two series of consultations with black women to discuss their concerns about the organization. Caucuses added their voices to the call for more employment of minorities. The idea was such a constant that it became part of our commitment when we thought about the future direction of the Racial Justice Program. We would continue to work on white racism, but would shift the major focus to empowerment of minorities, especially women. This, we felt, would move us forward toward the [Women's] Division's aim to be one inclusive organization.[12]

Commission on the Status and Role of Women (1972)

The general church commissioned a study of the status of women in the church. It revealed negative findings for Black women in church leadership. As a result, the Women's Division petitioned the 1972 General Conference, insisting that it create a Commission on Women that would give visibility to women's needs and concerns. In this way, the Commission on the Status and Role of Women (COSROW) was founded.

Black Women in the Front of the Bus

The Lord will see us through, The Lord will see us through,
The Lord will see us through today.
Oh,
Deep in our hearts we do believe
We shall overcome some-day.[13]
("We Shall Overcome," *The United Methodist Hymnal,* 533, v. 5; see also
Songs of Zion, "Negro Spirituals," 127)

In the leadership of Methodist Women, Black women never "sat in the back of the bus." They were actively involved in the Wesleyan Service Guild and in the Woman's Society of Christian Service (the predecessor organization of Methodist Women and United Methodist Women). The 1939 Plan of Union had brought together Black women from the North, South, East, and West, uniting them for the first time. These Black women came together to organize for mission and to lead the Central Jurisdiction of The Methodist Church in the development of a women's mission program. Even in the days when the church was racially segregated, Black women delegates were afforded seats on all the national boards and agencies. In the Woman's Society of Christian Service, Black women were board members. Among that distinguished group were Mary McLeod Bethune and Theressa Hoover. By the time the Methodist and EUB churches began their merger in 1968, Black women had already established a relationship with the Board of Missions and were recognized for their outstanding leadership both in the Central Jurisdiction and in the general church.

Black women have left enduring legacies in many mission endeavors, including international mission service, the deaconess movement, leadership training, fundraising for mission, membership cultivation, and consciousness raising. Most importantly, they made sure that their voices were heard in the development and implementation of *The Charter for Racial Justice.* These women were serious about mission. As the Task Group on the History of the Central Jurisdiction Women's Organization wrote:

> The early zeal to perfect the structures of the Central Jurisdiction was not busy-work dictated by organizational charts and by-laws. The organizational activities reflected a determination to make the unique black contribution to the achievement of the WSCS [Woman's Society of Christian Service] PURPOSE. That PURPOSE in 1940 was to: —Unite all women of the Church in Christian living and service; —Help develop and support Christian work among women and children around the world; —Develop the spiritual life; —Study the needs of the world; —Take part in such service activities as will strengthen the local church, improve civic, community and world conditions.
>
> Toward those ends, the organization pledged itself to: —Enlist women, young people, and children in this Christian fellowship; —Seek funds for the activities in the local church and support the work undertaken at home and abroad for the establishment of a world Christian community.[14]

The twenty-eighth and last meeting of the Women's Central Jurisdiction organization occurred in Nashville, Tennessee, in 1967. By this time, The Methodist Church had voted (in 1964) to dissolve the Central Jurisdiction, and the Evangelical United Brethren Church and The Methodist Church had been engaged in dialogue for almost a quadrennium on the restructure of the church. Black congregations were already being merged into the new structure. The Black Methodist Women chose as a theme for their last conference "Meeting the Tasks Ahead." Their thematic scripture was Revelation 3:8: "Look, I have set before you an open door, which no one is able to shut."

Christian Social Responsibility

In the early days of the twenty-first century, the organization of United Methodist Women (UMW) is still committed to racial justice. The Division monitors itself, the church, and society for signs of institutional racism. Its education programs are designed to teach inclusiveness and empowerment. Many strategies have been used, from boycotts of and disinvestments in South Africa during the Apartheid era to petitions and lobbying against racial profiling and corporate racism in the United States. UMW also monitors hate crimes and builds coalitions with other organizations that advocate equality for all. The Women's Division stands as a beacon as it develops leadership among women, helps young women find their place in the church and society, and uncompromisingly demands justice while, at the same time, advocating conditions leading to peace and harmony in the world.

Lessons From the Past

"The belief that African Americans can best serve the church by being all together is a keystone of racist thinking," wrote Charles Carrington, a young African American pastor, in 1936. "Therein, all identity and any unity depends on race lines," he continued. "The plan [for the Central Jurisdiction] violates the principles of brotherhood dominant in the life and teaching of Jesus and embodied in the church."[15]

Carrington, along with countless other African American Methodist leaders, raised questions about the segregationist Plan of Union for The Methodist Church. These are still questions for The United Methodist Church today as it explores the possibility of reuniting with historically Black Methodist churches.

The picture of the 1939 Plan of Union that comes into focus today shows the White supremacy and absolute authority of the slavery era persisting in another form. This White power would linger on in a newly created ecclesiastical authority that would utilize segregation as the new model whereby White Methodists could retain control. After Pharaoh lost control of the Hebrew slaves, he tried to chase them down with chariots and armed soldiers. Whites in the church were more successful. Though they had long since lost the power to enslave, they exerted power and dominion over African American Methodists for decades by implementing the objectives and culture of segregation.

Bishop Daniel A. Payne of the AME Church had thought all along that African Americans in the Methodist Episcopal Church would continue to be kept in a subjugated position by the dominant Whites. "The existence of the colored man in the Methodist Episcopal Church," he wrote, "always was, still is, and ever must be a mere cipher."[16]

An irony of this new Exodus was that some Black Methodist Episcopal members identified with those Old Testament Hebrew counterparts who believed that, since they were living in Pharaoh's house, they had to follow Pharaoh's rules. Other Black Methodists, like Moses in biblical times, heard a word of justice and equality and stood on the promise that their status would be improved in the new Methodist Church. Since this was not to happen, they rejected the Plan of Union, regarding the stigma of segregation as too humiliating to accept.

Making a Truly United Methodist Church

God is on our side, God is on our side,
God is on our side today.
Oh,
If in our hearts we do believe,
We shall overcome some-day.[17]
("We Shall Overcome," *Songs of Zion,* "Negro Spirituals,"
127, v. 5; see also *The United Methodist Hymnal,* 533)

Like the children of Israel, members of The Methodist Church needed to experience a transformation in order to spearhead societal change. As the Central Jurisdiction continued to strive for total inclusion in the church and as the wider society began to be influenced by the civil rights campaigns of the 1960s, The Methodist Church had to awaken and respond to the call. God was about to do a new thing with The Methodist Church.

The movement toward United Methodism took place during the years

1940-1967. At the end of World War I in 1918, Methodists, Evangelicals, and United Brethren had published strong statements condemning war. But with the advent of hostilities that thrust the world into the global conflict that was World War II, the strength of the former antiwar sentiment faded. Even so, many churches continued to express their rejection of war by declaring conscientious objection.

During the formative 28 years of 1940-1967, three important concerns occupied the churches that now make up United Methodism. First, they wanted to maintain ecumenism in church union, as was addressed in the 1946 merger of the Evangelical Church and the Church of the United Brethren in Christ that formed the Evangelical United Brethren (EUB) Church. Second, the church members demonstrated a growing uneasiness over the issue of racism, within both the church and society. Recognizing that racial segregation had been quilted into the fabric of their denominational structure deeply disturbed many people within The Methodist Church. They had to look no further than the Central Jurisdiction to see how insidious and unacceptable the separation had become. A third area of struggle was the right of women to participate fully, as clergy, in the life of the church. The limitation of women to a secondary role in the history of the churches became a painful reminder of how easily the iron bonds of prejudice could shackle God's people. These were shackles that the 1968 merger of The Methodist Church and the EUB Church was designed to undo.

On April 23, 1968, The United Methodist Church was created when Bishop Rueben H. Mueller, representing The Evangelical United Brethren Church, and Bishop Lloyd C. Wicke of The Methodist Church joined hands at the constituting General Conference in Dallas, Texas. With the words, "Lord of the Church, we are united in Thee, in Thy Church and now in The United Methodist Church," the new denomination was given birth by two churches that had distinguished histories and influential ministries in various parts of the world.[18]

After the 1968 merger in Dallas, the newborn United Methodist Church was able to design a unified structure without racial or ethnic boundaries.

Yet, while this was true in a legislative sense, it was not totally realized in a humanistic sense. Though free of a separate racial jurisdiction created by the action of a General Conference, The United Methodist Church still struggles with undoing the de facto segregation that takes place each Sunday morning in its local churches. The long shadow of the former Central Jurisdiction remains even now when one travels within the annual conferences and districts of the five U. S. geographic jurisdictions. For instance, in many cities one can observe two neighboring United Methodist churches, one with Black worshipers and one with White. A modern Exodus is needed to free the still separated United Methodist worshipers of the new millennium from the ghosts of their historical counterparts. For the name "United Methodist" did not automatically bring with it total inclusiveness in the church's pews, worship styles, or traditions.

What are the lessons and legacies of the past, as reflected in the Central Jurisdiction? How do we extract the painful sting of racist segregation that still plagues the multiracial, multinational United Methodist Church of today? There are no easy answers or quick legislative fixes that can rid us of the troubling undercurrent which our segregated history still brings to our worship and fellowship. Reconciliation and union will require that we deal with the following realities of race-based worship in our current United Methodist Church:

- The failure of the church to establish racial policies and practices that repudiate the societal barriers which create separate and unequal rights and privileges for African Americans and other racial/ethnic minorities.

- The assigning of lesser status and denominational presence to African Americans and other racial/ethnic minority constituents. Issues raised by individuals and groups of color are perceived and addressed as "special emphases," otherwise being ignored by the denomination.

- The continuing hesitation of Whites to confront other Whites on issues of race, as seen historically in the Northern and Southern branches of the Methodist Episcopal Church (1845-1939).

- The church's failure to change the fact that 11:00 on Sunday morning is the most segregated hour in America and the fact that all-White and all-Black churches can exist literally next door to one another.

- The failure of previous attempts at union with historically Black denominations because these efforts have been directed and designed by Whites without the full and equal participation of African Americans.

- The inadequate involvement of Black and other minority members in the overall future of The United Methodist Church.

In the final analysis, we do well to remember George Santayana's axiom: "Those who cannot remember the past are condemned to repeat it."[19] Nowhere was this truth more evident than in the reactions of Black delegates to the Service of Reconciliation and Healing at the 2000 General Conference. Like their predecessor delegates in 1939 when the Plan of Union was accepted and the Whites sang, "We're Marching to Zion," many African American delegates in Cleveland, Ohio, in May 2000 remained motionless as the service concluded.

There had been no recognition of those descendants of slaves and free Africans who had chosen to stay and work to transform Methodism from within. No recognition was voiced for the years of Black resistance to the Central Jurisdiction, which finally came to fruition in its disbandment nearly 30 years after its founding. No request for forgiveness was forthcoming for the neglect of historic Black schools and mission projects. Nor was there any apology for the suppression of Black leadership when the Central Jurisdiction was finally disbanded.

At the 2000 reconciliation service, some Black delegates bowed their heads as Whites clung to them and casually asked for forgiveness. Others wept quietly, wondering what, if anything, had been learned by the wider church in the 61 years that had elapsed since the 1939 action.

In a paper reflecting upon the history of Black people in the Methodist Church prior to 1939, Bishop Willis G. King provides a frank and intellectually honest assessment of the Central Jurisdiction. He sees it as a mere microcosm of the difficult and arduous journey of those of African descent in the Methodist Church. One statement of his in the 1967 *Central Jurisdictional Conference Journal* stands out as a key to understanding the problem of where to place the Black membership in the structure of American Methodism:

> To those who had believed in the possibility of the evangelization of people of all racial and national origins, and their inclusion in one Church of Jesus Christ, the plan of the Northern Church, while not ideal, had proven that the idea could be made to work.
>
> For those with the other point of view, namely that the two racial groups should remain in separate denominations, on the basis of race, the Negro membership in the Methodist Episcopal Church was a definite obstacle to Methodist Unification. The fact that the Negro membership in the Church numbered more than 300,000 did not make the problem any easier.
>
> It is evident then that one of the major issues in the negotiations on Methodist Unification from 1916...until 1939...was the status of the Negro membership in the re-organized Church.[20]

Symbolic gestures fail to take into account the oppressive decades that have confronted Methodist people of color since they first arrived in the American colonies and the United States. Mere "structural" arrangements cannot take the place of genuine and deliberate acts of confession and repentance as a means to right this egregious wrong. Dr. James P. Brawley addressed the subject of the Central Jurisdictional Conference of the former Methodist Church head-on:

> The Central Jurisdiction came into being as a reflection of the long-existing race problem in the Methodist Church. The race problem has been present since the establishment of the first Methodist societies and has been a vital issue from the organization of the church in 1784 to the present.[21]

For The United Methodist Church to make progress in resolving "the long-existing race problem" cited by Dr. Brawley, the greater power and superior status of White members must be consciously, willingly, and prayerfully relinquished. This can make it possible for Black members to take their rightful place as equals in the united church. Only then can the journey of Black and White United Methodists continue toward a freedom from differences and a celebration of diversity.

> We'll walk hand in hand, We'll walk hand in hand,
> We'll walk hand in hand some-day.
> Oh,
> If in our hearts we do believe,
> We shall overcome some-day.[22]
> ("We Shall Overcome," *Songs of Zion,* "Negro Spirituals," 127, v. 2; see
> also *The United Methodist Hymnal,* 533, v. 2)

Endnotes

1. G. Lane and C. B. Tippitt, pubs., *The Doctrines and Discipline of the Methodist Episcopal Church* (New York: Methodist Episcopal Church , 1844), pp. 82-83.

2. Karen Y. Collier, "A Union That Divides," in Grant S. Shockley, ed., *Heritage and Hope: The African American Presence in United Methodism* (Nashville: Abingdon Press, 1991), pp. 99-116.

3. Ibid., p. 103. The quotation is from Bishop Edwin Holt Hughes, cited in his autobiography, *I Was Made a Minister* (New York, Abingdon Press, 1943), p. 272. For the text of the Cape May declaration, see John M. Moore, *The Long Road to Methodist Union* (Nashville: Parthenon Press, 1943), p. 65.

4. John M. Moore, *The Long Road to Methodist Union* (Nashville: Parthenon Press, 1943), p. 91.

5. Karen Y. Collier, op. cit., p. 107.

6. Ibid., p. 109.

7. Ibid., p. 115, quoting James P. Brawley in *Journal of the Eighth Session of the Central Jurisdictional Conference of The Methodist Church* (Nashville: The Methodist Publishing House, 1967): "A membership of more than 320,000 Negroes had been legally segregated into the Central Jurisdiction." There are discrepancies of date and number in the sources reporting African American delegates' "no" votes to the Plan of Union, with Collier saying there were 36 "no" votes and 11 abstentions and Alice Knotts, in *Fellowship of Love,* citing 33 "no" votes and (presumably) 11 abstentions. The *1936 General Conference Journal* of the Methodist Episcopal Church provides no vote listing by individual delegates. Of about 18 African American conferences existing at the time, according to the Archivist at the General Commission on Archives and History, approximately 70 Black delegates (not including alternates) would have been attending, of whom at least 44 or 47 rejected the Plan of Union or abstained from the vote.

8. Alice G. Knotts, op. cit., p. 135. One of the delegates who objected to the plan for a segregated jurisdiction was the educator Mary McLeod Bethune, founder of Bethune-Cookman College (see chapter three).

9. Ibid., p. 249.

10. Ibid., p. 250.

11. Ibid., p. 246.

12. Peggy Billings, *Speaking Out in the Public Space: An Account of the Section of Christian Social Relations* (New York: General Board of Global Ministries, 1995), p. 32.

13. "We Shall Overcome," *The United Methodist Hymnal,* op. cit., no. 533, v. 5. See also *Songs of Zion,* op. cit., no. 127.

14. Task Group on the History of the Central Jurisdiction Women's Organization, *To a Higher Glory: The Growth and Development of Black Women Organized for Mission in The Methodist Church, 1940-1968* (New York: General Board of Global Ministries, no date), pp. 60-61.

15. Charles Carrington, "Methodist Union and the Negro," *The Crisis,* May 1936, p. 158.

16. See Daniel A. Payne, *History of the African Methodist Episcopal Church* (New York: Arno Press, Inc., and The New York Times, 1969).

17. "We Shall Overcome," *Songs of Zion,* op. cit., no. 127, v. 5; *The United Methodist Hymnal,* op. cit., no. 533.

18. *The Book of Discipline of The United Methodist Church 2000,* "Historical Statement" (Nashville: The United Methodist Publishing House, 2000), p. 9.

19. Elizabeth Knowles, ed., *The Oxford Dictionary of Quotations,* op. cit., p. 644, no. 9.

20. Address by Bishop Willis G. King (August 18, 1967) in *Journal of the Eighth Session of the Central Jurisdictional Conference of The Methodist Church* (Nashville: The Methodist Publishing House, 1967), p. 109.

21. Ibid., p. 120.

22. "We Shall Overcome," *Songs of Zion,* op. cit., no. 127, v. 2; *The United Methodist Hymnal,* op. cit., no. 533, v. 2.

5

SPEAKING FACE TO FACE

> *Now Moses used to take [a] tent and pitch it outside the camp, far off from the camp; he called it the tent of meeting. And everyone who sought the Lord would go out to the tent of meeting....When Moses entered the tent, the pillar of cloud would descend and stand at the entrance of the tent, and the Lord would speak with Moses....Thus the Lord used to speak to Moses face to face, as one speaks to a friend.*
> *(Exodus 33:7, 9, 11a)*

In order for our society to change, God has to call advocates from within the church to challenge the church. Only in this way can the church be brought to realize that, like the wider society, it, too, is committing the sin of racism. During the Civil Rights Movement of the 1950s and 1960s, God was calling on the church to go to the "tent of meeting" and to return with a different and radiant face, like the shining face of Moses after he returned from talking with God on Mount Sinai (Exodus 34: 29-35).

Around the mid-twentieth century, God was also shaping and calling American leaders from civic life, from the community, and from the government. God was calling leaders such as the Rev. Dr. Martin Luther King, Jr., Rosa Parks, Adam Clayton Powell, Jr., Daisy Bates, Medgar Evers, Roger Wilkins, and many other civil rights activists—calling them to teach the nation to honor a new covenant and to abide by renewed commandments. Like Moses, community leaders and church activists were willing to march, protest, and petition—in their case, often at the expense of beatings, jailings, and even death—for the full freedom, equal rights, and equal treatment of God's people.

Personal Note From the Rev. Bernard ("Skip") Keels

It is extremely important for powerful or privileged people to understand the societal sin they commit when they fail to recognize the personhood of others—especially the personhood of those unlike them. Recently, while returning to the United States from a vacation in the Bahamas, I witnessed a telling episode of unintended arrogance. It was committed by a White woman waiting in line in front of me to go through customs. Looking over at the huge gathering of Bahamians entering the U. S. Customs Service line, she frustratedly said to her male companion: "I can't believe all those Bahamians in the line! Why are so many of them coming into our country?"

Unable to resist the urge to seize this teachable moment, I introduced myself and apologized for overhearing the woman's comments. Then I mentioned the fact that the same question could be asked about us, as Americans, when we presented our cameras and showed our impatience to the Bahamian Customs officials. On numerous occasions, I witnessed the arrogance and surliness of Americans as they pushed and fussed their way through Bahamian Customs. Nevertheless, this woman could not recognize either her own rudeness or the hospitality shown by the many native Bahamians who had tended to our every need, always with a smile, courtesy, hospitality, and neighborliness.

Where Do We Go From Here?

During the great decades of struggle for civil rights in the United States, White Methodist clergy and laity were among the freedom riders who converged upon the segregated South. They withstood waves of violence as they demanded justice and equality for their Black brothers and sisters. Cries for justice today must first be wept in the segregated pews in which most of us still sit on Sundays.

From the time when Richard Allen dealt with the systematic exclusion of African American Methodists by creating the AME Church, until our time, when Black delegates quietly despaired at the 2000 United Methodist General Conference, there is a history from which we can learn if we have eyes to see and ears to hear. The United Methodist Church, which is multiracial but predominantly White, and the Black Methodist denominations are again beginning to discuss Pan Methodist Union—an effort of all branches of Methodism to seek union and reconciliation. However, any new attempt to open this dialogue must accept and acknowledge the long sojourn of separation and alienation, considering how it began and has continued.

Where Richard Allen (of the AME Church) and James Varick (of the AMEZ Church) were forced *out* of the Methodist Episcopal church pews, we must go *into* our churches to confront and combat the social and spiritual injustice of racism. We must call to account the organizational structures that exclude and discriminate. We must enter the political arena to challenge the systems that oppress the have-nots while excessively rewarding the haves. We must be active and vocal leaders in the church, demanding that our pews be places of sanctuary, welcoming all to come and experience the love of Jesus Christ. And, in so doing, we must assure a true hospitality that welcomes difference rather than merely tolerating it.

Shortly before his assassination, Martin Luther King, Jr., published a book called *Where Do We Go From Here: Chaos or Community?*[1] At that time, the Black Power movement, with its militant rhetoric, was making both Blacks and Whites uneasy. In fact, it was creating a strong backlash among many Whites—which was not surprising since even the most liberal Whites did not grasp the full enormity of racism. Dr. King was speaking out against the Vietnam war, recognizing the race- and class-based ideologies that sent poor Blacks and Whites to war against Vietnamese peasants. The label *Communist* was the red-herring accusation of the hour, and schemes were being hatched by modern-day pharaohs behind the scenes.

The life of Martin Luther King, Jr., and the lives of all those who have struggled against racism, before and after him, have made a difference. The further progress we see today was made by successors standing on the shoulders of these human-rights pioneers. But like Moses, Dr. King only glimpsed the promised land from a mountaintop. This vision showed that the journey, which was never promised to be easy, was not in vain. The road to the realization of the vision is still a narrow road, and it still stretches out before those who are willing to walk the walk—willing to take action rather than simply talking about it. In almost every situation, full awareness, true repentance, and open-hearted forgiveness are needed to amend the centuries-old wounds caused by the exclusionary rules and practices of the church.

The issues are more complex today than they have ever been. Overt racism, 1950s style, is no longer publicly acceptable. But new sets of codes have come into use, such as *reverse discrimination,* the claim that Whites are suffering unjustly because the pursuit of diversity by colleges and corporations has increased the participation of people of color in higher education and the workforce. Meanwhile, hate music by young White males is thriving even as it glorifies violence and spreads venom. Black churches and progressive White churches continue to be targeted for arson by right-wing extremist groups. Racial profiling by law-enforcement officers, who assume that people of color are more likely than Whites to commit crime, is a commonplace occurrence, if not the norm. Police have seen the courts excuse case after case of unprovoked violence against Blacks. And prisons are being built at record rates to hold the disproportionate number of people of color being incarcerated. Not only have African Americans in every strata and segment of the Black community been racially profiled or otherwise stereotyped, the church itself is not exempt from this practice. Often stereotyped ideas about liturgical and musical preferences will keep a church from reaching out to reflect the racial make-up of its community.

With television's insatiable appetite for visual news and with the availability of video cameras to millions of amateur reporters, some racist incidents have been caught on tape and telecast. The 1992 United Methodist General Conference in Louisville, Kentucky, began on May 5, less than a week after the acquittal of White members of the Los Angeles Police Department who had been videotaped beating a Black motorist, Rodney King. This shocking miscarriage of justice touched off a violent uprising—

and led the General Conference to create a "shalom zone" in Los Angeles, where a neighborhood could be rebuilt and renewed and where racial divisions could be healed. This shalom vision later led the church to create communities of shalom across the nation and around the world.

Personal Note From the Rev. Bernard ("Skip") Keels
Though I was a first-time delegate at the 1992 General Conference, representing what was then the Baltimore Annual Conference, I was one of four speakers selected by the General Conference to address the delegates on a critically important issue: how the church speaks when a major city is in the throes of racial upheaval and when the nation is in shock. What the General Conference ultimately learned is that the church must provide a strong contrast to the racism of society if it is to remain an authentic voice of Christian hope. This hope is freely given to all who call upon the name of Jesus Christ , seeking to become disciples of God's transforming love.

Beyond Schemes to Dreams

We have not reached the promised land, and, as always, the world is changing rapidly. Hard-won civil rights and personal rights to privacy are in jeopardy as a result of the attacks by Islamic terrorists against the United States on September 11, 2001, and the nation's subsequent war on terrorism.

Racism itself is not a topic of polite conversation. It is more upbeat to talk about multiculturalism in a "can't we all just get along" style of operation.[2] The schisms that have always haunted movements for freedom still haunt us today. Oppressed groups are pitted against one another. The successes of select individuals are spotlighted, implying that, since some people are succeeding, those who are not must somehow be at fault.

To counter the tendency for Whites and Blacks to stay—or to be kept—apart, whether at work or at worship, takes effort. Trust has to be built. Repentance, change, and forgiveness are constant motifs. Children of all races, but especially Whites, need to be taught not to fear racial differences.

This is difficult when features associated with people of color are used to symbolize evil in animated characters found in cartoons and video games.

The church continues to struggle to bring people of different races together in a just society free of favoritism, prejudice, and preconceptions. At the 2000 General Conference, as The United Methodist Church tried to open the door to conversations with historic African American denominations, its leaders forgot the African American families who had been part of their own denomination for decades. White people want to be forgiven, while African Americans and other people of color want to see change rather than give or receive consolation. Cries for reparations are heard from Pan African voices but often are discounted.

Like Moses and the first generation of Hebrews who escaped slavery in Egypt, those of us alive today will not see the promised land. Our hope is in the next generation, and the next, and the next. But that is no excuse for us to stop struggling. If we stop in the middle of the desert, we will surely die together. We must struggle on, even if our future of justice is still a dream. A dream is a powerful tool for changing lives. Dr. Martin Luther King, Jr., knew that when he proclaimed: "I have a dream!"

Dr. King also provided a powerful message to the church that is meaningful both in our understanding of past and present race relations and in our plans for charting the future. In his imaginative rendering of an invented manuscript called "Paul's Letter to American Christians," Dr. King said:

> Another thing that disturbs me about the American church is that you have a white church and a Negro church. How can segregation exist in the true Body of Christ? I am told that there is more integration within the entertaining world and other secular agencies than there is in the Christian church. How appalling this is![3]

Speaking as a modern-day Paul, Dr. King condemned as blasphemous and contrary to the Christian faith any attempt to use the Bible to "prove" Black inferiority. He reminded his readers of Paul's words to the churches of Galacia: "There is no longer Jew or Greek, there is no longer slave or free, there is no longer male and female; for all of you are one in Christ Jesus"

(Galatians 3:28). Expressing the hope that American churches would exercise leadership in ending segregation, Dr. King observed that "first, you must see that the church removes the yoke of segregation from its own body." Then he advocated more broadly based social action by the church to combat racism "in housing, education, police protection, and in city and state courts," while "keep[ing] channels of communication open between the races." The church, he said, must also bring its influence to bear in the struggle for economic justice.[4]

Continuing, he urged people of color "to work passionately and vigorously for your God-given and constitutional rights" but to "be sure that you struggle with Christian methods....using love as your chief weapon" and never turning to violence or yielding to bitterness. He advised Black and White Americans who "dare to speak for justice" to prepare themselves for condemnation, persecution, and sometimes jail. "Even if physical death is the price that some must pay to free their children from psychological death," he said, "then nothing could be more Christian."[5]

Personal Note From Christine Keels

When I was a child growing up in Memphis, my brothers and I would go to visit our grandmother in Mississippi. As a young person, I was afraid of the old washing machine that sat on her back porch, because when it reached the agitation stage, the entire house vibrated. You knew that the clothes were bound to be clean because of the effort the old washing machine took in twisting and turning the garments until they were spotless.

Similarly, we must twist and turn The United Methodist Church through forms of agitation until we cleanse the church of all racist thoughts and actions.

It is not enough simply to address the racial divide with Special Sunday emphases or resolutions adopted by the church. For true reconciliation, all parties must be involved and empowered to listen to one another's stories as a true community of faith. Such a community must be determined not to dismiss the pain of its oppressed and aggrieved sisters and brothers by searching for a quick fix to a deeply malignant spiritual disease. This disease—this sin of racism, which has led members of one body down a separate and unequal historical path—has had a catastrophic impact on the church's mission to make disciples for Jesus Christ. All who remain disengaged from the struggle are "Standing in the Need of Prayer."

Not my brother, not my sister, but it's me, O Lord,
standing in the need of prayer,
Not my brother, not my sister, but it's me, O Lord,
standing in the need of prayer. [6]
("It's Me, It's Me, O Lord," *The United Methodist Hymnal,* 352, v. 1.
See also "Standin' in the Need of Prayer," *Songs of Zion,* 110, v. 1.)

Personal Note From Christine Keels

I recently had the opportunity to attend an annual conference's Service of Reconciliation. It was part of the morning plenary. I arrived 30 minutes late that morning, owing to some disabilities I was experiencing at the time, and I walked in wearing a hand brace and a knee brace. As I approached an empty end seat, I asked an African American woman (sitting next to the seat) whether it was open, and I was told "no." Then, when I looked behind me, I saw two vacant seats three chairs into the next row, next to two White women. I asked the two women if the chair next to them was free. Since I did not get an immediate response, I asked the question again and was given a hesitant "yes." The two women stood up with seeming reluctance and gave me access. But given their less-than-warm response, I sat in the fourth seat and allowed for a seat between us. Then, as I listened to the business of the annual conference, I decided that I could not participate in the upcoming Service of Reconciliation without confronting what felt like discrimination. Was I experiencing racial prejudice? Was it my handicapping conditions that made me unwelcome? Or were the two women annoyed that I was late and was disturbing them?

Personal Note From Christine Keels (continued)

I could not be at peace until I knew the answer. The bishop (as if he knew my dilemma) called for a break in the business meeting so that people could become centered and prepare themselves for the spiritual service. I stood up next to the two women, placed my hand on the back of the one closest to me, and said, "Excuse me, my name is Chris." The woman greeted me with less than enthusiasm. Being the agitator, I stated: "I am not sure what I should be feeling. When I asked you if the seat was free, I did not get a welcoming response. Was it because I was late and disturbing you, or did you not want me to sit here? And, if so, why?" Both women looked shocked. The woman closest to the aisle turned away and pretended to be busy, looking in her tote bag. The woman closest to me stated that she was busy listening to the program because someone from her district was reporting. Therefore, she said, she was not focused on my question. I then asked the other woman what her reasoning was. She slowly turned to face me and said, "I was listening to the program." I said, "Oh, because the response I received, or my perception of the response, made me feel unwanted." The woman closest to me apologized and looked at my name tag. It had been made for another member of my church, who was not able to attend, and the original name had been scratched out and my name added. She read the scratched out name first and then said: "Oh, you are Chris Keels. I remember you from Regional School. I was not in your class, but I remember you." From that point on, we had a friendly exchange. But the woman who had turned away never attempted to engage in our conversation.

During the Service of Reconciliation, we were asked to go to stations within the hall to receive ashes as symbols of our sin. Both women left the auditorium when this process was explained. One could assume that they were ushers, or that they had to use the ladies' room, or that they needed to leave for some other reason. However, I don't think any of these possibilities was the case. When they returned, I tried to look for ashes on their foreheads or hands and could not distinguish any, possibly because of the lighting.

This example clearly shows why opportunities for reconciliation and repentance cannot be planned as ceremonial occasions, where superficial actions are supposed to erase the past. Sin cannot be overcome through the mere pretense of a planned "transforming experience." I am not against a true rite of passage toward reconciliation, but it must be much more than a shallow, scripted drama where most risks are skillfully avoided. We must confront and confess our sins, and repetition is an effective learning process. We must help people name their sins and then lead them through the process of healing. Our children are watching our behavior, and they are seeing that our actions often do not match our words. We are not living what we profess, sing about, or pray about on Sundays. We must help the privileged to understand that the special treatment they have enjoyed has often required the enslavement or exploitation of others.

Learning to Embrace and Welcome

On a recent vacation in Fort Lauderdale, the tour guide, who was showing us "millionaire alley," with its splendid mansions and moored yachts, observed: "It's hard now to imagine that the area where these magnificent homes now stand was once occupied by Indians living in covered platforms with no walls." Pointing to a particularly grand estate, he said: "This was the first *civilized* home to be built. Its original owner paid the local Indians about five dollars for 30 acres of land." He seemed totally unaware that some hearers might deem his comments offensive.

The church's confrontation with racism—whether blatant or subtle—must be like one raindrop that falls, followed by another, and another, until we have a puddle, a stream, a creek, a river, and finally an ocean of witnesses who allow love to overcome hatred, fear, and bigotry. In this confrontation, we must not only tell the African American story but also blend in the threads of racism from the histories of Native Americans, South and East Asians, Latinos, the peoples of the Middle East, and many other cultures so as to strengthen the fabric of our solutions. We can learn from one another's trails of tears and celebrate each other's victories as we determine our destiny.

As a church, how do we affirm our members of color who are the global majority but who are made to feel like the "ethnic minority"? How can we learn to embrace and welcome the gifts they bring to the community of the church? If we are truly to go to the table of reconciliation, we must return from that table calling on neighbors who appear to be different from us to come and be an equal part of us. We must say to them: "Come dance with me in the aisles, come sing with me in the pews, come read with me in Bible study, come lead with me in planning programs, and come bless me with your gifts and graces!

We can truly celebrate when there is individual change, local church change, institutional change, societal change, and global change. We need to seek one another out in order to begin our walk toward the promised land together. Our song for the road should be the "Canticle of Moses and Miriam" in *The United Methodist Hymnal.* For us, let racism be the horse and rider that the Lord has thrown into the sea.

Be exalted, Lord, in your strength! We will sing and praise your power.

Then Moses and the people of Israel sang this song to the Lord, saying,
"I will sing to the Lord, who has triumphed gloriously;
   the horse and its rider the Lord has thrown into the sea.
The Lord is my strength and my song, and has become my salvation;
this is my God whom I will praise.
   I will exalt my father's God who is a mighty warrior, whose name is the Lord.

Pharaoh's chariots and his host the Lord cast into the sea;
  and his chosen officers are sunk in the Red Sea.
The floods cover them; they went down into the depths like a stone.
Your right hand, O Lord, glorious in power,
  your right hand, O Lord, shatters the enemy."

Be exalted, Lord, in your strength! We will sing and praise your power.

"Who is like you, O Lord, among the gods?
  Who is like you, majestic in holiness, terrible in glorious deeds, doing wonders?
You stretched out your right hand, the earth swallowed them.
In your steadfast love, you have led the people whom you have redeemed;
you have guided them by your strength to your holy abode."

Be exalted, Lord, in your strength! We will sing and praise your power.

"You will bring them in, and plant them on your own mountain,
  the place, O Lord, which you have made for your abode,
  the sanctuary, O Lord, which your hands have established.
The Lord will reign for ever and ever."

Be exalted, Lord, in your strength! We will sing and praise your power.

Then Miriam, the prophet, the sister of Aaron, took a timbrel in her hand;
  and all the women went out after her with timbrels and dancing,
  and Miriam sang to them:

"Sing to the Lord, who has triumphed gloriously;
  the horse and its rider the Lord has thrown into the sea."

Be exalted, Lord, in your strength! We will sing and praise your power.[7]
(*The United Methodist Hymnal,* 135)

United Methodist Women must start the dance, must raise the timbrel, and must lead the songs as the church pursues its destiny on the path to freedom from racism. We need to pick up where Moses, Aaron, and Miriam left off—continuing the journey, with the past behind us, the present to motivate us, the future to challenge us, and the Lord of Abraham and Moses to lead and guide us along the way.

Endnotes

1. Martin Luther King, Jr., *Where Do We Go From Here: Chaos or Community?* (Boston: Beacon Press, 1967).

2. "Can't we all just get along?" was a question later asked by Rodney King, the Black motorist whose videotaped beating at the hands of White police officers touched off a violent uprising in Los Angeles in late April 1992, when the White officers were acquitted after a trial.

3. Martin Luther King, Jr., *Strength to Love* (Philadelphia: Fortress Press, 1981; original copyright 1963), p. 141.

4. Ibid., pp. 142-143.

5. Ibid., pp. 143-144.

6. "Standing in the Need of Prayer," *The United Methodist Hymnal,* no. 352; Songs of Zion, no. 110.

7. "Canticle of Moses and Miriam," *The United Methodist Hymnal,* no. 135.

HISTORICAL ARTICLES AND PRESENT-DAY INTERVIEWS

The following section includes two historical articles. One, by Bishop William Boyd Grove, has to do with the Pan Methodist Movement in the present, which seeks cooperation and some sort of union among The United Methodist Church and the historic Black Methodist denominations: the African Methodist Episcopal (AME) Church, the African Methodist Episcopal Zion (AMEZ) Church, and the Christian Methodist Episcopal (CME) Church. The other article, by the Rev. James Michael Culbreth, gives the history of a Black mission church founded in Mississippi at the end of the Civil War and still thriving today.

The remaining articles were written chiefly by UMW members in response to interview questions submitted by Christine and Bernard Keels. These questions were designed to elicit histories and memories of life in both predecessor and present-day Methodist denominations. They extend from slavery days to The United Methodist Church of the present, including information about the Methodist Episcopal Church; the Methodist Episcopal Church, South; the segregated Central Jurisdiction of The Methodist Church; and several of the historic Black Methodist denominations—specifically, the AME and CME churches. They include not only Black and White experiences and points of view but a response from a Korean American Methodist and Hispanic and Native American voices from the Rio Grande Conference and the Oklahoma Indian Missionary Conference. There are both points of unanimity and areas of difference. But all these voices are crying out for freedom and for a new equality in a promised land that sometimes seems discouragingly distant—and yet not impossibly far.

Pan Methodism

A Methodist Relationship

by William Boyd Grove

Pan Methodism is the relationship among the Methodist churches in the United States, namely, The United Methodist Church (UMC), the African Methodist Episcopal (AME) Church, the African Methodist Episcopal Zion (AMEZ) Church, and the Christian Methodist Episcopal (CME) Church. The word *pan* in this context means "inclusive" or "universal."

During the quadrennium 1996-2000, as Ecumenical Officer of the Council of Bishops, I was a member of the two Pan Methodist Commissions (the Commission on Cooperation and the Commission on Union). The two commissions were combined into one (the Commission on Cooperation and Union) by the most recent respective General Conferences. I have not been involved in the work of the Pan Methodist Commissions since 2000. Bishop Talbert, who is now Ecumenical Officer, succeeded me on the Commission in 2000.

The (united) Commission exists to enable the four churches to cooperate in mission and ministry and to move toward some form of union.

The churches are not committed to organic union at the present time but to union in some visible form, yet to be determined. In the present structure of movement toward one another, the three African American churches have a very strong voice—in part because they are three of the four churches involved and also because of the recognition of the reality of racism, past and present.

I think the African American churches were and are as scandalized by the creation of the Central Jurisdiction as all of us are now. I don't feel that I am the person to speak for them as to the status of African Americans in our church at the present time.

We are far from the organic union of these four churches, although more progress toward significant relationship has occurred in the last few years than in all the prior years of separation. When the time of full, organic union does come, as I believe it will (I believe it is not God's ultimate will that these four churches remain forever separate), African American leaders and members and White leaders and members will be integrated into the life of the church, perhaps as the conferences of the former Central Jurisdiction were and still are being integrated into the life and leadership of The United Methodist Church. I repeat that we are not anywhere near that point at present.

We must commit to a process that has integrity, continue to confront the issue of racism, and trust God to lead us to the fulfillment of this important mission.

United Methodist Women have always been in the vanguard of constructive Gospel change in the life of our church and its mission. That will be true in this journey as well. The same is true of the women's organizations in the other Pan Methodist churches. The Women's Division will lead prophetically in holding our church accountable for its racism—educationally, through its schools of Christian Mission, and relationally and pastorally, through development of deep and nurturing relationships with women in the other churches.

United Methodist Women can lead the conferences and local churches toward authentic repentance, including Services of Repentance in the annual conferences and local churches, as at the 2000 General Conference, teaching the histories of the other three churches and the reasons for separation and perhaps using the Study Guide developed by the General Commission on Christian Unity and Interreligious Concerns (GCCUIC) and approved by the 2000 General Conference. (This is only the beginning of an answer to this difficult but important question.)

Future directions for The United Methodist Church should include a strengthening of shared mission; a continuance of the conversations about the proper form of union for us to take, at least as a first step; and support of the Consultation of Methodist Bishops, an important meeting that brings the bishops of the four churches together about every five years.

I strongly recommend that local churches begin with a congregational use of the Study Guide, *Steps Toward Wholeness: Learning and Repent-*

ance, produced by the GCCUIC—wherever possible, in cooperation with members of congregations of the other churches.

William Boyd Grove, D.Min., a retired bishop of The United Methodist Church, was a member of the two Pan Methodist Commissions during the 1996-2000 quadrennium.

Reflection: Imagine a church that has repented of and left behind all traces of racism. What does it look like? Develop a timeline into the future that includes steps, events, and decisions which would lead up to a repentant and healed church.

Do an informal survey of United Methodists of various backgrounds. Ask if they have ever heard of the segregated Central Jurisdiction of The Methodist Church (1939-1968).

"What To Do With the Negroes"

by James Michael Culbreth

In 1864, one of the burning issues before the Methodist Episcopal Church, South (MECS), was: "what to do with the Negroes." This was a significant issue, because the time was rapidly approaching for Blacks to be set free from slavery. For 10 days during the General Conference of 1864, delegates debated about Blacks in the church. Three options were considered, according to the Rev. John Graham, who wrote a historical account of Asbury United Methodist Church, entitled *Our Templed Hills.* Those options were as follows:

- To encourage all Blacks in the church to unite with one of the African Methodist denominations, known as the African Methodist Episcopal Church and the African Methodist Episcopal Zion Church.
- To persuade Blacks to remain in the Methodist Episcopal Church, South, with full rights.
- To establish mission conferences for Blacks so that African Americans could have their own conferences, as in the other Black Methodist denominations.

The General Conference adopted the third option and proceeded to establish a mission conference. According to the Rev. Graham's historical account, the Mississippi Mission Conference was convened by Bishop Edward Thomson at Wesley Church in New Orleans, Louisiana. Although the conference was organized in Louisiana, it was named the Mississippi Mission Conference. Five White ministers were transferred into Mississippi from the northern conferences. Eleven Negro ministers were admitted into the conference on trial. Since only three Black churches already existed in the state, eight of the Black preachers were assigned to geographic areas in Louisiana, Mississippi, and Texas. Their mandate was to go and start new congregations.

On December 27, 1865, the Rev. Moses Adams began his work in

Mississippi. After a long trip, probably by horseback, Adams eventually arrived in Holly Springs, Mississippi. He was the first Black circuit rider to come to Holly Springs. Holly Springs was incorporated in 1837 and was named for the numerous holly trees in the town. Several springs were also present.

The Rev. Adams was warmly received into the community as a Methodist minister. He began working to establish a church soon after his arrival. Twenty-seven recently freed slaves became the first charter members of Asbury Methodist Church in 1865. The church was named Asbury in memory of the first American Methodist bishop, Francis Asbury. Since 1865, 40 pastors have been appointed to Asbury. My appointment as the current pastor began in June 1998.

In 1866, the historic Rust College was founded in the basement of Asbury Church, owing to the need to educate recently freed slaves. Since these early days, the church has undergone building renovations and expansions. Asbury is one of a few churches in Marshall County blessed with a ministry facility that consists of classrooms and a gymnasium.

Asbury currently claims a membership of more than 250. The church has an average worship attendance of 110. Asbury members are active in the political and social arenas of Holly Springs and Marshall County. The church also exists as a mission center for the community through such outreach efforts as Vacation Bible School, Summer Camp, Food Ministry, Scouting, United Methodist Men, United Methodist Women, Youth Ministry, Children's Ministry, and other ministry outlets.

According to the Rev. Israel Rucker, who served as Asbury's pastor from 1956 to 1960, the Central Jurisdiction years were years of struggle. The church made it through these years through acts of compassion and kindness. Rucker described the times by stating that "It was a period of sharing."

Despite the struggles associated with this time period, the church continued to progress slowly. During this time Asbury expanded its facility. Church members worked diligently, locally and nationally within the church.

Asbury welcomed the formation of The United Methodist Church. Asbury members served on various committees that helped to eradicate the

Central Jurisdiction. Rucker admits that working toward merger was difficult because there were people who wanted to maintain the status quo. Many Whites feared that the merger would pave the way for Blacks to integrate White churches. He praised the United Methodist Women, stating that "the United Methodist Women played a major role in the merger."

Now that we are all under one umbrella known as The United Methodist Church, some progress has been made. Blacks and Whites are gradually learning to work together within the church. Consequently, we have moved at a slow pace. There is still much distrust between the racial groups. Blacks still feel as if they are second-class citizens in the church. Numerous disparities exist between Black and White congregations. Too few White congregations will openly engage in fellowship with a Black congregation through pulpit exchanges, joint mission ventures, social events, and other cross-racial efforts. The question that is raised too often from White congregations is: "What's the agenda?" Many White pastors and congregations don't understand that destroying racism should be at the top of the church's agenda. Until we all are willing to relate to one another and to accept one another as people of God, things will remain unchanged.

In closing I offer this prayer for The United Methodist Church and its efforts toward eradicating racism. My prayer begins with the first two stanzas and refrain of the hymn "Many Gifts, One Spirit," by Al Carmines *(The United Methodist Hymnal, #114. Hymn composed for the Quadrennial 1973 Convocation of United Methodist Women):*

> God of change and glory, God of time and space, when we fear the future, give to us your grace. In the midst of changing ways give us still the grace to praise. God of many colors, God of many signs, you have made us different, blessing many kinds. As the old ways disappear, let your love cast out our fear. Many gifts, one Spirit, one love known in many ways. In our difference is blessing, from diversity we praise, one Giver, one Lord, one Spirit, one Word, known in many ways, hallowing our days. For the Giver, for the gifts, praise, praise, praise!

God, I thank you for being a God who honors diversity. I thank you for creating humankind as people of color. I thank you for the fact that, in your eyes, we are all your children, despite our differences.

Forgive us as your children for the fact that we allow skin color, economic status, and cultural differences to produce discord among us. Forgive us for the fact that we are responsible for causing people to experience turmoil because of their skin color. Forgive us, God, for the fact that we continue to practice racism in numerous forms in our nation, even in the twenty-first century.

God, help us who make up your United Methodist Church to realize that we displease you when we allow racism to prevail in our churches and communities. Help us to understand that it is your desire for us to exist as one. God, help us to deal with our racial hang-ups. Help us to learn how to appreciate and respect one another despite skin tone. Help us to work toward turning Dr. King's dream into reality.

God, it is my prayer that one day we, as United Methodists, will no longer identify our congregations as Black or White congregations but simply as congregations. God, I pray that the day will come when pastoral appointments will no longer be made on the basis of color or gender but on the basis of individual talents and abilities. Most of all, God, I pray that we, as your servants, will come to our senses and realize that we cannot enter your kingdom until we love one another as children of God. This is my prayer. Amen.

The Rev. James Michael Culbreth is pastor of Asbury United Methodist Church, which was founded in Holly Springs, Mississippi, in 1865, as a church for newly freed slaves.

Reflection: Write your own prayer for The United Methodist Church. What is the history of your congregation? What are the racial demographics in your area? How do you define your area?

We Would Not Be Left Behind
The Central Jurisdiction and Beyond

by Frances Dutton

I am a proud member of a church with a rich history of struggle, spiritual growth, and freedom in Jesus Christ. St. Luke's United Methodist Church is a symbol of The Methodist Church past and a beacon for The United Methodist Church of the future.

In 1843, 34 Negro slaves asked for and received permission to hold Sunday school in the Asbury Chapel (which is now known as Reisterstown United Methodist Church in Reisterstown, Maryland). This was the forerunner of St. Luke's Church. Out of the meetings that began here sprang two churches: Piney Grove and St. Luke's. In 1850, a few slaves gathered at Asbury to worship. This was the first integrated fellowship of this church, as a White class leader led them. Soon they had many converts and then they met at 'Uncle' Charles Brown's house until a church could be built. In 1855, a generous White donor gave Blacks community ground for a cemetery and a schoolhouse. Religious services were held in the schoolhouse, and many services were held during the summer in camp meetings. Camp meetings often lasted three weeks. Later, the same generous White donor gave permission to build a church as long as it didn't interfere with the school.

Money was raised through subscriptions and donations from another generous White donor for the building and development of the Colored Methodist Episcopal (CME) Church of Baltimore County, Maryland. This church became part of a circuit. The original building remains to this day. We—my family and church members—proudly worship in the church because it stands as a memorial to slaves, Black pioneers, and people of the post-Industrial Revolution who carved out a place for us to worship and congregate.

As with most churches, we eventually purchased an organ, developed a choir, and purchased a parsonage. Our continued financial progress led to liquidation of our debt. Under our current pastor, the Rev. Roosevelt Oliver, we have launched a progressive building fund that will help to house our growing congregation and our expanding programs.

Although we have always been separate from the White church, about 20 years ago, a series of Sunday-night hymn sings began with members of our sister White Methodist churches. We were on a charge with Piney Grove Church for about 60 years. About 1969, after the merger of the Washington Conference (of the Central Jurisdiction) and the Baltimore Conference, we became part of the Glyndon Parish until 1994. At that time, we became an independent church served by one pastor.

In earlier times, it was not easy to get and pay a full-time pastor. Many times, our pastor had to work at other jobs, not always having time for training and for full-time involvement in developing ministries for the church. This was our most difficult struggle during the Central Jurisdiction period [1939-1968]; however, there was more fellowship time among Blacks at conference and district meetings then than there is now.

When St. Luke's learned of the merger [of The Methodist Church with the Evangelical United Brethren Church] and of the new 'United Methodist Church,' we felt that our church would become part of a larger body and would not be left behind to struggle along.

The merger brought better training for Black pastors and laypeople. Also, we benefited from better leadership, more ministries within the local church, and outreach programs. When we became United Methodists, the women at St. Luke's could focus our mission efforts beyond our communities and local churches; however, it was not until later that we became a charter unit of United Methodist Women. At that time, a director of the Women's Division joined our church and advised us that we did not need to send our pledge to mission through a White church but that we could become chartered and independent. We are now the St. Luke's United Methodist Women, enjoying full membership in the organization, with representatives attending the Women's Assemblies in Orlando and Philadelphia.

I offer this prayer as a lifelong Methodist and a proud member of United Methodist Women:

Praise God for love and healing. Praise God that people can come together and worship. We must praise God and magnify God's name in harmony for all of God's blessings.

Frances Dutton lives and worships in Reisterstown, Maryland. Her United Methodist church was formerly a CME church and then became part of the segregated Central Jurisdiction of The Methodist Church.

Reflection: How has your congregation been "...a symbol of the Methodist Church past and a beacon for The United Methodist Church of the future?"

Have you ever been the recipient or giver of great generosity? Are there issues with giving and receiving? What gifts are needed for a whole future?

Hurtful? Oh Yes!

Life in the CME, the Central Jurisdiction, and The UMC Today

by Dorothy Boyd

Growing up in Woodlawn Missionary Baptist Church, in Chicago, Illinois, with a history of Baptist preachers in my family, I married the assistant pastor of St. Paul Colored Methodist Episcopal (CME) Church in Chicago in 1940. My marriage was accompanied by serious warnings from both friends and family of what my role would be as a preacher's wife in the CME Church.

This was the beginning of a serious period of adjustment for me, undertaken so that I could assist my husband in the development of his ministry. The CME worship style was known to differ from that of the Baptists. It was modeled after the former Methodist Episcopal Church, South (MECS), which became part of The Methodist Church in 1939. The Baptist worship style was emotional and bold in its expressions, as worshipers communicated with God by using both the heart and the spiritual body. I had never heard of the CME Church until I met my spouse.

The CME church was organized on December 16, 1870, as the Colored Methodist Episcopal Church in America. The "in America" was dropped from the name by 1930, and in May 1954, the name was changed to the Christian Methodist Episcopal Church. At its beginning, the CME Church consisted of Negroes who, while slaves, had been members of the Methodist Episcopal Church, South, but who, having gained their freedom, requested from the church of which they were members their own separate and independent religious organization. The Methodist Episcopal Church, South, granted this request. Consequently, the CME Church is the only independent Black Methodist body organized with the full cooperation, including the ecclesiastical and legal authority, of the church from which it came: the Methodist Episcopal Church, South.

As a result of my spiritual upbringing, I quickly joined the women's group and took on the task of learning the history of the CME Church. The more I learned about this church, the more intrigued I became by its past, and I began to explore the history of Methodism. What intrigued me most was how the three historically Black Methodist churches came into being. The African Methodist Episcopal (AME) Church is the oldest independent group, formed by the first Blacks to leave the Methodist Episcopal Church. [In 1787, Richard Allen and Absalom Jones led a group of African Americans out of St. George's Methodist Episcopal Church in Philadelphia after White trustees had dragged Black worshipers from their knees, demanding that they move to another part of the church. Later, Allen founded the AME Church. In 1844, the Methodist Episcopal Church, South, split from the mother church over the issue of slavery.] An overload of disgust, passion, and emotion probably contributed to the Black worshipers in Philadelphia's simply walking out of the Methodist Episcopal Church. I am sure they were tired of the isolation, the embarrassment, and the persistence of negative racial attitudes in the church.

Later, in the South after the Civil War, some of the former slaves, soon to form the CME Church, preferred to remain in the Methodist Episcopal Church, South. In 1870, they received their requested dowry (land grants, possessions, and ecclesiastical and legal authority) and were set up as their own denomination, while considering themselves still a branch of the "Mother Methodist" tree.

Doubtless because the full story was not known, the CMEs have remembered the AMEs throughout the years as "hot-headed renegades." The CMEs see themselves as a proud people who have maintained a peaceful relationship with the "mother church." They strongly believe in and advocate on behalf of their educational institutions. In the South, CME history is well preserved at the National Headquarters in Memphis, and the CME's funding of educational institutions is documented in Nashville. Although they are saddened by the polarization of Black Methodists, the CMEs believe, to this day, that they did the right thing in their partial separation.

Later in life, my family and I left the CME Church and joined The Methodist Church under the segregated Central Jurisdiction. Shortly thereafter, we supposedly were reunited and became United Methodists. Well, personally, I think we have yet to reach the promised land as Methodists. I believe we are still in a period of exodus. We are human, and that very "humanness" will not allow us to get to the promised land. Bias, prejudice, bigotry, hatred, and racism continue to hold us back. I have survived thus far by not taking everything personally, and I would advise people not to allow themselves to dislike and mistreat others because of the color of their skin.

It seems to me that Blacks are more accepting of everything in the church and a bit more easygoing than they should be—just in order to get along, to keep the peace, and to be accepted. I think the Whites in the church still need to reach a point where they can practice "individualized acceptance." Instead, they tend to view all Blacks as one, assuming falsely that all members of a given group are the same. For example, in selecting our church leadership, we choose Blacks not because of their individual skills but to balance the ethnicity of the slate.

John Wesley's teachings were the main attraction to the "mother Methodist church" for me. However, we do not seem to be able to follow such teachings. We are dealing with people and their perceptions and attitudes about race—some of which are contrary to the Wesleyan position. I recognize that if we were to have full Black leadership, we would be isolating the White Methodists and laying a foundation for reverse racism. Voting along color lines either way is not productive for the body of Christ.

Racism still lives in The United Methodist Church, and we manage to keep it alive by holding people back based on color or on jealousy. Apparently, we lack what it takes to confront racism at its core—thinking that, if we do so, we will lose friends. The new face of racism is to set people up to fail, if they are of a different race, by failing to provide the appropriate resources and support to make their involvement or leadership successful. Today, racism is more covert than overt in The United Methodist Church. We must confront this problem as it exists. If we separate ourselves and wear blinders to hide the truth, we will lose our souls.

In United Methodist Women, it seems that diversity can only be maintained through a forced system of alternate leadership, which again does not always allow for the most qualified people to take office. It discourages much-needed new growth when the premise on which actions are taken is: 'It is not your turn, because we need a Black or White person this time around. Wait until your color code is needed.' Hurtful practices are taking place in the way we teach diversity. For example, the year we had the Caribbean study at the Schools of Christian Mission, one of the instructors decided to serve ginger beer (an island drink made from herbs). Our White sisters said that they were unable to find ginger beer, so they served ginger ale instead. This was hurtful because no one thought to discuss the problem with some of the Black UMW members, who have no problem purchasing ginger beer at supermarkets in their communities. You don't have to visit an ethnic grocery store to find it.

To cite another example, we had a West Indian celebration at my church. A group of older United Methodist Women refused to drink the ginger beer that was served, indicating: "We are Methodists and do not drink alcohol." In order to preserve my standing in the church, I was forced to search the trash for an empty bottle to prove that I was not serving alcohol at a UMW meeting in the church. Was this hurtful? Oh yes!

My family and I are of mixed ancestry. When I have certain grandchildren with me, I am confronted by people—usually strangers—asking personal questions concerning their heritage or blood line. Is this hurtful? Oh yes! I don't think there is any place in the world that is so focused on color and the use of color as a means of separating people as we are here in the United States. If we would focus on more productive concerns, racism would not be such a problem. But, unfortunately, the color of one's skin tends to be a problem even within families that are mixed. This kind of attitude can spill over into every facet of our lives, if we allow it.

Dorothy Boyd of Tacoma Park, Maryland, has been a pastor's wife in the Colored (later Christian) Methodist Episcopal (CME) Church; a member of The Methodist Church in the segregated Central Jurisdiction; and a member of The United Methodist Church and UMW.

Reflection: What hurtful experiences of race have you seen in the church?

We Got What We Asked for but Lost What We Had

The Central Jurisdiction and The United Methodist Church

by Hattie Hamilton

My husband was a Methodist pastor during the Central Jurisdiction period [1939-1968]. As a clergy couple, we had nothing with which to compare our experiences in the Central Jurisdiction because it was our way of life. African American pastors in the Central Jurisdiction took care of one another and developed strong bonds that carried them through the difficult period of segregation in the church. After the dissolution of the Central Jurisdiction, my husband used to say that "we (Black Methodist clergy) got what we asked for but lost what we had." As a result of pastoral itinerancy and the need to spread out African American pastors, the bond and fellowship that had developed during the Central Jurisdiction period was lost and is almost extinct.

In addition, African American pastors who had full clergy rights in the segregated Central Jurisdiction found that their credentials suffered in the reunited church. Those who were not formally educated were reduced to the status of local pastors. My husband was very upset by this and felt that most of the local pastors were fully qualified for the ministerial role.

Pastors from the Central Jurisdiction were excited about the merger, but they were also anxious because they knew that the playing field would never be level. So they compromised and found themselves "in the same picture"—as victims of covert racism—"but placed on a different easel." My husband and many other African American United Methodist pastors felt lonely and alienated. In our conference, for example, there were approximately 554 appointments and there were only 31 African American pastors.

My husband felt that things could have been different for African Americans in The United Methodist Church if we had worked together for equality instead of developing separate organizations for Blacks and other ethnic minorities in the denomination. Such action allowed institutional racism to continue to breed.

As members of the historic Tindley Temple Methodist Church in Philadelphia, we had some exposure to the culture of White Americans because of our slightly mixed congregation. In fact, in 1973, White Americans were coming to Tindley Temple because it was known for its inspirational music, stimulating preaching, and social-outreach ministry (a soup kitchen). People enjoyed hearing the hymns written by Charles Albert Tindley (1851-1933) that were performed regularly in my church.

Although Tindley Temple is in Philadelphia, where the African Methodist Episcopal (AME) Church began, we have not had a strong relationship with "Mother Bethel," the first AME church. My husband was originally an AME pastor before becoming a mainline Methodist. We lost a lot of friends during this time because of our decision to pursue unity among the races. We felt The Methodist Church offered great possibilities and opportunities. A very close friend of mine who is African Methodist Episcopal periodically asks me: "What are you doing in the White man's church?"

I don't know about the Pan Methodist Movement. The African Methodist Episcopal (AME), African Methodist Episcopal Zion (AMEZ), and Christian Methodist Episcopal (CME) church members know what is going in The United Methodist Church and that things are not right. They feel that we want them to join us to increase the voting pool at General Conference (to sway votes) and that we want to acquire their property and resources. The big dilemma for The United Methodist Church in any type of merger will be how to share power and relinquish power.

I serve on the Episcopacy Committee and know that it is difficult to change hearts to reflect written policies. The committee has always had to struggle with racism in the appointing of pastors to our churches. I have never had a problem with racism in my leadership in the church; however, I have noticed that White friends of mine will come and put their arms around me while refraining from speaking to the African American sitting next to me.

The first time I was selected to attend General Conference, I was the only African American selected. The committee was debating about providing me a single room when a White female delegate spoke up and volunteered to be my roommate. It was an isolating feeling to have my fate debated without regard for my presence, my feelings, or the fact that my status was equal to that of the other people in the room. The woman who volunteered and I continued to be roommates each time I was elected because of our personal choice and our commitment to each other.

I feel that the racism which exists in The United Methodist Church causes ethnic minorities to compete against one another. A member of an ethnic minority who rises to the top is compelled to keep other ethnic minority members in a lower status in order to maintain her or his own leadership position. Institutional racism promotes this attitude and, in fact, thrives because of it. African Americans have to stop holding one another back, particularly in election processes. We have been made to feel that only one African American name should be placed in nomination, thereby denying the rights of others who are interested and qualified and denying the church the full breadth of talent and abilities. We should vote for the most qualified person, no matter what the person's color is or how many members of a particular race appear on the ballot. African Americans in predominantly White denominations are afraid of one another's achievements. Mass achievement appears threatening, because White society has designated only a small piece of the pie to ethnic minorities.

We need to let The United Methodist Church know that we can do more than "sing and usher." Because of these stereotypes of African Americans, I have consciously refused to assume such roles in the church. African Americans and other ethnic groups have to learn to lift one another up. False images of African Americans' supporting one another while speaking against one another in the presence of Whites is unacceptable if we are to affirm all of God's children. Because African Americans have been made to feel inferior, we continue the "house boy-plantation mentality" in the life of the church. We must ask whether we have been "set up" not to be together and not to love one another.

In United Methodist Women and in other committees and organizations, we stack the deck of cards against ourselves by scheduling meetings in the daytime only. Again, this denies many members a seat at the table of leadership and power.

I think heaven is the promised land, and I hope and trust that we will not be segregated there. I hope and trust that heaven will include and welcome Blacks and Whites and that there won't be any signs posted that say: "Whites only."

Hattie Hamilton of Philadelphia, Pennsylvania, is the wife of a former AME pastor who joined The Methodist Church and served in both the Central Jurisdiction and The United Methodist Church. She continues to experience racism in the church today.

Reflection: How do we train and promote diverse leadership? What does sharing power look like in the church? How do we go beyond "singing and ushering" as roles for African Americans?

Feeling "Less Than"

Within and Outside the Rio Grande Conference

by Ilda Vasquez

I was born a Methodist and have been one all my life. The whole time I was growing up and attending the Hispanic Methodist Church in Elsa, Texas, I never even thought of racism or experienced it. We even had a pastor, the Rev. Weaver, a White Anglo, who served our church for several years, and we never looked on him as "different." He had been a missionary in Mexico and spoke Spanish very well—with a definite accent, but well nevertheless. The congregation accepted him and made him feel welcome. However, when my husband retired from the Army in 1981 and we moved to Weslaco, Texas, we immediately visited the La Santísima Trinidad Methodist Church in the Rio Grande Conference because I wanted to sing and pray and hear the Word in my native tongue.

But my husband and two children did not enjoy the service there, so we visited First United Methodist Church. When we walked into the sanctuary that first Sunday, you would have thought we would have been welcomed with open arms—a young family (my husband was only 40 when he retired from the Army) with two children. But no one spoke to us or even smiled at us. I left that service *knowing* that I would not be back to that church!

However, my husband and children enjoyed the service and wanted to return. I fought it and tried to convince them that La Santísima Trinidad would grow on them and that they would learn to love it, but I was not successful. I struggled with this and prayed about it and finally decided that our worship as a family was more important than the church in which the worship took place. So I decided to join First Church along with the rest of my family, and we've been members of First Church ever since.

At First UMC, we were patient and persevered and kept coming back and did not say much for a while about the racism that existed. Then, as opportunities presented themselves, such as in Sunday school, at United Methodist Women's meetings, and in other settings in the church, my husband and I would point out some of the ways in which the church could be more inviting to *all* people and not make them feel the way we had felt when we had first visited the church.

When I was a junior in high school and was the campaign manager for a Hispanic boy whom we wanted to get elected as Student Council president, I was called into the principal's office and was reprimanded and threatened with expulsion from school because I was campaigning for this particular young man. I was so frightened about being expelled that I went to my mother and told her all about it. My mother, although she had only a fifth-grade education, said the principal could not do that. She said that we would go and speak to one of the School Board members, who happened to be Hispanic, and see what could be done. Mr. Gonzalez, the School Board member, assured us that he would handle this concern, and he did. I continued to campaign for Saul Silva and all went well. I learned from this experience that if I ever encountered situations such as this in the future, I needed to be patient and seek assistance from those who had some power and who might be able to help. So I guess my answer to this question of racism is to be patient, to persevere in whatever situation you are in, and always to ask for guidance from God. By the way, my candidate for Student Council president did win—and won well!

Because Hispanic and Native American churches were developed as part of missionary conferences, there is a feeling of their being "less than" other churches because their members are not considered to be full "United Methodists." This is not a good feeling! For example, it is my understanding that the Central Jurisdiction was created in The Methodist Church so that African Americans would be segregated into their own jurisdiction, no matter where any particular Black church was located, and they would not be a part of the rest of The Methodist Church.

When the Central Jurisdiction was eliminated, I believe the Hispanics were a bit concerned. The understanding was that the African American churches would now be integrated and would become one with the rest of the church. And yet the Rio Grande Conference was looked upon as solely for Hispanics and was not to be a part of the rest of the church. The feeling was that the Hispanics were being left out because, politically, they were not strong.

I think the common link between African Americans and Hispanics is the fact that we have suffered many of the same forms of discrimination. Because our color, cultures, names, or styles of worship happen to be different from those of the dominant culture, we have struggled with many of the same prejudices. We would not be served in restaurants because of who we were. We were segregated in school and given "less than" the White children. We were often not allowed to speak out publicly, and we were not given the leadership positions because we were African Americans or Hispanics.

We must truly open the doors to our churches and accept whoever walks in through those doors. We need to stop saying that so-and-so visited us and that these visitors were "Black" or they were "Hispanic." Why do we have to say they were Black or Hispanic? They were simply *visitors.* We have got to stop thinking of people in the same way as in the past. We are all God's children. God doesn't distinguish us by color or race.

As a UMW leader, I feel the organization needs to voice our concerns whenever equality in the church is not present. We must be more vocal about this whole issue. Even in our election process, we must be more vigilant. In UMW, when I was first asked to serve at the conference and district levels, I really believed that I had been asked because a balance was needed. However, in my present position, I truly believe I was selected because of my talents and skills. At the district level, I was asked to serve as Coordinator for Christian Social Involvement. At that time, this district looked upon the position as one of not much responsibility. I felt that I had to prove myself in order to be "allowed" to serve in a position that was considered "more important." But now I don't have those feelings—I guess because I was given so many opportunities to learn and grow, and the women embraced me, and I really do believe they love me because I'm Ilda—not Hispanic or anything else, but just me—a child of God.

I don't feel that the Charter for Racial Justice is enough to get UMW to deal with racism within our organization and the church. I serve on the General Commission on Religion and Race; and when I mentioned the Charter for Racial Justice as a tool to help as we try to eliminate racism, there was only one person, a pastor from Alaska, who knew what I was talking about! Obviously, the Charter for Racial Justice is not enough!

On the concept of ethnic congregations' renting space from predominantly White congregations, I ask: How can we be "united" when we are not willing to give to one another—all of us being United Methodists? In 1968, the little church I grew up in, Elsa Methodist Church, was being rebuilt by a group of Methodists from the Indiana Conference. So the First United Methodist Church in a neighboring city "allowed" us to rent space at their church for a nominal cost. We could use only the sanctuary, and then only one side of the sanctuary. Hymnals and Bibles and other things in the church were off-limits. Sunday school for all ages had to be held in the allotted space. Obviously no fellowship activities could be held during that time because the kitchen facilities could not be used. The whole concept of one congregation's renting space to another [in the same denomination] does not sit well with me because this is not being united!

I feel that African Americans and Hispanics are placed in a position of competing for leadership in the church because of designated "ethnic" spaces. My personal experience has been that, especially when the election for delegates to General Conference and Jurisdictional Conference comes about, once a person of color is elected—and it's usually after all the other places except one or two have been filled—then the quota has been met and no one else of color will be elected. So, in essence, we do compete for that one place or position of leadership.

Ilda Vasquez is a lifelong Methodist who grew up in a Hispanic Methodist church in the Rio Grande Conference and who, as an adult, has been part of a United Methodist congregation that is predominantly White.

Reflection: Where do you see competition between racial and ethnic groups happening in the church? How can this dynamic be addressed?

What Are You Doing in My Church?

A Response From the
Oklahoma Indian Missionary Conference

by Josephine Deere

I was born into The United Methodist Church. My father was a local pastor in the Oklahoma Indian Missionary Conference (OIMC). However, remaining a Methodist when I became an adult was my choice, because I have a firm belief in our doctrine.

As I think about my particular ancestors, and about how the church was brought to this part of the country, and about the significant role that my ancestors played in the church's being here, it makes me sad and happy at the same time. To know that the Native Americans were the ones who brought the Methodist church to Oklahoma gives us a sense of pride. But knowing what they went through to *get* here and how they were treated after they arrived—even by some of our own people—is the sad part. Although our conference is older than some, we were not given a vote at General Conference until 1976. Has this been a form of racism in our church? I don't know.

I have been very fortunate to be a part of the Oklahoma Indian Missionary Conference, where all of our congregations are Native American. I have attended non-Native churches only as a visitor. In the churches I have visited, the majority of the congregation members accepted us well. There were a few—and I imagine there will always be—that gave us a look which spoke for itself: "What are you doing in my church?"

Having been a part of the Oklahoma Indian Missionary Conference, I have not had to face the prejudice and the racism that some of my Native brothers and sisters have had to face in conferences where there are no Native American congregations.

I have been attending large gatherings of the church for a number of years. No matter what event I am attending, there is always a portion of institutional racism or simply racism. This is an issue that has been faced for generations and will continue to be. Just keeping the issue in front of the church instead of burying our heads in the sand will help for a better understanding.

So far our churches within the Oklahoma Indian Missionary Conference have been able to hold on to our tribal identities, with our liturgy and hymns in our own languages. But how long will we be able to hold on to our status as a missionary conference? Each generation of the church will strive to hold on to that status for as long as the river flows. Yet we are losing our languages, our customs, and our traditions as changes come over time and through inter-marriages with other races. So our churches are no longer predominantly made up of one tribe, as was the case in years past.

We have come a long way in the church in dealing with racism, but we still have a long way to go. I think we are used to looking at or dealing with racism as a matter of Black and White. Now that our church has such diversity in its minority membership, we have to look at racism not as a Black and White issue but as an issue involving all people of color.

I heard about the Central Jurisdiction only after becoming an adult. Even then, I did not understand the connection of those churches that had "Methodist" in their names but were not a part of the mother church.

One avenue the church has taken to try to deal with issues of separatism and racism has been the establishment of Native American Awareness Sunday (NAAS). However, with this observance needs to come some education on the traditions, practices, and customs of the predominant tribe in the area or region. All tribes are different. When observing NAAS, use local church members who are Native American instead of inviting Native Americans from the OIMC in to "perform" for a congregation. Native Americans have a spirituality about them that is unexplainable but can be felt.

I don't think we are doing a very good job of being inclusive. I see other minorities being lifted up (if that is how you want to say it), but I am still concerned about the Native American women's being a part of United Methodist Women—not from my particular conference but across the denomination.

Our children know no color—only what we teach them, and I think we can learn more from our children than they can learn from us. A child truly believes that "red and yellow, black and white, they are precious in His sight." So if a child can believe that, why can't we, as adults, believe like a child?

Josephine Deere is a member of the Oklahoma Indian Missionary Conference of The United Methodist Church.

Reflection: When you see someone in church who is "different," how do you react? What is your way to make people feel welcome?

What Native peoples populated your area historically? Today? See if you can find census data on line or call a local official to find out how to access that information.

For Whites Only

An Asian American Response

by Charlyn (Sung) Suh

I was born as the daughter of a pastor serving a Methodist church in Korea. Therefore, I automatically joined The United Methodist Church without looking into other denominations. I also like the fact that The United Methodist Church is liberal.

I remember reading and hearing that, for a long time, the leadership of The United Methodist Church was for Whites only. So Blacks struggled to have leadership within our denomination. There was no chance for them to speak up in main meetings and conferences, because Blacks were not allowed.

We Asian Americans have common bonds with African Americans in their struggles against racism in The United Methodist Church. We feel that we're ignored and separated. We have the same struggles even when we share facilities with White churches. There are Whites who do not want to see us or to communicate with us. They don't even want to smell the scent of anyone who is not White. There has to be a way that both of us—African Americans and Asian Americans—can create together and share together so that we do not feel so easily ignored.

The first time I experienced racism was during a worship service, where the language of worship represented "dark" as "evil" and "white" as "good." Being blond and blue-eyed is presented as beautiful [in American culture]. For example, White children who have blond hair and blue eyes are considered to be perfect.

Inclusiveness in United Methodist Women is oftentimes only a window dressing. The United Methodist Women talk about racism and inclusiveness, but they are addressing only the "Black and White" issues. What about people of other colors?

We Asian Americans came here to receive and appreciate the opportunities that this new land provides. Therefore, our culture survives the forced assimilation of our society by ensuring that we work hard to be educated in order to survive. We support our churches with lots of money—tithes, special offerings, and support for missionaries—in order to keep our culture alive and well. Our priorities are church and our children's education.

I think the greatest accomplishment toward the eradication of racism that has been made by The United Methodist Church is our establishment of educational programs to get rid of ignorance. At least, if there is a problem related to racism, then those who have been educated do not ignore it. The church has started to interpret scripture in a way that links the issue of racism with a refusal to continue tolerating White domination over other ethnic groups.

I believe each congregation needs to look within its membership for balanced leadership that links the Bible with other concerns of the community. There also needs to be an intentional effort toward event sharing with other ethnic groups, including women, men, and children, rich and poor. There needs to be fellowship. For Asians, it is risky to speak up, and we feel that others do not understand our culture. For example, we often don't speak the first time we attend a meeting, out of respect for the leader. This expression of courtesy is often interpreted as an unwillingness to share and a lack of interest. Eric Laws, an author and social-justice advocate, has written a book entitled, *The Wolf Lies Down with the Lamb,* indicating that we need to find ways to allow all voices to be heard, even if it means taking turns in meetings, intentionally inviting each voice to share.

If I were able to look into the future 20 years from now, I would hope that we would have moved forward and that the church would have a record of never giving up. Inside The United Methodist Church, there needs to be a real mutuality and real equality. This concept should be flourishing among all the different ethnic groups at all levels of the church.

As a mother, I learn from my children that they do not see people from the outside. When they see the people, they see who they are and what they can do. They do not see the colors of the people at all. They see people from a different perspective, and I know that God wants me to have this perspective when I see members of other ethnic groups.

I was ashamed learning about the history of [some of the predecessor denominations of] The United Methodist Church. Many of the preachers could not preach against the slavery system because the church was secured by money that came from slave holders. I share the parable below as a reflection on what we need to do to respond to God's call when riches interfere with the ability to seek justice and to be righteous in our actions.

> Then someone came to [Jesus] and said, "Teacher, what good deed must I do to have eternal life?" And he said to him, "Why do you ask me about what is good? There is only one who is good. If you wish to enter into life, keep the commandments." He said to him, "Which ones?" And Jesus said, "You shall not murder; You shall not commit adultery; You shall not steal; You shall not bear false witness; Honor your father and mother; also, You shall love your neighbor as yourself." The young man said to him, "I have kept all these; what do I still lack?" Jesus said to him, "If you wish to be perfect, go, sell your possessions, and give the money to the poor, and you will have treasure in heaven; then come, follow me." When the young man heard this word, he went away grieving, for he had many possessions." (Matthew 19:16-22)

So I learned that we, as Christians—even if we lose everything we have—should do justice and should show love toward our neighbors, whether they are black, brown, yellow or white.

Charlyn (Sung) Suh is a United Methodist who was born in Korea and now lives in Los Angeles, California.

Reflection: How can you avoid using words such as *black* or *darkness* to denote "evil" and *white* or *whiteness* to mean "good"? What alternative words of contrast might you choose?

How would you structure a fair and supportive arrangement for congregations sharing a church facility?

They Have a Different Style of Worship

by Sally Ernst

My father was United Presbyterian and my mother was Methodist Episcopal. As a child, I went to the Methodist Episcopal Church, first attending Sunday school and then eventually joining the church. It was a struggle for me because our church was very conservative and the ministry was based on instilling a fear of God in the parishioners.

At age 17 or 18, I went away to school and did not attend any church for five years. I also moved away from my hometown and settled in Pittsburgh, Pennsylvania, in the Bethel Park community. I was attracted to Bethel Park because of its openness and the type of social-justice ministries the church was involved in. However, I did not believe everything I heard coming from the pulpit. My faith was built on what I read and studied.

Blacks were not welcomed in my church because of the actions of Richard Allen in the St. George Methodist Episcopal Church years ago in Philadelphia. [In 1787, after Black members of the congregation who were praying in the balcony were dragged from their knees and ordered to move, Allen led a group of African Americans out of the church. Later, Allen established the African Methodist Episcopal (AME) Church.] Blacks have never been equal in the Methodist Church, and White parishioners refused to accept their presence. However, this form of racism was never discussed formally in the church.

When I was in the sixth or seventh grade, a Black family was living across the street from our church. When I asked my Sunday school teacher why they did not attend our church, I was told, "They have a different style of worship." My parents stated that people did not want this Black family to attend our church. Others told me that "we don't have them in our churches; it's not acceptable." I heard and observed that their worship style was more emotional, celebratory, and joyful than our more subdued and formal style of worship. They seemed to "know God better."

I feel that The United Methodist Church is still in a period of Exodus. We blame the victims of racism, "the Black Church," rather than examining the entire church. We White Methodists pacify ourselves by saying, "They did not want to join us." We have used this argument as our excuse to avoid doing the right thing. I knew Black people in the segregated Central Jurisdiction [of The Methodist Church], and we were willing to build one church; however, we White Methodists were encouraged not to accept Blacks. I remember Doris Handy, who was a strong advocate for unity. She told me how, in the Central Jurisdiction, she had to travel from Pennsylvania to Baltimore, Maryland, for meetings and conference attendance instead of being allowed to attend local Methodist church meetings. With limited funds, she had to travel enormous distances to worship and take part in church planning because the White Methodist Church told her "she was not good enough" to be a member of the mainline church.

I strongly believe that racism is still alive today—and for several reasons. First, White people are in denial. They fear the loss of leadership positions, power, and control. Secondly, White people like things the way they are. They fear change. White people feel that it is difficult to change traditions. Heritage is used as an excuse for not being fully inclusive. Lastly, our clergy are encouraged to keep the membership numbers up; therefore, they compromise the social-justice ministry of fighting racism to maintain their current all-White congregations. Evangelism in The United Methodist Church is deeply affected by our bias, prejudice, and racism. God is not interested in the number of people who consider themselves superior to others.

Lots of people who are members of minority ethnic groups would not choose to attend my church and other predominantly White congregations because of our lack of effort toward inclusiveness. My local church is only one example of the church's unwillingness to accept all people. Gays, lesbians, and bisexuals are admitted only as token members.

Young people are more involved in inclusiveness in our society and are therefore the beacon of hope in our churches. They are more open to contemporary worship services. For example, in my church we have a contemporary service that 300 to 400 young people attend on Sunday nights. They faithfully attend this service, but they do not want to become a part of the larger church. Church members complain that it is an expensive ministry to support and promote. They fear and predict that, without sincere efforts at evangelism, these young people will not join the church and will not make and pay a pledge—therefore only using the church and not supporting it by paying their fair share of the church's expenses.

We will continue to exist in a period of Exodus, delaying our arrival in the promised land, just as the Israelites did, as long as we fail to have an open church and thus deny ourselves the gifts, values, and cultures of others, which would make our journey much, much richer.

Sally Ernst is a White United Methodist who lives in Pittsburgh, Pennsylvania. She is a former president of the Women's Division of the General Board of Global Ministries.

Reflection: What do you see in the next generation? How does the denial of racism play out among Whites?

From Overt to Covert Racism

An Interview With Carole and Boyce Cook

Carole: My family had always attended a large, predominantly White church in Birmingham, Alabama, because it was our family tradition and just the way things were when I was growing up in the 1940s and 1950s. I was raised Methodist; my husband was Baptist.

Boyce: My family attended the largest Baptist church in town. Later in life I joined the Methodist Church. Still later, when I returned to the Baptist Church and Carole joined, we participated annually in pulpit exchanges and congregational lunches with Black churches and in Martin Luther King, Jr., celebrations. I grew up in Anniston, Alabama, and had been indoctrinated to believe that "Dr. King was the closest thing to the devil." My eyes were opened to the social-justice ministry of Dr. King during these shared celebrations. I also learned that White people can't sing—at least, not with the volume and enthusiasm of the African Americans whom I heard sing during these celebrations.

I have never attended a predominantly White church that had a close relationship with an African Methodist Episcopal (AME), African Methodist Episcopal Zion (AMEZ), or Christian Methodist Episcopal (CME) church. I was Baptist for most of my childhood and early adult years. In 1961, I attended a Methodist church (thanks to the influence of my wife) when we moved to Knoxville, Tennessee. We returned to the Baptist Church during the turmoil of the early 1960s. Then we left the Baptist Church during the 1990s because of the turmoil there.

Carole and Boyce: We do not remember the Central Jurisdiction.

Carole: When I was growing up, I knew that African Americans worshiped in their own churches in their own way. Racism and segregated congregations did not become an issue for me until racism became a national social issue. My family in Birmingham did not see a need for change. My parents were traditionalist and set in their ways; however, they respected the rights of others through not participating in racist jokes or violent oppressive actions. My mother had an African American maid who came in once a week, but Mother was not concerned about civil rights as long as her way of living was not affected. Meanwhile, the maid, Alma, and her husband were raising their children and sending them to college. We lived in the suburbs. My parents wanted their community, church, and country club to remain the same and would not look at the problem. They avoided discussing racial relations with me because it always led to questions and arguments.

My father was a vice president of a savings and loan bank in downtown Birmingham. After years of heated discussion with me on the subject of racial equality, he experienced an incident that he could not get out of his mind. One day, an older Black woman was standing in front of a large hotel drug store as he approached. She asked him whether she "was allowed" to go into the store. He was shaken. It had never occurred to him that she could *not*. Suddenly he saw her as a real person who was put at a great disadvantage. He took her arm and escorted her into the drugstore. But he never forgot that moment of realizing what it might be like for her.

Boyce: Carole's father was a loan officer at the bank in earlier years and had many dealings with African Americans who applied for loans. He was uneasy with the inequity in our society, but he had felt that was simply the way life was. Similarly, White folks had no opinion about Black people's being forced to worship in a different setting because it's just the way things were.

When White folks learned of the merger [of The Methodist Church and the Evangelical United Brethren Church] and the new church called "United Methodist," there were mixed reactions. I remember that my insurance agent, who had been a big wheel in The Methodist Church, became a big wheel in the Baptist Church because of the merger. His wife always stated that they left The Methodist Church because it was not teaching from the Bible.

Carole: I think congregations are still separated by color because people fear the unknown and they are conformists to their traditions. People are resistant to change. They are unwilling to share power, resources, and leadership.

I believe that women have the unique ability to bring people together. Because of the commitment on the part of churchwomen to the issues of family and children, there is a natural sense of solidarity that transcends color.

Boyce: We were attracted to the church we attend now because it is near a university.

Carole: We like university church settings because they encourage and allow for the diversity that the colleges or universities attract. It is refreshing to encounter open-minded attitudes and to have a mixture of ideas and nationalities as part of our worship service and ministry.

Boyce: In America, we have to be careful not to move toward "a community of common beliefs." Look at the backlash against Arabs as a result of America's suspicions since the 9/11 attacks. In the church, we have tried interracial committees and pulpit exchanges. However, it feels like we are swimming upstream. People are too used to their traditions. As a result, programs like these phrase out because they are simply a token intent. For example, when we received our first African American senior pastor, members of the church felt that the bishop had it in for us or suspected that there was another problem since the pastor was Black and coming from another conference.

In spite of such reactions, I do feel that race relations in America have come a long way since 1954. But, in some cases, the rules of the game have changed from overt to covert racism. The church and the social activists must realize that some of the strategies used in the Civil Rights Movement will not work against today's racism.

I have an African American friend, Ken, that I would do anything for, and he would do anything for me. We were fellow employees at a company in Florida and began our friendship through shared lunches and breaks. He later became my close friend and business partner. However, we had a problem with family relationships because of his wife's past experience. She had a sister who was married to a military man who was lynched. The emotional pain and loss of this family deeply affected my friend's wife and understandably influenced her response to me and to Whites in general.

Because of Ken's love for me, he came to our Baptist Church to help us start a mission in "the projects" and he became its head deacon. When that mission effort failed, Ken led many of its members to join our church. However, his wife remained a member of their original church. Ken is an exceptional leader; he is president of the local NAACP, and he quickly became a deacon and then head of the board of deacons. Through the warmth and visitation program of that church and their love for Ken, they eventually drew his wife into the church, where she became superintendent of the Sunday school. Last summer, after 15 years, we had a personal breakthrough in that Ken and his wife came up from Florida to Delaware and stayed with us. The barrier is coming down. Both Ken and his wife feel at home in that predominantly White Southern Baptist Church in Florida because of the love and affirmation that church gives them.

Carole: The Florida church is a very unusual Southern Baptist Church. For instance, when we joined, they had had female deacons among the male ones for 20 years. I was very active in the church and became a deacon myself. When Boyce left Florida to begin a new position and look for a home in Delaware, I remained in Florida to sell our house. During that time, I invited Ken's wife to many activities at our church and had them both to our home for dinner. She seemed at home with me, but she was very shy.

I was pleased to see that Boyce was attending a United Methodist church in Delaware and soon joined it along with him. We could not take the increasing narrow-mindedness of the Southern Baptist Church in general, though we loved our Florida church.

Boyce: When I lived in Knoxville, Tennessee, I was a member of the

Jaycees [Junior Chamber of Commerce]. An African American man joined our organization, and I showed him the ropes. I had to work with him in fighting for integration. When I confronted my White club members, they stated that "the Black man's presence would lower the prestige of the club." Nowadays, White people might be more willing to assist with confronting racism, but they are more concerned about what is in it for them and there is a fear of disturbing the status quo.

Carole enjoys genealogy research. In this hobby, she recently heard from a young African American man seeking to find out whether they are related.

Carole: Yes, I am doing everything I can to see if we have relatives in common. My mother's great-great-grandfather, Zebulon, was born in Cecil County, Maryland. When he died in Lowndes County, Alabama, in 1855, he had included in his will a bequest to "my mulatto grandson, Jack." I have not been able to identify Jack's parents with any documentation, but the old man's word counts for something. I hope that we can find some documentation somewhere. Genealogy, at its best, is history and does not judge. Therefore, genealogists at their best are looking for the truth, whatever that may be. I welcome all my kinfolk, regardless, and I have a feeling Jack would say the same.

Carole and Boyce Cook are White natives of Alabama who currently live in Newark, Delaware, where they worship at a United Methodist church.

Reflection: Is there racial diversity in your family? If you discovered relatives of a different racial identity, how would you feel?

Did you know about the Central Jurisdiction before this study? Did you know of the origins of the historically Black Methodist denominations? Who should know about these things, and why?

STUDY GUIDE FOR

Exodus

THE JOURNEY TO FREEDOM

by Loretta Williams, Joe Agne, and J. Ann Craig

INTRODUCTION TO THE STUDY GUIDE

Welcome to the study guide portion of *Exodus: The Journey to Freedom.* The exercises and background pieces in the following pages will help us take a few more steps on the road to freedom. Freedom from slavery is the foundation for the entire Jewish and Christian traditions. Moses serves as the saving figure in the Hebrew text and is the authority to which Jesus refers. After his crucifixion, Jesus is understood to be the new Moses leading his people into faith and out of the bondage of sin. Freedom from bondage of any kind is inherent in the good news of the Bible.

The study guide will help leaders and participants in this spiritual growth study engage the material in a way that leads to freedom. In this guide, Loretta Williams, Joe Agne, and Ann Craig worked together to incorporate the specifics of the Exodus text and the Methodist family history as well as to develop the group process. Each member of the team has a long history of assisting groups and individuals in addressing the issues of racism. You are now part of the larger team of United Methodists who are willing to face the reality that our ideas about race and power affect our spiritual lives.

As in many families, there have been splits and injuries that many would prefer to keep swept under the rug. In the Methodist family, splits have created new denominations, such as the African Methodist Episcopal (AME), African Methodist Episcopal Zion (AMEZ), and Colored Methodist Episcopal (CME) churches. The White leaders of the Methodist Episcopal churches of the North and South mirrored the sin of Jim Crow laws when, in creating The Methodist Church in 1939, they segregated all Black Methodist churches into one race-defined Central Jurisdiction, which lasted until The United Methodist Church was formed in 1968.

Today, the AME, AMEZ, CME, and United Methodist denominations are in conversation about the possibility of reunion. Knowledge, wisdom, honesty, and sensitivity are only a few of the characteristics participants in these discussions will need to bring to the table. The extent to which women are involved will be a predictor of success, since women make up around 75 percent of the membership of the churches. Women have historically understood relationships, as well as law, to be foundational to any lasting social changes.

In the context of Christian churches, we draw from creeds and theology that affirm our full humanity and that place repentance, forgiveness, and confession of Jesus Christ at the heart of spiritual growth. We must let God free us of the burden of guilt or anger, shame or hatred, that we might be carrying. But this cannot be done without honest repentance. Our time studying this history is not designed to shame individuals. Instead, it allows us to inspire one another to work to resist racism. It also empowers us to be honest with one another so that we can confront racism with confidence, knowing that we are not alone in the journey.

Things to Remember in Groups Dealing With Racial Issues

1. Dealing With Race as a Subject

Many of us have been taught that race is a taboo subject for polite conversation. Do not be surprised if the subject is uncomfortable at times. Stay with the conversation, practice breathing deeply, and, if conflict emerges, keep your voice in a conversational tone to avoid escalating a difficult discussion into an argument. Arguing, accusing, crying, pouting, and other emotional responses reinforce the taboo against talking about racial issues.

2. Strategies for Racially Mixed Groups

a. African Americans will need to employ effective coping mechanisms in a racially mixed group dealing with race. Avoid being cast in the role of an expert on racial questions or on Black churches. Encourage participants from the dominant culture to work out their own answers or do their own research rather than shift the attention and the burden to you.

b. Members of other racial or ethnic minorities need to bring in their own stories, as they relate to the history of African Americans in the United States. This study is not intended to reinforce a view of race as a "Black and White" issue only, but there are specifics that must be dealt with as the historically Black Methodist denominations discuss merger with The

United Methodist Church. Prejudice against people of African descent is widespread in Latin American, Asian, European, and even African contexts. Bring those experiences, observations, and realities to the conversation and also include experiences of cross-racial and multiracial resistance to racial oppression.

c. White participants and others who are not African American need to avoid asking Black participants to tell them about racism or to warn them when they are speaking or acting in racist ways. This is like asking the question of those judged by Jesus in Matthew 25: "Lord, when did we see you hungry...?" Members of the dominant culture know plenty about racism but are taught by the culture to pretend that they never see it or know anything about it. In reality, the experience of White privilege is like the experience of fish in water—it is assumed and it is everywhere. Do not wait for a minority person to confront a racially loaded situation. Instead, take the lead, take the risk, and name the situation out loud. If you need help, ask another White person for assistance. Do your homework, but don't expect to have your consciousness raised all at once; keep at it, even if it gets frustrating.

3. Strategies for Racially Homogeneous Groups

a. All-White groups will be tempted to say that there is no problem since there are no members of minority groups present. This is a particularly self-reinforcing form of racism. Because racial segregation is still an important pillar of racism, many groups, communities, and even whole towns are largely made up of one race. Because racism is so institutionalized that same-race groups are the norm does not indicate that race is not an issue. On the contrary, racism is a painfully present issue, even if you think there is no one of a different race within 100 miles of you. Study the history of race and ethnicity in your area, as well as the current demographics; don't assume that you already know this information. For example, did you know that 25 percent of the cattlemen in the old West were of African descent? Where did they settle?

b. Racial and ethnic groups that are not of African or European descent may think this study has little to do with their own realities, but they should take time to think about the impact of racially or ethnically defined congregations. What history and dynamics do people who are not from either White or Black cultures have in common? What are their differences? What are their relationships with White and   Black cultures?

c. African American groups may be tempted to think that there are no new issues in this study, but do not hesitate to take another look. What were the dynamics leading to the establishment of the segregated Central Jurisdiction and to its disbandment 30 years later? What are the vested interests of the various groups in the current conversations about Pan Methodist union?   How do differences of race, class, attitude, and theology play out in the different Methodist denominations? How would the conversation of those in historically Black denominations change if there were White participants?

4.   General Guidelines for Class Participation

(Adapted from Nancy Carter's book, *Matthew: Who Do You Say I Am?*)
a.   Listen with respect. Allow each person room to express opinions.
b.   Speak long enough to convey your point but not so long that others do not have enough time to speak or respond.
c.   Monitor how many times you talk. Make a mark on your paper. If you are a big talker, once you reach three times, give it a rest until others have a chance. If you are shy, make it a goal to talk at least twice; people like to know what you are thinking.
d.   Do not attack a person, but be willing to be honest. Ask speakers to clarify or rephrase their statements before you contest them. Share your perspective with first-person statements rather than "you" statements (e.g., "I feel..." or "My experience is...").
e.   Do your best not to talk about group conversations outside the classroom. Try to keep both the content of discussions and the issues raised within the group. If there is tension, deal with it in the group during a class session. If the dynamics become too intense, invite a mediator whom everyone in the group trusts.

f. Be sensitive to one another. For example, some people like to hug, but others do not. Avoid asking everyone to hug someone. Use a less intimate gesture, such as holding hands for prayer or shaking hands in greeting. Saying "Greet each other in a sign of peace" allows people to choose their actions.

Leading or Facilitating a Spiritual Growth Study

Advance Preparation
1. Pray for God's guidance and for each participant.
2. Use the Internet for research: <http://gbgm-umc.org/umw/exodus>
3. Do a search on "Moses" using biblegateway.com. Moses is a central figure in the Bible.
4. Read widely on Exodus and on the Black Methodist denominations.
5. Go through the student text and the study guide and create a timed, detailed outline of sessions.
6. Print the summary timeline at the following web address: <http://www.gcah.org/UMC_timeline.htm>. Or, better yet, order a detailed Methodist Timeline for $2 from:

> The General Commission on Archives and History
> The United Methodist Church
> P.O. Box 127, 36 Madison Avenue
> Madison, NJ 07940

7. Prepare or copy a brief outline of sessions, including your name and assignments.
8. Work through the opening and closing worship for each session. Involve others.
9. Collect items for worship centers; a class member can volunteer to prepare them.
10. Pack your Bible, an assortment of related books, and, if possible, *The United Methodist Hymnal* and *Songs of Zion* (Supplemental Worship Resources 12).
11. Bring room decorations related to the topic.
12. Identify audiovisual material, such as videos or music CDs (compact disks), that relate to the topic.

13. Arrange for equipment, such as a VCR, CD player, computer projector, and the like.
14. Plan for a class assistant who helps set up the room and handles audio-visual equipment.
15. Secure markers, newsprint, and other materials, as needed.
16. Arrive early to set up the seating in a configuration that enhances participation.
17. Create the first worship center; have class members take over after that.
18. Identify or post a graffiti wall where people can write questions or comments on a chalkboard or on newsprint

Curriculum Development

1. Adults need a variety of activities designed for different learning styles.
2. Alternate large-group activities with small-group activities.
3. Incorporate words, music, visuals, movement, reports, and the like in each session.
4. Use assignments, reports, and projects to tap group resources.

Classroom Implementation

1. Welcome the group.
2. Do housekeeping items: identify bathrooms and sources of water and snacks.
3. Provide nametags.
4. Take attendance by passing around a paper to sign. This will give you a list from which you can learn names. If people want to be certified or to get credit for Continuing Education, attendance records are necessary.
5. Introduce yourself and any volunteer assistants.
6. Facilitate the introduction of all participants.
7. Ask the talkers to talk a maximum of three times and then to listen for a while.
8. Ask the non-talkers to set a goal of talking at least two times.
9. Ask the group to monitor gender and race dynamics, such as:
   a. not responding to statements made by minorities or women.

b.   interrupting and negating.

c.   using such expressions as "you people," "they," or "those people."

10. Affirm each person who contributes, using such responses as "Yes"; "Thank you"; "Interesting point"; or "Great." If you disagree with someone's opinion, ask others to provide different opinions. You can also affirm a person for stating her or his position well and then offer another viewpoint. If you are ever attacked, ask if anyone else in the group wants to comment before commenting yourself. Stay positive.

SESSION 1

Goals

*   Introduce participants to the scope of the study and give the assignments.
*   Establish ground rules for interaction.
*   Outline the Book of Exodus in terms of history and religious ritual.
*   Define *racism* (see Appendix D and the Glossary) and state its spiritual consequences.
*   Use Exodus to explore stereotyping and power structures. (Pertinent passages are quoted in chapters 1 and 3 of the Keels' book.)
*   Explore the identities of class members and the role of the Exodus story in various cultures.

Special Assignments for Upcoming Sessions

Small Group: Work on the timeline. Select and post key events.
(Sessions Two-Four)

Four People: Summarize the histories of the Methodist denominations.
(Session Two; see Keels' text, chapters 2 and 4)

One Person: Report on the costs of the Civil War.

(Session Three; see Keels' text, chapter 2, and websites in the Session Three lesson plan)

<u>Three People:</u> Perform vignettes of women leaders. (Session Four)

- Ask two women to dramatize a conversation between Ida B. Wells and Jessie Daniel Ames, using information from the following websites: <http://womhist.binghamton.edu/aswpl/intro.htm> and <http://www.ku.edu/kansas/crossingboundaries/page6d2.html>
- Ask one participant to take on the character of Virginia Durr, wife of a prominent White lawyer, Clifford Durr, in Montgomery, Alabama, in the 1950s during the bus boycott. (See Appendix K.)

<u>Small Group:</u> Create a closing worship service based on the Jewish Seder. (Session Four; see Appendix L)

Study Book Reading Assignments for All Students

- Chapter 1 of the Keels' book (Session Two)
- Chapters 2 and 3 of the Keels' book (Session Three)
- Chapters 4 and 5 of the Keels' book (Session Four)
- Read the articles on pp. 123-160 as time allows.

Bible Reading Assignments for All Students

- Read or skim Exodus to identify three types of material: story, law, and religious ritual. (Session One)
- Read Exodus looking for points of decision. (Session Two)
- Read Exodus 32:25-35. (Session Three)
- Read Exodus 21:1-10, 15:1-21. (Session Four)

Outline for Class

Introduction and Assignments .... 5 minutes
Worship .... 5 minutes

Room Ideas

- Photocopy and post pictures showing conditions under slavery. (Such photos are available on the Internet as part of the Library of Congress Exhibit, "African American Odyssey," to be found at the following website: <http://memory.loc.gov/ammem/aaohtml/exhibit/aointro.html>
- Post a picture of John Wesley and William Wilberforce, the recipient of Wesley's last letter, which called slavery an "execrable villainy." (See Keels' book, chapter 1.)
- Post the map of the Exodus journey.
- Post the map of the Atlantic slave trade.
- Post the definition of *racism* from Appendix D and cover it with newsprint.
- Post Professor Banks' world view diagrams from Appendix E.

Introductions

- Introduce yourself. Explain that you are a leader, not a teacher.
- Review the "General Guidelines for Class Participation" in the "Introduction to the Study Guide," above.
- Use the "Knowledge Pursuit!" game (Appendix A) to have people introduce themselves and to learn about the knowledge present in those gathered, as well as absent knowledge. Each of the two is relevant for understanding the lenses through which we view our world. When someone completes the 25 squares or when a set time (5-10 minutes) runs out, ask the group if there were any "Aha!" moments. Ask if there were points at which the limits of your particular cultural background were apparent.

Worship

"Go Down, Moses"	*The United Methodist Hymnal*, #448 (verse 1)
Scripture:	Exodus 1:8-14
"Go Down, Moses"	#448 (verse 2)
"Freedom in Christ"	#360 (unison prayer)
Prayer for the Class by a Participant	
"Go Down, Moses"	#448 (verses 3-4)

Note: *Christine and Bernard Keels use African American spirituals, such as "Go Down, Moses," throughout their text as an interpretive tool. See Appendix M for more information about spirituals and gospel music.*

Group Building

* Summarize "Things to Remember in Groups Dealing with Racial Issues" in the "Introduction to the Study Guide," above. Have the class identify which elements apply to the composition of their group. Are there other pertinent issues that are not listed in this section?

* If the desire to be "colorblind" comes up, work through appendix G with the class.

* Let the group know that racism is a difficult topic to deal with. People may have comments or questions that they might not feel comfortable stating in public. Point out the graffiti board as a place where people may write questions and comments. Assure participants that their graffiti may be positive, negative, or simply expressions of curiosity. All will help the class to grow.

Bible Exercise

Working in groups of two, divide the book of Exodus into sections grouped under three heads: story, law, and religious ritual. Under the *story* heading, place the sections that deal with the Hebrew people's escape from slavery.

Under the *law* head, include sections dealing with laws to govern the people's common lives. And under the *religious ritual* head, include sections dealing with proper worship. (Hint: Use the section heads in the Bible, which appear at the bottom of pages in the NRSV, and skim quickly. Half the class can begin in the middle of Exodus if time is short.) Then work as a large group to identify the sections and to write them on newsprint.

In small groups, discuss the following:
- Do the three types of content overlap? Which type seems the oldest, and why?
- Tradition long held that Moses wrote the first five books of the Bible. Why could this be true? What works against the belief?
- What authority do the three types of material hold for you?
- What effect does the authority of Exodus have on the practice of slavery and issues of race?

Defining "White Privilege" and "Racism"
- Suggest: "Instead of beginning with a traditional definition of *racism,* let's begin with a definition of *White privilege.* Working individually, write a two-sentence definition of *White privilege.* Then stand up and find others who have a definition similar to yours. Working with them, refine your definition. Then we'll share several definitions in the large group."
- Ask the class to brainstorm a list of privileges from which White people benefit. Then have them consult Robert Jensen's article on "White Privilege" in Appendix B.
- Next, ask class members to work individually on a two-sentence definition of *racism* and then to work with others who have similar definitions to refine the definition in a small group. Share several definitions in the large group.
- Unveil the definition of *racism* posted earlier or turn to Appendix D. Compare the book's definition with the group's definitions.

Stereotyping and World View

- Read Exodus 1:15-22. Ask: "What are the stereotypes of Hebrews and Egyptians? What is the reality of power in this account?" Have participants relate the definition of *racism* in Appendix D to this Exodus excerpt.
- Have the class look at Professor James Banks' chart on monocultural and multicultural world views in Appendix E. Ask: "In what ways do you participate in the middle diagram? What would participation in the third diagram be like?"
- Affirm the group members for their hard work.
- Make or confirm upcoming assignments to class members.

Closing

"Oh, Freedom!"   *Songs of Zion,* #102

Oh, freedom! Oh, freedom! Oh, freedom all over me! When I am free!
And before I'd be a slave, I'll be buried in my grave,
And go home to my Lord and be free.

(Negro Spiritual, circa 1830)

SESSION 2

Goals

- Begin a timeline for slavery, racism, and Methodist denominations. Include the founding of the historically Black Methodist churches and the founding of the Central Jurisdiction of The Methodist Church.
- Focus the Bible study on points of decision by the various people in Exodus.

- Use the Bible to explore how Exodus functions in cultural contexts.
- Analyze how both the oppressed and the oppressor lose from oppression, though in differing measure and substance.
- Identify examples of how the Bible has been misused to reinforce slavery and racism.
- Introduce John Wesley's position on slavery.

Outline for Class, With Video

Worship...5 minutes
Timeline..10 minutes
Points of Decision...10 minutes
Video...20 minutes
Discussion..25 minutes
Scripture to Free or Enslave..................................15 minutes
Wesley's Letter to Wilberforce.............................15 minutes
Closing..5 minutes

Outline for Class, Without Video

Worship...5 minutes
Timeline..10 minutes
Points of Decision...10 minutes
Sacrifice..10 minutes
Scripture to Free or Enslave..................................15 minutes
Myth of Ham...15 minutes
Wesley's Letter to Wilberforce.............................15 minutes
Closing..5 minutes

Room Ideas

- Post a long sheet of newsprint with a timeline developed by the small group given this assignment.
- Also post the entire Methodist Timeline so the class can reference it and select additional items to post.
- Post Key Scriptures, such as "Slaves, obey your earthly masters...." (Ephesians 6:5)

Worship

"O Mary, Don't You Weep"   *The United Methodist Hymnal*
                                                     #134 (verses 1-2)
"The World Methodist Social Affirmation"   #886
"O Mary, Don't You Weep"   #134 (verse 3)

Decisions and Their Consequences

*   Have the class gather by the timeline. Ask the small-group members who worked on the timeline to highlight the key points they have identified thus far. Invite the remaining members of the group to add significant events when such events come to their attention.

(If there is insufficient time for class members to prepare a timeline in advance, make a blank timeline and put timeline items on separate strips of paper so that participants can begin taping them to the timeline as they come to class. Have them be ready to point out one or two items that they posted. Or, after posting, you may ask participants to look over the posted events, with volunteers lifting up one or two that seem central to the study.)

Bible Exercise 1: Points of Decision

*   Brainstorm a list of points of decision in the Exodus account.
*   Brainstorm points of decision in the history of Methodism's treatment of Black people.
*   Brainstorm a list of decisions the church has to make about race today.

Video

*   Show a 20-minute excerpt on "Mother Bethel" from the video "Brotherly Love," part of the PBS Series *Africans in America.* This four-part series is $39.95 per tape or $150 per set. Call your conference UMW to borrow a tape or contact PBS toll-free at 877-727-7467.
*   Have the class members work in small groups to discuss the differences

between *consequences, punishments,* and *sacrifices.* Compare the events of Exodus and the situation in Philadelphia (see chapter 2). After 15 minutes, the small groups should report to the large group.

If you do not have access to the video, use the following Bible study process:

Sacrifice is a major theme emerging from Exodus.
— The Hebrew midwives, Pharaoh's daughter, Moses' mother, and Miriam were willing to sacrifice their security to save the child.
— Moses sacrificed his peaceful life to return to Egypt.
— Those in power were willing to sacrifice their own people and family members to maintain control.
— The Hebrews were willing to sacrifice the predictability of slavery for the uncertainty of freedom.
— A lamb is sacrificed at Passover, and Jesus later became identified with the Passover lamb.

Ask:
— What sacrifices can you identify in the struggles against slavery and racism?
— What sacrifices (plagues?) did the Egyptian oppressors suffer in Moses' time?
— What are the differences between consequences, punishments, and sacrifices?

Have class members work in small groups and then report to the class as a whole. For the third question, have a dictionary available to consult. For example, *consequences* are simply the effects or outcomes resulting from a cause, though the connotation may often be negative, as in "face the consequences." *Punishments* are undesired consequences, or penalties, imposed for forbidden behavior. *Sacrifices* are chosen hardships endured to advance a cause, or things given up to gain something of greater value.

Bible Exercise 2: Interpreting Exodus in Its Cultural Context

Read Acts 7:17-53
- What is missing from the Exodus account given by Stephen?
- Who was Stephen addressing, and what was his agenda?
- How is the Exodus story used in your racial or ethnic group?
- Are there characters or events missing in your account?
- Does your account come from the Bible? From your church? From a movie?

Use of Scripture to Free or Enslave

- List scriptures that have been used to rationalize and enforce slavery and racism. Examples: Ephesians 6:5, Colossians 3:22, Titus 2:9, I Peter 2:18.
- How do you deal with the fact that parts of the Bible seem to support slavery?
- Brainstorm scriptural passages that compel us to advocate for freedom and justice.

The Ham Myth

Summarize the Keels' discussion of Noah's curse on his son Ham.
- Ask how many people have heard of the Ham myth's being used to enforce racism.
- Is there a difference between racial groups as to who has heard the Ham myth used in this way?
- Why would Noah curse the son who discovered his drunken stupor?
- What are the implications of this story and its use to explain, justify, or excuse racism?

John Wesley was totally committed to the Bible as the Word of God, communicating the good news of salvation. The myth of Ham and the scripture saying, "Slaves, obey your earthly masters" were operating in his day to support the slave trade. How could Wesley call himself "a man of the Book" while resisting slavery until his dying day? What does this say about interpretations of scripture?

The last letter John Wesley ever wrote was sent to William Wilberforce protesting slavery (see the Keels' text, chapter 1). Have participants work in groups of two to write a short letter to a person in a position of authority, expressing their feelings about racism and suggesting what should be done to eradicate it.. Then combine them into groups of four to share their letters. Finally, read two or three examples to the whole class.

Assignments for Next Session

- Read chapters 2 and 3 of *Exodus: The Journey to Freedom.*
- Select four people to summarize the histories of these Methodist denominations: the AME, AMEZ, CME, and UMC (including its Methodist predecessors: the MEC; the MEC, South; and The Methodist Church). See the Keels' text, chapters 2 and 4.
- Report on basic facts about the cost of the Civil War. (See Session Three websites.)
- Ask the whole group to continue adding important events to the timeline.

Closing

"There Is a Balm in Gilead" *The United Methodist Hymnal, #375*

SESSION 3

Goals

- Explore Exodus as the spiritual autobiography of a people.
- Discuss how resistance to oppression is part of spiritual growth.
- Consider history as a spiritual journey—a metaphor bringing insight.

Outline for Class

Room Ideas

- Post pictures of early Black bishops.
- Post pictures of leaders against racism in churches.

Worship

"Stand by Me"	*The United Methodist Hymnal,* #512 (verses 1-2)
Scripture:	Psalm 72:1-17 p. 795 (read antiphonally)
"Stand by Me"	#512 (verse 3)
Prayer "For Overcoming Adversity"	#531
"Stand by Me"	#512 (verses 4-5)

Graffiti Board Review

Review any messages posted on the graffiti board, with discussion and comments as appropriate.

Bible Exercise

- Brainstorm the elements of a spiritual autobiography.
- Read Exodus 32:25-35.

—Work in groups of three or four to identify how this troubling passage functions as part of a spiritual autobiography for the Hebrew people.
—Individually outline five or six events in your life—both positive and negative—that have been key points of spiritual growth for you.
—Now brainstorm about 10 events in the history of the United States that could be included in a spiritual autobiography of the nation.

Denomination Histories

Call on the four presenters who were assigned to summarize the histories of the Methodist denominations now discussing possible union: the AME, AMEZ, CME, and UMC. Invite them to provide their respective summary histories. The UMC reporter should include pertinent information about predecessor Methodist denominations, specifically, the Methodist Episcopal Church; the Methodist Episcopal Church, South; and the reunited Methodist Church of 1939-1968. As they report, ask the Timeline Group to add any dates to the timeline that might be missing..

Timeline Review

- Are there a few key moments in Methodism's spiritual autobiography?
- Is there a general character to these events? What do they have in common?

Presentation on the Costs of the Civil War

Present data taken from the two websites that follow:
<http://www.civilwarhome.com/warcosts.htm> and
<http://www.germantown.k12.il.us/html/deaths.html>.
Also see the Keels' text, chapter 2, pp. 45-46, 50.

Quiz on African American History

Work through the quiz on African American History in Appendix F. After completing it and checking against the information in Appendix H, ask the class why it is important to have a working knowledge of these historical realities. What realities of today are impacted if we don't know this information? What does this kind of information have to do with denominational histories?

Leader: We've looked at some of the history around the Civil War. Like the story of Moses coming down from the mountain and commanding half the Hebrew camp to kill the other half (see Exodus 32: 25-28), this country spent billions of dollars and shed lakes of blood to eliminate the golden calf of slavery and White supremacy. The abolition of slavery was a powerful movement of Whites and Blacks. Emancipation of the slaves came at great cost. Freedom from racism is yet to come.

We've touched upon the potential impact of ignorance through our quiz. The journey to freedom remains. The Israelites wandered in the desert, and the church is not finished with rebellion against the fact that all humanity was created in God's image. Thus we have a history to learn and a history to create.

Shortly after the Civil War, during the Reconstruction Period when Southern White men who had supported the Confederacy lost their right to vote, the South Carolina legislature had a majority of African American elected officials. But not long after that, Ku Klux Klan terrorism and Jim Crow laws reinstated White racism in the South. Although slavery had been outlawed, the idolatry of race lived on.

Post-Emancipation Realities

Read aloud to the class the following scenarios illustrating some post-emancipation realities. They are excerpted from Patricia C. Click, *Time Full of Trial: The Roanoke Island Freedmen's Colony, 1862-1867* (Chapel Hill: University of North Carolina Press, 2001), pp. 110-111, 125.

In December 1865 an editorial in the *Christian Recorder,* the journal of the African Methodist Episcopal Church, denounced missionary teachers "who while in the North made loud pretension to Abolition, [but] when they get South partake so largely of that contemptible prejudice that they are ashamed to be seen in company with colored men....The missionaries came South believing that the freedpeople's years in slavery had left them bereft of self-discipline and purpose—that their experience in slavery led them to lie and steal without compunction....The teachers truly believed that education would lift the freedpeople to their proper position in the "New Social Order" that was to replace the slave system.

...In the spring of 1862, after the Ninth New York [Regiment] had settled into occupation duties on Roanoke Island, the regiment's Zouave Minstrel and Dramatic Club found it difficult to procure hair for wigs for its minstrel chorus. Matthew Graham of the Ninth New York later described the ensuing events. Concluding that the freedmen were a ready source of the desirable tresses, the soldiers tried to talk them into cutting their hair and donating it to the club for its theatrical endeavors. A few of the former slaves cooperated, but apparently not enough to fill the club's needs, so the soldiers resorted to force. Graham recounted that the freedmen "who were the owners of the kind of head covering coveted" by the dramatic corps "were kidnapped, carried to a squad-room, [and] kept quiet by dire threats," until "a Zouave armed with a pair of shears" cut their hair and sent them "on their way as bald as babies."

What, from a modern perspective, seems to have been cruel and thoughtless behavior did not strike the [White] soldiers as inappropriate. In many ways the hair incident serves as a metaphor for the military's treatment of the freedpeople....

- Have class members work in small groups to discuss comparable situations in church and society today.
- In the large group share any examples of comparable racially loaded situations.

Leader: These historical accounts are part of the spiritual autobiography of the United States. A pivotal moment in our journey through the wilderness was Rosa Parks' act of resistance on a bus in Birmingham, Alabama, in the 1950s. But history is written in snippets and from various perspectives. Even the Exodus account was written by a people who had developed enough wealth to create an opulent temple. The details of their journey that have come down to us are amazing, but do you ever wonder what parts of the story might have been missing? We'll never know but we do know that history is often filtered through the perceptions of the powerful.

Class Activity

Distribute copies of the coloring-book drawing of Ms. Rosa Parks (Appendix I). Ask the participants to work in small groups to identify the main points of the story that they would tell a 12-year old godchild about this woman. Give no other clues in making the assignment. Allow eight minutes for the groups to come up with their stories.

Then have two or three readers read aloud the full story in Appendix I. In the large group, have participants respond to the following questions:

- What similarities and differences do you see in the stories?
- Which version—your group's or the version read aloud—might inspire your godchild?
- Why do you think so many of us didn't really know the full story?
- From whose perspective did we gain our information before today?
- What are we called to do, now that we know the real story?

Assignments for Next Session

- Read Chapters 4 and 5 of *Exodus: The Journey to Freedom.*
- Have the three assigned women prepare the vignettes of women leaders that they will perform.
- Have the class work through the quiz: "Women's Leadership Against Slavery and Racism."
- The group planning the closing Seder should be ready.

Closing:

"The Battle Hymn of the Republic" *The United Methodist Hymnal,* #717

Note: Julia Ward Howe wrote these lyrics and set them to the tune of "John Brown's Body Lies a' Moulderin' in the Grave." For further facts and for the "John Brown" lyrics, see the following websites:
http://womenshistory.about.com/library/weekly/aa013100c.htm
http://www.fortunecity.com/tinpan/parton/2/jbrown.html

SESSION 4

Goals

- Raise class members' awareness of the significant roles played by women in the Book of Exodus.
- Spotlight women's leadership in the long struggle against slavery and racism.
- Focus the class on the issues to be resolved in Pan-Methodist union (involving the AME, AMEZ, CME, and UMC) and the impact of these decisions on Methodism in the future.
- Learn some of the symbolic details involved in the Seder (the Hebrew Passover feast).

Outline for Class

Worship...5 minutes
Review Graffiti and Timeline Additions......................................5 minutes
Bible Study on the Women of Exodus.......................................20 minutes
Quiz: "Women's Leadership Against Slavery and Racism"....10 minutes
Dramatized Vignettes of Women Leaders.............................15 minutes

Issues for AME, AMEZ, CME, and UMC Reunion ....20 minutes
Write a Spiritual Biography of Methodism in the Future........10 minutes
Worship Service Modeled on the Seder and Methodist
    History..15 minutes
Evaluation..5 minutes

Worship

"Let My People Seek Their Freedom"   *The United Methodist Hymnal*
                                            #586 (verse 1)

"Canticle of Moses and Miriam"   #135 (See also Keels' text,
                                            chapter 5, pp. 120-121)

"Let My People Seek Their Freedom"   #586 (verse 3)

Bible Exercise 1: Women of Exodus

- Read Exodus 2:1-10.
- Identify the power relationships in the story. What were the social rules and laws at work?
- List the female characters and the actions and risks each took.
- With whom do you identify—Miriam? the baby Moses? Pharaoh's daughter? the maids?
- What happens when you read the story as if you were one of the other characters?
- What is God calling you to do? .

Bible Exercise 2: Miriam and the Triumph Song

- Read Exodus 15:20-21; then read Exodus 15:1 and skim through the rest of the song (see the Keels' text, chapter 2, pp. 43-44).
- Why do you think the opening phrase is repeated? Why does the text first say Moses and the Israelites sang and then portray Miriam picking up a tambourine and singing the opening phrase of the same song? Whose song is this? Are there two separate songs? What are the possibilities of interpretion for these parallel texts?

- What is the importance of Miriam's being called a prophet (in the NRSV)? In your group, look at several different translations. Do some versions of the Bible, especially older ones, say "prophetess" instead of "prophet"? What different impact do the two words have?
- As an additional exercise related to Miriam, read Numbers 12 to explore her leadership role and the dynamics between her and her brothers, Moses and Aaron. Note that the people did not leave until Miriam was brought back into the camp. You can also explore the account of Miriam's death in Numbers 20:1.

Women's Leadership against Slavery and Racism

Match the names below to the correct descriptions that follow (pp. 186-188).

1. Harriet Tubman
2. Harriet Beecher Stowe
3. Julia Ward Howe
4. Susan B. Anthony
5. Sojourner Truth
6. Ida B.Wells-Barnett
7. Billie Holiday
8. Thelma Stevens
9. Theressa Hoover
10. Charter for Racial Justice
11. Lena Doolin Mason
12. Leontine Kelly
13. Pauli Murray
14. Peggy Billings

A. Black orator who spoke against slavery and for women's rights. In her famous "Ain't I a Woman" speech, she said: "If the first woman God ever made was strong enough to turn the world upside down all alone, these women together ought to be able to turn it back and get it right-side up again. And now that they are asking to do it, the men better let them."

B. Document first developed by the Woman's Division in 1952 and later adopted by The Methodist Church as a whole in 1966.

C. Dubbed "Black Moses" for her multiple trips into the South to lead escaped slaves to their freedom.

D. Mississippi-born White woman who was serving as a missionary in Korea when Martin Luther King, Jr., began to lead marches in the South. She returned to the United States to fight against racism.

E. Founding member of the NAACP who wrote a series of articles called "Lynch Laws in Georgia" and ran for public office in Illinois.

F. White woman who wrote *Uncle Tom's Cabin,* a powerful fictional portrayal of Blacks in slavery. When she was introduced to President Lincoln, he said: "So you're the little woman who wrote the book that made this great war!"

G. Famous jazz and blues singer who sang "Strange Fruit," a haunting song depicting and protesting lynching in the South.

H. White Methodist Episcopal woman who witnessed a lynching in the South as a child and became a passionate advocate for racial justice.

I. First African American staff member in the Women's Division. She served for more than 30 years and became Deputy General Secretary of the General Board of Global Ministries.

J. She fought for the abolition of slavery and for women's right to vote. When Black men were given the vote under the Fourteenth and Fifteenth Amendments, but women were denied the franchise, she focused on women's voting rights.

K. African American Methodist evangelist who preached to all-White and racially mixed congregations from 1887 into the 1900s. Her poem, "The Negro Was In It," documents historic leadership of Blacks.

L. White woman who wrote the words to "The Battle Hymn of the Republic" in 1861 to inspire the Union forces in the Civil War.

M. First African American woman to be a United Methodist bishop.

N. Black woman who wrote *States' Laws on Race and Color,* with funding from the Woman's Division. Published in 1950, the book was used by legislators, activists, and others as a tool for changing race laws.

See Appendix J for the key to the quiz.

Activity: Dramatized Vignettes of Women Leaders

- Ask two women (assigned in Session One) to dramatize a conversation between Ida B. Wells and Jessie Daniel Ames, using information from:
  <http://womhist.binghamton.edu/aswpl/intro.htm>
  <http://www.ku.edu/kansas/crossingboundaries/page6d2.html>

- Ask one woman (assigned in Session One) to take on the character of Virginia Durr, wife of a prominent White lawyer, Clifford Durr, in Montgomery, Alabama, in the mid-1950s during the bus boycott. (See Appendix K for Virginia Durr's oral history, and use the discussion questions in the appendix.)

Issues for Pan Methodist Reunion

Play the 10-minute segment on the Central Jurisdiction of The Methodist Church from the video *Crossing Borders,* available through your Conference UMW. Or ask group members what they know about the Central Jurisdiction. Refer them to chapter four of the Keels' text and the supplemental articles on pp.123-160. Also provide the following background.

The Central Jurisdiction and the Conversation About Reunion With Historic Black Denominations

When the Civil War ended, the Industrial Revolution went into full swing in the North, but instead of finding wider opportunities open to them, Blacks were generally relegated to the most menial tasks. In the South, signs of hope—such as a Black majority elected to the South Carolina legislature—were soon crushed by White terrorism in the form of the Ku Klux Klan and by entrenched racism.

Leaders of the Methodist Episcopal Church in the North; the Methodist Episcopal Church, South; and the Methodist Protestant Church began to discuss reunion shortly after the end of the Civil War. Karen Y. Collier in "A Union That Divides" (a chapter in *Heritage and Hope: The African American Presence in United Methodism*) documents that, from 1891 through 1939, General Conferences debated the place of Blacks in the church. In 1919 a commission spent 13 days straight talking about the role of Black clergy and bishops in the proposed union of the three Methodist bodies. Eventually, a "compromise" was made with the Methodist Protestant Church and the Methodist Episcopal Church, South—which united with the Methodist Episcopal Church in 1939 to form The Methodist Church. This compromise was to establish a nongeographic and segregated "Central Jurisdiction" for the new church's Black congregations. African Americans were not consulted about this proposal. The Women's Mission Council had been meeting with Black women in the Black churches and resisted the formation of the Central Jurisdiction.

Finally, with the formation of The United Methodist Church in 1968—thanks to pressure from African Americans, the Woman's Division, key leaders of the Evangelical United Brethren Church, and other antiracist Whites—the Central Jurisdiction was disbanded.

Today the discussion of a United Methodist union with three historically Black Methodist denominations (Pan Methodist Union) has some parallels with the formation and the dissolution of the Central Jurisdiction. Work in groups of four to identify some of the parallel issues and dynamics. Consider these questions:

- Who will gain by the merger? Will anyone lose?
- What might be some arguments against the reunion?
- What are the arguments in favor of reunion?

Then come back together. In the large group, list on newsprint the pros and cons of reunion. Are there concerns that might have racial prejudice involved?

- What gains and losses might be felt?
- What might the groups have to give up and what might they gain?
- How would you imagine an effective process for coming to a meaningful reunion?

Spiritual Biography of Methodism

Have class members work individually, each writing a one- or two-paragraph spiritual biography of the future Methodist church or churches. Hold these for the class's closing Seder.

Closing Worship

Close with a Seder based on the journey from slavery toward freedom in American history and the history of Methodism. See Appendix L for basic instructions for preparing the Seder. Build in an opportunity for participants to share their visions for the future, as expressed in their spiritual biographies of Methodism.

Appendix A

KNOWLEDGE PURSUIT!

1) Read through the questions, seeing which ones you can answer with certainty. Sign your name by those.

2) The object of the game is to find the answers within the group and to be the first to completely respond to the questions with names of knowledgeable people. Find such a person for each question. Write in her or his name.

3) Let the facilitator know when you complete the 25 questions.

FIND SOMEONE WHO....

Knows when the UMC Charter for Racial Justice Policies was adopted.

Knows whether the 13 original colonies in what became the U.S. condoned slavery in the 17th and 18th centuries.

Knows where to find: "Blessed are those who hunger and thirst for righteousness, for they will be filled."

Knows what Rosa Parks did.

Knows at which General Conference an Act of Repentance and Reconciliation re racism in United Methodism took place.

Has had her or his name mispronounced.

Knows whether Abraham Lincoln supported colonization of freed slaves outside the U.S.

Knows who Stephen Biko was.

Knows whether, when Maine entered the Union in 1819, its state constitution restricted voting rights to White men only.

Knows the significance of Cinco de Mayo celebrations.

Knows the year the World Missionary Conference began a program on racism after deciding in 1910 that race was an ecumenical concern.

Knows what the term *Han* means.

Knows the significance of eagle feathers.

Knows why the Irish immigrated to the United States in the 1800s.

Has been misunderstood by a person from a different culture.

Can name at least 5 Caribbean countries.

Knows where "Mother Bethel" church is.

Can speak more than one language.

Knows who said that power concedes nothing without struggle.

Knows when The Philippines was declared no longer a colony of the United States.

Can name the West Coast equivalent to Ellis Island.

Can name five state names that reflect our Mexican and Spanish roots.

Has an *abuela*.

Knows who said that "No one has a right to sit down and feel hopeless. There's too much work to do."

Knows what *Mahatma* means.

Appendix B

WHITE PRIVILEGE by Robert Jensen

The following article, copyright © 1998 by Robert Jensen, is reprinted by permission. It first appeared in the *Baltimore Sun* on July 19, 1998. See <http://uts.cc.utexas.edu/~rjensen/freelance/whiteprivilege.htm>. Jensen is a professor in the Department of Journalism at the University of Texas at Austin. His e-mail address is rjensen@uts.cc.utexas.edu.

Here's what white privilege sounds like:

I am sitting in my University of Texas office, talking to a very bright and very conservative white student about affirmative action in college admissions, which he opposes and I support.

The student says he wants a level playing field with no unearned advantages for anyone. I ask him whether he thinks that in the United States being white has advantages. Have either of us, I ask, ever benefited from being white in a world run mostly by white people? Yes, he concedes, there is something real and tangible we could call white privilege.

So, if we live in a world of white privilege—unearned white privilege—how does that affect your notion of a level playing field? I ask.

He paused for a moment and said, "That really doesn't matter."

That statement, I suggested to him, reveals the ultimate white privilege: the privilege to acknowledge you have unearned privilege but ignore what it means.

That exchange led me to rethink the way I talk about race and racism with students. It drove home to me the importance of confronting the dirty secret that we white people carry around with us every day: In a world of white privilege, some of what we have is unearned. I think much of both the fear and anger that comes up around discussions of affirmative action has its roots in that secret. So these days, my goal is to talk openly and honestly about white supremacy and white privilege.

White privilege, like any social phenomenon, is complex. In a white supremacist culture, all white people have privilege, whether or not they are overtly racist themselves. There are general patterns, but such privilege plays out differently depending on context and other aspects of one's identity (in my case, being male gives me other kinds of privilege). Rather than try to tell others how white privilege has played out in their lives, I talk about how it has affected me.

I am as white as white gets in this country. I am of northern European heritage and I was raised in North Dakota, one of the whitest states in the country. I grew up in a virtually all-white world surrounded by racism, both personal and institutional. Because I didn't live near a reservation, I didn't even have exposure to the state's only numerically significant non-white population, American Indians.

I have struggled to resist that racist training and the ongoing racism of my culture. I like to think I have changed, even though I routinely trip over the lingering effects of that internalized racism and the institutional racism around me. But no matter how much I "fix" myself, one thing never changes—I walk through the world with white privilege.

What does that mean? Perhaps most importantly, when I seek admission to a university, apply for a job, or hunt for an apartment, I don't look threatening. Almost all of the people evaluating me for those things look like me—they are white. They see in me a reflection of themselves, and in a racist world that is an advantage. I smile. I am white. I am one of them. I am not dangerous. Even when I voice critical opinions, I am cut some slack. After all, I'm white.

My flaws also are more easily forgiven because I am white. Some complain that affirmative action has meant the university is saddled with mediocre minority professors. I have no doubt there are minority faculty who are mediocre, though I don't know very many. As Henry Louis Gates, Jr., once pointed out, if affirmative action policies were in place for the next hundred years, it's possible that at the end of that time the university could have as many mediocre minority professors as it has mediocre white professors. That isn't meant as an insult to anyone, but is a simple observation that white privilege has meant that scores of second-rate white professors have slid through the system because their flaws were overlooked out of solidarity based on race, as well as on gender, class and ideology.

Some people resist the assertions that the United States is still a bitterly racist society and that the racism has real effects on real people. But white folks have long cut other white folks a break. I know, because I am one of them.

I am not a genius—as I like to say, I'm not the sharpest knife in the drawer. I have been teaching full-time for six years, and I've published a reasonable amount of scholarship. Some of it is the unexceptional stuff one churns out to get tenure, and some of it, I would argue, actually is worth reading. I work hard, and I like to think that I'm a fairly decent teacher. Every once in a while, I leave my office at the end of the day feeling like I really accomplished something. When I cash my paycheck, I don't feel guilty.

But, all that said, I know I did not get where I am by merit alone. I benefited from, among other things, white privilege. That doesn't mean that I don't deserve my job, or that if I weren't white I would never have gotten the job. It means simply that all through my life, I have soaked up benefits for being white. I grew up in fertile farm country taken by force from non-white indigenous people. I was educated in a well-funded, virtually all-white public school system in which I learned that white people like me made this country great. There I also was taught a variety of skills, including how to take standardized tests written by and for white people.

All my life I have been hired for jobs by white people. I was accepted for graduate school by white people. And I was hired for a teaching position at the predominantly white University of Texas, which had a white president, in a college headed by a white dean and in a department with a white chairman that at the time had one non-white tenured professor.

There certainly is individual variation in experience. Some white people have had it easier than me, probably because they came from wealthy families that gave them even more privilege. Some white people have had it tougher than me because they came from poorer families. White women face discrimination I will never know. But, in the end, white people all have drawn on white privilege somewhere in their lives.

Like anyone, I have overcome certain hardships in my life. I have worked hard to get where I am, and I work hard to stay there. But to feel good about myself and my work, I do not have to believe that "merit," as defined by white people in a white country, alone got me here. I can acknowledge that in addition to all that hard work, I got a significant boost from white privilege, which continues to protect me every day of my life from certain hardships.

At one time in my life, I would not have been able to say that, because I needed to believe that my success in life was due solely to my individual talent and effort. I saw myself as the heroic American, the rugged individualist. I was so deeply seduced by the culture's mythology that I couldn't see the fear that was binding me to those myths. Like all white Americans, I was living with the fear that maybe I didn't really deserve my success, that maybe luck and privilege had more to do with it than brains and hard work. I was afraid I wasn't heroic or rugged, that I wasn't special.

I let go of some of that fear when I realized that, indeed, I wasn't special, but that I was still me. What I do well, I still can take pride in, even when I know that the rules under which I work are stacked in my benefit. I believe that until we let go of the fiction that people have complete control over their fate—that we can will ourselves to be anything we choose—then we will live with that fear. Yes, we should all dream big and pursue our dreams and not let anyone or anything stop us. But we all are the product both of what we will ourselves to be and what the society in which we live lets us be.

White privilege is not something I get to decide whether or not I want to keep. Every time I walk into a store at the same time as a black man and the security guard follows him and leaves me alone to shop, I am benefiting from white privilege. There is not space here to list all the ways in which white privilege plays out in our daily lives, but it is clear that I will carry this privilege with me until the day white supremacy is erased from this society.

Frankly, I don't think I will live to see that day; I am realistic about the scope of the task. However, I continue to have hope, to believe in the creative power of human beings to engage the world honestly and act morally. A first step for white people, I think, is to not be afraid to admit that we have benefited from white privilege. It doesn't mean we are frauds who have no claim to our success. It means we face a choice about what we do with our success.

Appendix C

BEING AN ANTI-RACIST WHITE PERSON

The following guidelines were modified from Paul Kivel's book *Uprooting Racism: How White People Can Work for Racial Justice.* (Philadelphia: New Society Publishers, ©1995), pp. 102-104.

Every situation is different and calls for critical thinking about how to make a difference. [However, here are] some general guidelines:

Assume racism is everywhere, every day. Notice who speaks, what is said, how things are done and described. Notice who isn't present. Notice code words for race and the implications of the policies, patterns, and comments that are being expressed.

Notice who is the center of attention and who is the center of power. Racism works by directing violence and blame toward people of color and consolidating power and privilege for white people.

Notice how racism is denied, minimized, and justified. Strategies of dismissal abound.

Understand and learn from the history of whiteness and racism. Note the price that has been paid for giving up one's connection to a particular land or country of [one's] ancestors.

Understand the connections between racism, economic issues, sexism, and other forms of injustice. Oppression is about power and is about dominant/subordinate relationships.

Take a stand against injustice. Build courage. Take risks.

Be strategic. Decide what is useful to challenge and what is not. Attack the source of unbalanced power.

Don't confuse a battle with the war. Racism is flexible and adaptable. Remember: "Step by step, the longest march…."

Don't call names or be personally abusive. Attacking people does not address the systemic nature of racial oppression.

Support the leadership of people of color. Do this consistently, but not uncritically.

Don't do it alone. Build support networks and allies.

Talk with your children and other young people about racism. Build on their sense of fairness and justice.

Appendix D

RACISM: HOW IT WORKS AND OPERATES

Racism is a system of prejudice through which one race maintains supremacy over another race by means of a set of attitudes, behaviors, social structures, and ideologies. It involves four essential and interconnected elements:

POWER
The capacity to make and enforce decisions is disproportionately or unfairly distributed.

RESOURCES
There is unequal access to such resources as money, education, information, safe neighborhoods, safe drinking water, and the like.

STANDARDS
Standards for appropriate behavior are ethnocentric, reflecting and privileging the norms and values of the dominant race or society.

PROBLEM DEFINITION
Reality is misdefined when "the problem" is incorrectly named and thus misplaced away from its perpetrators onto its victims.

In the United States, racism can best be understood as a system of White supremacy, that is, a system that differentiates between Whites (or Anglos) and people of color based on the four elements above. Because the social systems and institutions in the United States are controlled by White Anglo elites, Whites have the power to make and enforce decisions and have greater access to resources. White standards for behavior are considered superior and are the standards by which the behaviors of other groups are judged. When speaking about racism, Whites often talk about a "Black" or "Hispanic" or "Asian" or "Indian" problem, thus defining "reality" incorrectly and misplacing the problem of racism away from its perpetuators—members of White society—onto those it victimizes—people of color.

(Adapted from Women's Theological Center/ Racial Justice Connection, Inc.)

Appendix E

FROM A MONOCULTURAL TO A MULTICULTURAL WORLD VIEW

Professor James Banks, who advocates an authentic multicultural approach in the schools, talks about the need to move from a monocultural to a multicultural perspective. He argues that those of us educated in the United States were taught from a singular perspective:

ANGLO AMERICAN PERSPECTIVE

In more recent years, educators have been encouraged to pay more attention to the diversity of backgrounds represented in the student population. This is progress, Banks says, but an additive approach is limited—necessary, but not sufficient.

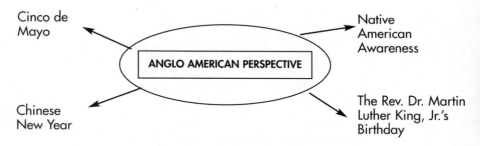

Cinco de Mayo

Native American Awareness

ANGLO AMERICAN PERSPECTIVE

Chinese New Year

The Rev. Dr. Martin Luther King, Jr.'s Birthday

Banks promotes a more authentic multiculturalism—-a multiethnic approach.

EVENT FOCUSED VIA ALL OF THE STAKEHOLDERS AND THEIR SOCIAL HISTORIES.

Appendix F

AFRICAN AMERICAN HISTORY QUIZ

1. African Americans were the only people who were enslaved in the colonies that became the United States.

____True   ____False

2. In the United States, slaves were clearly divided into two classes of people: house Negroes and the field Negroes who bore the brunt of slavery's brutality.

____True   ____False

3. During and after slavery, light skin predicted the highest social status within the Black community.

____True   ____False

4. During slavery it was illegal to teach a slave to read.

____True   ____False

5. Most lynching that occurred started when a Black man was accused of a sexual incident involving a White woman.

____True   ____False

6. The Civil Rights Movement began in 1955 and is a magnificent example of a spontaneous uprising that freed an oppressed people.

____True   ____False

Appendix G

SHOULD A COLOR-BLIND SOCIETY BE THE GOAL?

Fact: U.S. society is racially structured, from top to bottom.

Fact: The recipients of the "worst" and the "best" are determined on the basis of color (e.g., life expectancy, infant mortality, access to higher education, poverty, income, and the like).

Judgments made about race by the dominant society are a profound determinant of one's rights, one's location in the labor market, and one's life chances.

The resiliency and adaptability of the color line can be discerned throughout the history of the United States. Skin color carries social meanings that, in turn, provide the basis for societal structuring. People of color daily experience the imbalance of power that exists in the way that the society is structured.

Fact: "Color-blindness" is usually invoked when a person gets uncomfortable with the pervasiveness and impact of racism in U.S. history and in social structures today.

The answer to the question "Should a color-blind society be the goal?" No. Color-blindness is problematic and is a denial of reality. The centrality of race in U.S. life must not be camouflaged.

We must keep our eyes open to the facts that racism is founded on historical practices that continue to this day. Examples:

- Native American peoples have had to survive continued genocidal systems.

- African Americans have had to survive being expropriated, enslaved, and colonized.

- Mexicans have had to survive invasion, annexation, exploitation, and alienation.

- Asians have had to survive slave wages, exclusion, and use as a buffer against Blacks.

For extensive links and analyses of disparities based on race, visit the website: <http://www.trinity.edu/mkearl/race.html>

Appendix H

ANSWERS TO AFRICAN AMERICAN HISTORY QUIZ

Numbers 1-6 are neither true nor false. All are half-truths. Consider the following:

1. Millions of Native Americans, particularly in South America, were enslaved. To cite one example, in 1730, more than 35 percent of the slaves in the Carolinas were Cherokee, Creek, or members of other indigenous populations.

2. The house-field distinction has been overemphasized. Current research has found no distinct classes among the enslaved but instead blurred lines. Most Blacks who worked in the master's house were women, and they often suffered sexual and other abuses. Also there were slaves who worked neither in the fields nor in the house: for example, tanners, blacksmiths, and other artisans.

3. Status based on skin shade was, at best, a half-truth. During slavery, free Blacks came in all shades and held the highest status. Otherwise, the relationship between skin color and status has always been complex, varying by region. In the Deep South plantation country, having lighter skin meant the person might be related to a wealthy White person. However, in the upper South, lighter skin was likelier to indicate a relationship with poor Whites. Still, the "lighter is better" theme moved to the North with the early twentieth-century migrations of African Americans from the Deep South to the North.

4. There were no laws concerning the education of slaves during the period 1619-1820. These restrictions came later, as a few Southern states made it illegal to teach a slave because some slave rebellions were led by people who could read the Bible and the Declaration of Independence.

5. Actually, more than 70 percent of lynchings occurred when the victims tried to vote, purchased land, or owned successful businesses. Journalists gave more attention to sexually motivated lynchings.

6. In truth, Blacks had long brought court cases to defend their rights and had long organized and resisted oppression.

(Modified from Paul Ruffin, "Ten Myths, Half-Truths, and Misunderstandings about Black History," *Black Issues in Higher Education,* February 6, 1997.)

Appendix I

ROSA PARKS

Script:

THE ROSA PARKS STORY AS IT MIGHT BETTER BE TOLD

Rosa Parks
1913-
Birthplace: Tuskegee, Alabama

It was 1955.

Everyone in the African American community in Montgomery, Alabama, knew Rosa Parks. She was someone that people admired for her courage and commitment. All through her life she had been involved in community activities and in trying to eliminate discrimination.

In her state, and in much of the South, African Americans were prevented by law from using the same public facilities as White people. In addition, the Black facilities were vastly inferior to those reserved for Whites.

Public buses were divided into a front section and a back section. On these buses, the law said that Blacks had to sit in the back rows only. They could be made to give up their seats if any White person needed a seat. Even an elderly Black person had to give up a seat for a White adult or child. If not, the Black person would be arrested by police officers for breaking segregation laws. In bus stations, there were separate restrooms and water fountains, and less money was spent on keeping facilities clean for Black people.

One day, Ms. Rosa Parks got on the bus. She sat down in the colored section, as she typically did each time she rode back and forth to work. She sat in the first row of the colored section. As the bus got crowded, she was asked to give up her seat to a White man. She refused. It was not the first time this had happened. In the past, she had refused and the bus driver had simply put her off the bus. Ms. Parks, along with many other

Blacks, was opposed to segregation and its unfair rules. She refused to move back, staying in her seat, looking straight ahead.

This time, the bus driver got angry. He was tired, hot, and very stubborn. So he called a police officer who arrested Ms. Parks. She was not the first Black arrested in Montgomery for not moving back. In fact, during the months leading up to this event, at least three others refused and were arrested.

Black leaders and some of their White allies had been talking about ways to end the legalized racism that was segregation. One option identified by the Women's Political Council, an African American women's professional organization, was to pressure the bus company. They had studied the ridership of the buses, finding that the majority of bus riders in Montgomery were African Americans. So if African Americans did not ride, then the bus company would lose money.

This plan had been talked about and prepared over a number of years and was ready to be put into action when the right time came. The U. S. Supreme Court had finally ruled that having separate school facilities for Blacks and Whites was unconstitutional. The time was right for another stand against segregation..

The Women's Political Council watched what was happening. Some people had been arrested, but none thus far had the kind of community base and supportive family that helps a person to be strong.

The day Ms. Parks was arrested, the leaders called a meeting at Dexter Avenue Baptist Church. They talked about what to do and agreed that now was the time for action. Ms. Parks had the courage and staying power needed. So the Montgomery bus boycott began.

There was a young new minister in town who got involved. His name was Martin Luther King, Jr. People in the community thought that he would lend fresh energy to the plan of action. At first he said no—he wasn't sure that he had the time or that he knew enough people. But, yes, he did want to end segregation. So when he met with people at a community meeting, he heard what they wanted to do and understood that he had strengths as a trained minister and newcomer. So he agreed to play a spokesperson's role.

For more than a year—381 days, to be exact—Black people stayed off the bus, even though it was a real hardship. Some walked. Some bicycled. Some shared rides. Some people organized car pools, sharing their own cars with others for shopping and to go to and from work. These African Americans knew what they were doing and why. They were determined that they would not ride until they were treated as equals.

All that walking! All that organizing! All that sharing!

What determination, courage, and commitment were shown by Ms. Parks, the Rev. King, and the men, women, and children on the street. The folks who wrote the leaflets and those who handed them out were all determined agents of freedom. What an effort! These people took risks to make democracy begin to work for all of us!

The buses were desegregated after 381 days of the boycott.

This was but one step in a long and continuing struggle to end racism in the United States.

(From resources developed by Loretta Williams.)

Appendix J

ANSWERS TO QUIZ: WOMEN'S LEADERSHIP AGAINST SLAVERY AND RACISM

A-5, B-10, C-1, D-14, E-6, F-2, G-7, H-8, I-9, J-4, K-11, L-3, M-12, N-13

Appendix K

ORAL HISTORY FROM VIRGINIA DURR

The oral history material is excerpted from *VOICES OF FREEDOM: An Oral History of the Civil Rights Movement from the 1950s Through the 1980s,* by Henry Hampton and Steve Fayer, copyright © 1990 by Blackside, Inc. Used by permission of Bantam Books, a division of Random House, Inc.

Part 1: The Montgomery Bus Boycott

<u>Facilitator:</u> Introduce Virginia Durr as the wife of a prominent lawyer, Clifford Durr, who was the White attorney who bailed out Ms. Rosa Parks when she was arrested in Montgomery, Alabama, in 1955 for not giving up her seat on a segregated bus to a White male. Virginia Durr accompanied her husband to the jail on that day. She describes her perspective on the boycott.

"The strange thing that happened was a kind of a play between White women and Black women, in that none of the White women wanted to lose their help. The mayor of the town issued an order that all the Black maids had to be dismissed to break the boycott. Well, their reply was, 'Tell the mayor to come and do my work for me, then.' So the White women went and got the Black women in the car. They said they did it because the bus had broken down or any excuse you could possibly think of. And then the Black women, if you picked one of them up who was walking, they'll tell you that they were walking because the lady that brought them to work, her child was sick.

"So here was this absurd sort of dance going on. I saw a woman that worked for my mother-in-law, and they were asking her, 'Do any of your family take part in the boycott?' She said, 'No, ma'am, they don't have anything to do with the boycott at all.' She said, 'My brother-in-law, he has a ride every morning and my sister-in-law, she comes home with somebody else, and they just stay off the bus and don't have nothing to do with it.' And so when we got out of the room, I said to Mary, 'You know, you have been really the biggest storyteller in the world. You know everybody in your family's involved in the boycott.' And she says, 'Well, you know, when you have your hand in the lion's mouth, the best thing to do is pat it on the head.' I always thought that was a wonderful phrase."

Activity

- Invite "Virginia Durr" to stay in character and to sit down to have coffee with her next-door neighbor, Jane Smith, on the day after Ms. Durr went with her husband to bail Ms. Parks out of jail. Choose a participant to play Jane Smith, who is scandalized by what Virginia Durr had done. Ask the two participants to act out a conversation in which Virginia supports Ms. Parks' action and Jane opposes it. If the conversation becomes stilted, invite others from the audience to drop by as other neighbors, or have one come in as the Black cleaning woman of the house.
- When the conversation seems to languish, invite Ms. Durr to send her neighbors home. Have her move to another place in the room, announce that it is 10 years later, and read the following:

"The boycott took off some of the terrible load of guilt that White Southerners have lived under for so many generations, such a terrible load of shame and guilt that we won't acknowledge. But you can't do things like that to people and pretend to love them too. It has created such a terrible schizophrenia, because when you're a child, particularly if you have Blacks in the house, you have devotion to them. Then when you get grown, people tell you that they're not worthy of you, they're different. And then you're torn apart, because here are the people you've loved and depended on. It's a terrible schizophrenia. That's why I think so much of the literature of the South is full of conflict and madness, because you can't do that to people. You can't do that to children. At least under the Nazis they never even pretended to like the Jews, but in the South it was always that terrible hypocrisy. You know. We love the Blacks and we understand them and they love us. Both sides were playing roles which were pure hypocrisy. So I thought the boycott was absolutely marvelous."

Discussion Questions

- Could you identify with what Virginia Durr was saying? Why, or why not?
- What feelings did you experience as the women were talking together?
- Had you heard Virginia Durr's story before?

Part 2: Another Experience Described by Virginia Durr

"I had to take some sweet Southern ladies with the Woman's Society for Christian Service of The Methodist Church to see Jim Eastland in Washington one day. The WSCS was one of the poll tax committee's greatest supporters [in opposing the poll tax, which was used to keep Blacks from voting], and these were very fine church women. A Mrs. Arrington from Mississippi was head of the WSCS. She came to Washington with eight or nine other women and they stopped by the poll tax office. It was hot summer and they were dressed like the ladies in Mississippi and Alabama dress, which I think is very pretty—light voile dresses, white shoes, white gloves, white beads, and white hats with flowers on them. They looked very lovely, I thought—very Women's Society.

"They wanted to go to the Methodist Building for lunch. We tried to find some Negro women to take with us because the ladies from Mississippi wanted to integrate the building. They thought it was terrible that the Methodist Building wasn't integrated, and it wasn't for years and years. These were really remarkable women. And they wanted to go to see Jim Eastland, their senator.

"Now this is an absolutely true story—a nasty story, but a true story. We went to Jim Eastland's office. Of course, I didn't want to go with them. By this time I had come to hate him, but they insisted that I go because they didn't know how to get around in Washington. So we walked into Jim Eastland's office, and his secretary saw these nice ladies from Mississippi all dressed up and ushered us right in to Jim Eastland. There he was, sitting at his desk. He rose when they came in and he shook their hands. Mrs. Eastland's sister-in-law was a great worker in the Women's Society for Christian Service of Mississippi. In fact, she was the secretary. There was something said about Mrs. Eastland's sister-in-law being a great friend and so forth. Everything started off very pleasantly until they came to the poll tax. And then do you know what he did? He jumped up. His face turned red. He's got these heavy jowls like a turkey and they began to turn purple. He screamed out, 'I know what you women want—Black men laying on you.' That's exactly what he said.

"We left promptly and went to the Methodist Building for lunch. It was so embarrassing to these ladies that their senator had said such a thing. They tried to apologize to me, [saying,] 'Well, now, Mrs. Durr, you know the Eastlands. I don't know whether you know it, but they don't come from southern Mississippi. They come from northern Mississippi.' That didn't mean anything to me, so I said, 'What do you mean?' They said, 'They come from the hill country, not the delta, you see. And they are not really, well, ah, they have made their money quite recently.' What they were saying was the Eastlands were poor White trash who had only recently made money, that Jim Eastland was common as pig tracks and that was just the kind of remark he would make. They were so embarrassed for him and kept apologizing to me. They couldn't imagine that a Mississippi senator would say what he did...."

Discussion Questions

- Virginia Durr does not tell in her oral history whether or not the WSCS ladies from Mississippi integrated the Methodist Building. Can we assume that they did not since the luncheon there is described as consumed by embarrassment over the crudeness of the senator?

- How can we find out when the Methodist building was integrated? Who could tell us that story?

- What was offensive to the women? The sexual reference? The racism? Both?

Appendix L

BASIC SEDER INSTRUCTIONS
(Adapted from JewishEncyclopedia.com)

The Seder Plate

The *Seder plate* helps to set the stage for the centerpiece of the celebration: telling the story of Exodus. The plate is placed on the table in front of the leader. A special Seder plate or a large regular platter may be used.

The items on the Seder plate are placed in a very specific order. Starting from the bottom, and going clockwise, the order is: *chazeret* (lettuce), *karpas* (vegetable), *beitzah* (roasted egg), *zero'ah* (roasted bone), and *charoset* (nuts and dates). In the center is *marror* (bitter herbs). The Talmud states a concept of *Ain ma'avrin al hamitzvot*—we shouldn't "pass over" any *mitzvah* (rite) that is in front of us. For this reason, the Seder plate is arranged to follow the order of the *Haggadah* (the book containing the story of the Exodus and the ritual of the Seder).

1. *Chazeret/Chazeres.* Romaine lettuce.
2. *Karpas.* Parsley, celery, lettuce, or potatoes may be used.
3. *Beitzah/Baytzah.* Hard-boiled egg. It represents the festival sacrifice brought at the Holy Temple.
4. *Zero'ah/Z'roah.* Roasted shankbone of lamb or chicken neck. It symbolizes the paschal sacrifice at the Holy Temple in Jerusalem on the afternoon before Passover.
5. *Charoset/Charoses.* A mixture of finely chopped dates or apples, nuts, and cinnamon moistened with wine. It resembles the mortar used by the Israelites to make bricks while they were enslaved in Egypt.
6. (center) *Marror/Morror.* Bitter herbs or fresh grated horseradish for the suffering in Egypt.

Other Items on Your Seder Table

Three Matzos. (crisp flat unleavened bread) This symbolizes bread baked in haste, without leaven, so that the people would be ready for a quick escape.

Wine. Wine (or grape juice) symbolizes the blood shed during the plagues of Egypt. Each time a plague is mentioned, a drop of juice is splashed on a cloth.

Salt Water. A dish of salt water symbolizes the tears shed by the Israelites while under the oppression of the Egyptians.

Cup of Elijah. A large goblet of wine is placed near the center of the table, representing the fulfillment of the prophesies.

Pillow. A pillow, cushion, or other symbol of physical comfort represents the pleasures of freedom.

There are actually seven different *mitzvot* (acts reminding us of right-eousness) that we perform at the Seder. Two are from the Torah:
1. telling the Exodus story
2. eating matzo

The other *mitzvot* are rabbinical:
3. eating *marror* (bitter herbs)
4. eating the *Afikomen* (an extra piece of matzo for dessert as a reminder of the Passover offering)
5. saying *hallel* (a chant of praise: Psalms 113-118)
6. drinking wine
7. demonstrating acts of freedom, for example, sitting with a pillow cushion and leaning as we eat and drink.

Appendix M

SPIRITUALS AND GOSPEL MUSIC

There is a significant difference between spirituals and gospel in the African American musical tradition. The first difference is in the time that each appeared. Spirituals are the music that chronicles the era when Africans were enslaved in the American colonies and the states. Spirituals take many forms, were sung a cappella (without accompaniment), and typically focused on getting out of slavery. The good life would come in death and the afterlife.

At the dawn of the twentieth century in the large-scale African American migration north, some Blacks took the a cappella spirituals and attempted to make them more palatable to the musical sensibility of Whites. This change correlates with class formation within the Black community.

Gospel music came about as a protest against some African Americans' making the spirituals "too White," by which "frozen and stagnant" was meant. The drum was reintroduced into musical improvisation through the influence of the blues. *Gospel* stands for the good news laced with protest and the struggle for freedom and liberation. There is optimism in gospel music—a belief that people have the insight to comprehend oppression, the courage to confront it, and the wisdom to find transformative new solutions.

For an excellent overview of the music of people of African descent, listen to *The Long Road to Freedom: An Anthology,* a collaboration compiled by Harry Belafonte. It can be obtained at local music stores and on the World Wide Web.

Mahalia Jackson (1912-1972) is considered by many to be gospel's superstar. Her photo may be scanned from the Web at the following website: www.loc.gov/exhibits/odyssey/archive/09/0916001r.jpg

Glossary

African Methodist Episcopal Church (AME) The first African American denomination in the United States, founded by Richard Allen in 1794 as the Bethel African American Methodist Church and united with other AME churches in 1816. Allen and Absalom Jones, both free Blacks, had led Black worshipers out of the St. George Methodist Episcopal Church in Philadelphia in 1787 after White trustees dragged Black members up from their knees in prayer to move them from a section of the newly built balcony that the Whites decided to segregate.

African Methodist Episcopal Zion Church (AME Zion or AMEZ) An African American Methodist denomination founded in New York City in 1796, when about 30 Black members withdrew from the John Street Methodist Episcopal Church in order to escape the "constant humiliation and restriction" imposed on them. They went to worship in an "African Chapel" called Zion that was granted to them by Bishop Francis Asbury.

AME The African Methodist Episcopal Church.

AMEZ The African Methodist Episcopal Zion Church.

bondage The condition of being bound as a slave; slavery.

carpetbagger A White Northern opportunist who moved to the South after the Civil War to seek financial gain or political power.

Central Jurisdiction The specially created, nongeographic jurisdiction of The Methodist Church (1939-1968) into which 320,000 Black Methodists in African American churches in the United States were segregated for three decades.

Christian Methodist Episcopal Church (CME) An African American Methodist denomination, originally named the Colored Methodist Episcopal Church, set up in 1870 by the Methodist Episcopal Church, South, for its former slave members.

Church of the United Brethren in Christ (1800-1946) A predecessor denomination of The United Methodist Church, which united with the Evangelical Church in 1946 to form the Evangelical United Brethren (EUB) Church.

Civil War The 1861-1865 war in the United States fought between the Union (the United States; the North) and the Confederacy (the 11 Southern states that seceded) over slavery, commerce, property, and "states' rights."

CME The Christian Methodist Episcopal Church (originally, the Colored Methodist Episcopal Church), an African American Methodist denomination founded in 1870.

Colored Methodist Episcopal Church see Christian Methodist Episcopal Church; CME.

Compromise of 1850 A series of bills passed by the U. S. Congress that outlawed the buying and selling of slaves in Washington, D. C., but also instituted fugitive slave laws (see below).

Confederacy The 11 Southern states that seceded from the United States in 1860 and 1861 to form the Confederate States of America, defeated by the Union in the Civil War (1861-1865).

covenant 1. A formal and binding agreement. 2. God's promise to God's people.

Curse of Ham see Ham, Curse of

Emancipation Proclamation A document issued by President Abraham Lincoln on Jan. 1, 1863, freeing the slaves living in the Confederacy. Though the Union then lacked the power to enforce it, it encouraged slaves to escape and join the Union Army, and it heralded an end to slavery.

EUB The Evangelical United Brethren Church (1946-1968).

Evangelical Church (1922-1946) A predecessor denomination of The United Methodist Church, which united with the Church of the United Brethren in Christ in 1946 to form the Evangelical United Brethren (EUB) Church.

Evangelical United Brethren Church (EUB) (1946-1968) A predecessor denomination of The United Methodist Church, which united with The Methodist Church (1939-1968) to form The United Methodist Church in 1968.

execrable villainy Hateful, accursed evil: John Wesley's description of slavery.

Freedmen's Bureau An agency (1865-1872) set up by the U.S. government after the Civil War to prepare former slaves for a life of liberty. Its work included public education, hospitals and medical centers, food relief, restoration of the economy, and protection of Black civil rights.

fugitive slave laws Laws that called for the return of slaves who escaped from a slave state to a free state. The Compromise of 1850 (see above) included severe penalties for anyone helping a slave escape or interfering with a slave's recapture.

Ham, Curse of The myth that Noah's curse on his son Ham and grandson Canaan (Genesis 9:18-27) caused Ham's descendants to be Black. This myth was used for centuries as a "justification" for considering Blacks cursed and for disparaging and enslaving them.

Hebrew A descendant of Abraham, Isaac, and Jacob (renamed Israel); hence, a member of God's chosen people; an Israelite, or Jew.

hermeneutical Interpretive.

indentured servant A person contracted to work for another without pay for a limited period, with freedom guaranteed at the contract's end. Some Whites and Blacks came to the American colonies as indentured servants in exchange for the payment of their passage to the New World.

institutional racism Racial prejudice that is so deeply ingrained in and furthered by the social, economic, and political systems of a society as to be a fundamental part of the established order.

Israel 1. Jacob. 2. Jacob's descendants. 3. The Hebrew people, believed to be God's chosen people through God's covenant with Jacob.

Israelite 1. A descendant of Jacob, renamed Israel by God. 2. One of the Hebrew people.

Jim Crow Laws and practices that White power elites set up to maintain the subordination of Blacks and to deprive them of their rights as citizens after Reconstruction ended in the South in 1877. The name Jim Crow, which became synonymous with segregation, came from a minstrel show character portrayed by a White man who would blacken his face and hands with cork, dress in shabby clothes, and pretend to be an uneducated, happy-go-lucky, lazy Negro.

jubilee, year of In the Hebrew scriptures, an observance that was to take place every fiftieth year, during which slaves were to be set free and debts forgiven (see Leviticus 25:8-17).

lynching The execution, usually by hanging, of someone suspected or accused of wrongdoing, without due process of law. Most victims of the lynchings in the South after Reconstruction were Black men. More than 70 percent of the victims of White mob violence had committed such "offenses" as trying to vote, purchasing land, or owning successful businesses.

MEC The Methodist Episcopal Church (1784-1939).

MECS The Methodist Episcopal Church, South (1844-1939).

Methodist Church, The (1939-1968) A predecessor denomination of The United Methodist Church, formed in 1939 through the union of the Methodist Episcopal Church, the Methodist Episcopal Church, South, and the Methodist Protestant Church.

Methodist Episcopal Church (MEC) 1. The main branch of Methodism in the United States from 1784 to 1844. 2. The Northern branch of mainstream Methodism (1844-1939) after the Methodist Episcopal Church, South, formed a separate denomination over the issue of slavery.

Methodist Episcopal Church, South (MECS) A branch of Methodism that broke away from the Methodist Episcopal Church in the North in 1844 over the issue of slavery. It reunited with the MEC as part of The Methodist Church (1939-1968).

Methodist Protestant Church A branch of Methodism that united with the MEC and the MECS in 1939 to form The Methodist Church (1939-1968).

Middle Passage The forcible transporting of captive Africans to the Americas by cramming them into the holds of ships under cruel, inhuman, and often unsurvivable conditions.

Pan Methodism The relationship among the Methodist churches in the United States, namely, The United Methodist Church (UMC), the African Methodist Episcopal (AME) Church, the African Methodist Episcopal

Zion (AMEZ) Church, and the Christian Methodist Episcopal (CME) Church. The word *pan* in this context means "inclusive" or "universal."

Pan Methodist Union A proposed future reconciliation and union, in some yet-to-be-determined form, of The UMC and the three African American Methodist denominations: the AME, AMEZ, and CME.

Pharaoh A king of ancient Egypt: used like a proper name.

poll tax A tax on people instead of property, charged as a requirement for voting and used in the past to keep African Americans from exercising their right to vote.

racial profiling The assumption by law-enforcement officers that people of color are more likely than White people to commit crimes.

racism A system of prejudice through which one race maintains supremacy over another race by means of a set of attitudes, behaviors, social structures, and ideologies. The controlling race has the power to make the decisions, to set the standards, to access the most resources, and to blame the victims of prejudice for the racial "problem."

Reconstruction The period from 1865 to 1877 when the 11 former Confederate states were under U. S. government control and were forced to modify their political and social institutions to gain readmission to the Union.

redlining The refusal of financial services, such as home mortgages or home insurance, to people living in minority neighborhoods because of stereotypes labeling these people as poor financial risks.

reverse discrimination The claim that White people suffer unjustly because the pursuit of diversity by colleges and corporations has increased the participation of people of color in higher education and the workforce.

scalawag A White Southerner who prospered during the Reconstruction Period by working for or supporting the U. S. government during its occupation and military rule of the South.

Service of Reconciliation A worship service in which Whites repent of their racism, confront and confess their sins, and ask forgiveness of Blacks for slavery, segregation, ongoing racial prejudice, and other wrongs. To begin a process of healing, such a service should be more than a superficial ceremony or shallow, scripted drama where most risks are avoided.

shalom zone/communities of shalom A United Methodist mission initiative created by the 1992 General Conference in response to uprisings in Los Angeles after the acquittal of White police officers who had been videotaped beating a Black motorist. A shalom zone or community is an area that the church seeks to rebuild and renew, while healing racial divisions that exist there.

sharecropper A tenant farmer who works another's land, giving the landlord a share of the crops raised instead of paying rent.

slave A person who can be bought, sold, and owned as "property" by a "master" and who must obey, work without pay, and suffer whatever mistreatment or punishment the master may decree.

spiritual One of the songs sung a cappella by African slaves in America, telling the history of their bondage and their dream of liberation, typically in the afterlife.

Temperance Movement A movement of women who advocate total abstinence from all alcoholic beverages. It began in 1874 with the founding of the National Woman's Christian Temperance Union.

tent of meeting In Exodus 33:7-11, a tent that Moses would pitch outside the Hebrew camp during the journey to the Promised Land and in which the Lord would speak with Moses face to face. "Everyone who sought the Lord would go out to the tent of meeting."

ultraism Extremism, as in government or politics.

Uncle Tom Though the name "Uncle Tom" has come to mean "a subservient Black person, deferential to Whites," the character Uncle Tom in Harriet Beecher Stowe's novel *Uncle Tom's Cabin* was dignified and brave, choosing to die rather than betray slaves trying to escape.

Underground Railroad A secret, strategically organized network of escape routes and safe havens that enabled many slaves to escape to the North before the Civil War. The "passengers" traveled on foot by night, guided by a "conductor," and would hide and sleep during the day in secret places (called "stations") provided by law-defying sympathizers.

Union The United States during the Civil War, after the secession of the Confederate states.

United Methodist Church, The (UMC) The global church formed in 1968 by the union of The Methodist Church and the Evangelical United Brethren Church.

White privilege The many unearned benefits and advantages derived from being White in a society run mostly by White people.

year of Jubilee see jubilee, year of

Zion 1. The Hebrew people. 2. Their homeland. 3. A religious community devoted to God. 4. The city of God. 5. Any utopia.

Bibliography

Compiled by Ernest Rubinstein, librarian of The Interchurch Center, with additional entries by the editors. Thanks are due to the librarians of Union Theological Seminary for granting access to the stacks of Burke Library.

Out-of-print books are often easily obtained through online used-book search services, such as the following three: http://www.bookfinder.com, http://www.alibris.com, and http://www.addall.com. In addition, inter-library loan services are almost always available at local public libraries.

I. Exodus Commentaries

Ashby, Godfrey. *Go Out and Meet God: A Commentary on the Book of Exodus.* (International Theological Commentary). Grand Rapids, MI: Eerdmans, 1998.

Binz, Stephen. *The God of Freedom and Life: A Commentary on the Book of Exodus.* Collegeville, MN: Liturgical Press, 1993.

Brueggemann, Walter. "The Book of Exodus." In Vol. 1 of *The New Interpreter's Bible*. Nashville: Abingdon Press, 1994.

Cassuto, Umberto. *A Commentary on the Book of Exodus*. Jerusalem: Magnes Press, 1983.

Childs, Brevard S. *Book of Exodus: A Critical, Theological Commentary*. (The Old Testament Library). Louisville, KY: Westminster John Knox Press, 1974.

Clements, Ronald. *Exodus*. (Cambridge Bible Commentary). Cambridge, UK: Cambridge University Press, 1972. Out of print.

Coggins, Richard. *Book of Exodus* (Epworth Commentaries). London: Epworth Press, 2000.

Cole, R. Alan. *Exodus: An Introduction and Commentary*. (Tyndale Old Testament Commentaries). Westmont, IL: Intervarsity Press, 1973.

Craghan, John F. *Exodus*. (Collegeville Bible Commentary). Collegeville, MN: Liturgical Press, 1985.

Dunnam, Maxie. *Exodus*. (The Communicator's Commentary). Nashville: Thomas Nelson, 1987.

Dupertuis, Atilio. *Liberation Theology and the Exodus: A Study in Its Soteriology*. (Seminary Doctoral Dissertation Series). Berrien Springs, MI: Andrews University Press, 1987. Out of print.

Durham, John. *Exodus* (Word Bible Commentary). Nashville: Word Books, 1987.

Dykstra, Laurel A. *Set Them Free: The Other Side of Exodus*. Maryknoll, NY: Orbis Books, 2002.

Ellison, H. L. *Exodus*. (The Daily Study Bible Series). Louisville, KY: Westminster John Knox Press, 1982.

Exodus: A Lasting Paradigm. Ed. by Bas. Van Iersel and Anton Weiler. (Concilium 1987/no. 1). London: SCM Press, 1987. Out of print.

Exodus: The Egyptian Evidence, Ed. by Ernest Frerichs and Leonard Lesko. Warsaw, IN: Eisenbrauns, 1997. Out of Print.

Feminist Companion to Exodus to Deuteronomy. Ed. by Athalya Brenner. New York and London: Sheffield Academic Press, 1994.

Fretheim, Terence E. *Exodus*. (Interpretation: A Bible Commentary for Teaching and Preaching). Louisville, KY: John Knox Press, 1991.

Goldberg, Michael. *Jews and Christians: Getting our Stories Straight: The Exodus and Passion Narratives*. Harrisburg, PA: Trinity Press International, 1999. Out of print.

Janzen, J. Gerald. *Exodus* (Westminster Bible Companion). Louisville, KY: Westminster John Knox Press, 1997.

Janzen, Waldemar. *Exodus*. (Believers Church Bible Commentary Series). Scottdale, PA: Herald Press, 2000.

Larson, Bruce. *The Presence: The God Who Delivers and Guides*. New York: HarperCollins, 1988. Out of print.

Larsson, Goran. *Bound for Freedom: The Book of Exodus in Jewish and Christian Traditions*. Peabody, MS: Hendrickson Publishers, 1999.

Mittman, Barbara K. *Exodus: Leaving Behind, Moving On*. (Bible Study for Young Adults, 20-30). Nashville: Abingdon Press, 1999.

Nicholson, Ernest W. *Exodus and Sinai in History and Tradition.* Louisville, KY: John Knox Press, 1973. Out of print.

Pixley, George. *On Exodus: A Liberation Perspective.* Maryknoll, NY: Orbis, 1987. Out of print.

Propp, William H.C. *Exodus 1-18.* (Anchor Bible series). New York: Doubleday, 1999.

Richards, Larry. *Freedom Road: Studies in Exodus, Leviticus, Numbers, and Deuteronomy. (*Bible Alive series). Elgin, IL: David C. Cook Publishing Co., 1976.

Sarna, Nahum. *Exodus: The Traditional Hebrew Text with the New Jewish Publication Society Translation.* Philadelphia, PA: Jewish Publication Society, 1991.

Sarna, Nahum. *Exploring Exodus: The Origins of Biblical Israel.* New York: Schocken Books, 1996.

Stiebing, William H. *Out of the Desert? Archaeology and the Exodus/Conquest Narratives.* Buffalo, NY: Prometheus Books, 1989.

Vizotzky, Burton. *Road to Redemption: Lessons from Exodus on Leadership and Community.* New York: Crown, 1998.

Walzer, Michael. *Exodus and Revolution.* New York: Basic Books, 1985.

Zakovitch, Yair. *And You Shall Tell Your Sons: The Concept of Exodus in the Bible.* Jerusalem: Magnes Press, 1991.

II. Historical Overviews of African Americans in Methodism

Crum, Mason. *The Negro in The Methodist Church.* New York: Division of Education and Cultivation, Board of Missions and Church Extension, The Methodist Church, 1951. Out of print.

Lane, G. and C. B. Tippitt, Pub. *The Doctrines and Discipline of the Methodist Episcopal Church.* New York: Methodist Episcopal Church, 1844.

Outler, Albert, Ed. *John Wesley and Slavery.* New York: Oxford University Press, 1964.

Richardson, Harry V. *Dark Salvation: The Story of Methodism as It Developed Among Blacks in America.* New York: Doubleday, 1976. Out of print.

Shaw, J. Beverly F. *The Negro in the History of Methodism.* Nashville: Parthenon Press, 1954. Out of print.

III. African Americans in the Predecessor Bodies of The UMC

Billings, Peggy. *Segregation in the Methodist Church.* Cincinnati, OH: Board of Missions, The Methodist Church, 1967. Out of print.

Brawley, James P. *Two Centuries of Methodist Concern: Bondage, Freedom, and Education of Black People.* New York: Vantage Press, 1974. Out of print.

Carrington, Charles. "Methodist Union and the Negro." In *The Crisis* (May 1936).

Carter, Ruth G., et al. *To a Higher Glory: The Growth and Development of Black Women Organized for Mission in The Methodist Church, 1940-1968.* New York: Women's Division, Board of Global Ministries, The United Methodist Church, 1978. Out of print.

Collier, Karen Y. "A Union That Divides." In *Heritage and Hope: The African American Presence in United Methodism.* Nashville: Abingdon Press, 1991.

Collins, Donald E. *When the Church Bell Rang Racist: The Methodist Church and the Civil Rights Movement in Alabama.* Macon, GA: Mercer University Press, 1998.

Culver, Dwight W. *Negro Segregation in The Methodist Church.* New Haven, CT: Yale University Press, 1953. Out of print.

Current, Angella P. *Breaking Barriers: An African American Family and the Methodist Story.* Nashville: Abingdon Press, 2001.

Findlay, James E. *Church People in the Struggle: The National Council of Churches and the Black Freedom Movement, 1950-1970.* Oxford: Oxford University Press, 1993.

Heritage and Hope: The African American Presence in United Methodism, Ed. by Grant S. Shockley. Nashville: Abingdon Press, 1991.

Hildebrand, Reginald. *The Times Were Strange and Stirring: Methodist Preachers and the Crisis of Emancipation.* Durham, NC: Duke University Press, 1995.

Knotts, Alice G. *Fellowship of Love: Methodist Women Changing American Racial Attitudes, 1920-1968.* Nashville: Abingdon Press, 1996.

Loescher, Frank S. *The Protestant Church and the Negro: A Pattern of Discrimination.* Westport, CT: Greenwood Publishing Group, 1948. Out of print.

McClain, William. B*lack People in The Methodist Church: Whither Thou Goest?* Nashville: Abingdon Press, 1984.

McDowell, John Patrick. *The Social Gospel in the South: The Woman's Home Mission Movement in the Methodist Episcopal Church, South, 1886-1939.* Baton Rouge: Louisiana State University Press, 1982. Out of print.

Moore, John M. *The Long Road to Methodist Union.* Nashville: Parthenon Press, 1943.

Murray, Pauli. *States' Laws on Race and Color.* Cincinnati, OH: Women's Division of Christian Service, 1950. And Supplement, 1955. Out of print.

Thomas, James S. *Methodism's Racial Dilemma: The Story of the Central Jurisdiction.* Nashville: Abingdon Press, 1992.

Weatherford, Willis Duke. *American Churches and the Negro: An Historical Study from Early Slave Days to the Present.* Hanover, MA: Christopher Publishing House, 1957. Out of print.

Wilson, Robert L. and James H. Davis. *The Church in the Racially Changing Community.* Nashville: Abingdon Press, 1966. Out of print.

IV. African Americans in The United Methodist Church

Davis, James H. and Woodie W. White. *Racial Transition in the Church.* Nashville: Abingdon Press, 1980. Out of print.

Dunagin, Richard Lee. *Black and White Members and Ministers in The United Methodist Church: A Comparative Analysis.* Ph.D. Dissertation, University of North Texas, 1991. 252 p. (Available for purchase through Bell and Howell: 1-800-521-0600.)

Experiences, Struggles, and Hopes of the Black Church. Ed. by James S. Gadsden. Tidings, 1975. Out of print.

Graham, John H. *Black United Methodists: Retrospect and Prospect.* New York: Vantage Press, 1979. Out of print.

Hunt, C. Anthony. *The Black Family: The Church's Role in the African American Community.* Bristol, IN: Wyndham Hall Press, 2000.

Jones, Major L. *Black Awareness: A Theology of Hope.* Nashville: Abingdon Press, 1971.

Our Time Under God Is Now: Reflections on Black Methodists for Church Renewal. Ed. by Woodie W. White. Nashville: Abingdon Press, 1993.

Sano, Roy I. *From Every Nation Without Number: Racial and Ethnic Diversity in United Methodism.* Nashville: Abingdon, 1982. Out of print.

Shockley, Grant; Earl D. C. Brewer; and Marie Townsend. *Black Pastors and Churches in United Methodism.* Atlanta: Center for Research in Social Change, Emory University, 1976. Out of print.

V. The Black Church

Afro-American Religious History: A Documentary Witness. Ed. by Milton Sernett. Durham, NC: Duke University Press, 1985.

Black Christian Worship Experience, The. Ed. by Melva Wilson Costen and Darius Leander Swann. Atlanta: Interdenominational Theological Center, 1992.

Collier-Thomas, Bettye. *Daughters of Thunder: Black Women Preachers and Their Sermons, 1850-1979.* San Francisco: Jossey-Bass, 1998.

Cone, James H. *Black Theology and Black Power.* New York: The Seabury Press, 1969.

Du Bois, W. E. B. *The Souls of Black Folk.* New York: Bantam, 1989 (first published 1903).

Frazier, Franklin E. *The Negro Church in America.* New York: Schocken Books, 1963.

Hersovits, Melville. *Myth of the Negro Past.* Boston: Beacon Press, 1990.

Hough, Joseph C. *Black Power and White Protestants: A Christian Response to the New Negro Pluralism.* Oxford: Oxford University Press, 1968. Out of print.

ITC/Faith Factor Project 2000 Study of Black Churches. Atlanta: Interdenominational Theological Center, 2001. 7 seven-page pamphlets.

Lincoln, E. Eric and Lawrence H. Mamiya. *The Black Church in the African American Experience.* Durham, NC: Duke University Press, 1990.

Mays, Benjamin E. and Joseph William Nicholson. *The Negro's Church.* Manchester, NH: Ayer Company Publishers, 1973. (first published: Russell and Russell, 1933).

Mays, Benjamin E. *The Negro's God as Reflected in His Literature.* Westport, CT: Greenwood Press, 1970. (first published: Russell and Russell, 1938).

Mays, Benjamin E. *Seeking to Be Christian in Race Relations*. Cincinnati, OH: Friendship Press, 1964. Out of print.

Montgomery, William E. *Under Their Own Vine and Figtree: The African American Church in the South, 1865-1900*. Baton Rouge: Louisiana State University Press, 1993.

Myrdal, Gunnar. *An American Dilemma: The Negro Problem and Modern Democracy*. 2 vols. Somerset, NJ: Transaction, 1996. (first pub.1944).

Pinn, Anne H. and Anthony B. Pinn. *Fortress Introduction to Black Church History*. Minneapolis, MN: Fortress Press, 2002.

Pinn, Anthony B. *The Black Church and the Post-Civil Rights Era*. Maryknoll, NY: Orbis, 2002.

Raboteau, Albert J. *Canaan Land: A Religious History of African Americans*. Oxford: Oxford University Press, 2001.

Recovery of Black Presence: An Interdisciplinary Exploration: Essays in Honor of Charles B. Copher. Ed. by Randall C. Bailey and Jacquelyn Grant. Nashville: Abingdon Press, 1995.

Thurman, Howard. *Jesus and the Disinherited*. Boston: Beacon Press, 1996 (first published 1949)

Thurman, Howard. *The Luminous Darkness: A Personal Interpretation of the Anatomy of Segregation and the Ground of Hope*. Richmond, IN: Friends United Press, 1997. (first published 1965).

Washington, Joseph R. *Black Religion: The Negro and Christianity in the United States*. Lanham, MD: University Press of America, 2002.

Watley, William D. *The African American Churches and Ecumenism: Singing the Lord's Song in a Strange Land.* Grand Rapids, MI: Eerdmans and WCC, 1993.

Wilmore, Gayraud S. *Black Religion and Black Radicalism.* New York: Doubleday, 1972. Out of print.

Woodson, Carter. *History of the Negro Church. 3rd ed.* Washington, DC: The Associated Publishers, 1992.

VI. The Historically Black Methodist Churches

Allen, Richard. *The Life Experience and Gospel Labors of the Rt. Rev. Richard Allen.* Nashville: Abingdon Press, 1960. Out of print.

Angell, Stephen. *Bishop Henry McNeal Turner and African American Religion in the South.* Knoxville, TN: University of Tennessee Press, 1992.

Black Itinerants of the Gospel: The Narratives of John Jea and George White. Ed. by Graham Russell Hodges. Hampshire, UK: Palgrave Macmillan, 2002.

Bradley, David Henry. *A History of the A.M.E. Zion Church.* 2 vols. Nashville: Parthenon Press, 1956, 1970. Out of print.

Campbell, James T. *Songs of Zion: The African Methodist Episcopal Church in the U.S. and South Africa.* Oxford: Oxford University Press, 1995. Out of print.

Claiming Our Heritage for the 21st Century: 125th Anniversary of the Christian Methodist Episcopal Church: Commemorative Essays. Memphis, TN: CME Church, 1995. Out of print.

Dodson, Jualynne E. *Engendering Church: Women, Power, and the AME Church*. Lanham, MD: Rowman and Littlefield, 2002.

Dvorak, Katharine. *An African American Exodus: The Segregation of the Southern Churches*. Brooklyn, NY: Carlson, 1991. Out of print.

George, Carol V. R. *Segregated Sabbaths: Richard Allen and the Emergence of Independent Black Churches, 1760-1840*. Oxford: Oxford University Press, 1973. Out of print.

Gregg, Robert. *Sparks From the Anvil: Philadelphia's African Methodists and Southern Migrants, 1890-1940*. Philadelphia, PA: Temple University Press, 1993.

Henry, Thomas W. *From Slavery to Salvation: The Autobiography of Rev. Thomas W. Henry of the AME Church*. Ed. by Jean Libby. Jackson, MS: University Press of Mississippi, 1994. Out of print.

Holsey, Lucius H. "The Colored Methodist Episcopal Church." In *Afro-American Religious History: A Documentary Witness*. Durham: Duke University Press, 1985.

Hood, James Walker. *One Hundred Years of the African Methodist Episcopal Zion Church*. New York: A.M.E. Zion Book Concern, 1895. Out of print.

King, Bishop Willis G. "Address: August 18, 1967." In *Journal of the Eighth Session of the Central Jurisdictional Conference of The Methodist Church*. Nashville: The Methodist Publishing House, 1967.

Lakey, Othal Hawthorne. *The History of the CME Church (Revised)*. Memphis, TN: The CME Publishing House, 1996. Out of print.

Lakey, Othal Hawthorne and Betty Beene Stephens. *God in My Mama's House: The Women's Movement in the CME Church.* Memphis, TN: The CME Publishing House, 1994. Out of print.

Little, Lawrence S. *Disciples of Liberty: The African Methodist Episcopal Church in the Age of Imperialism, 1884-1916.* Knoxville, TN: University of Tennessee Press, 2000.

Martin, Sandy Dwayne. *For God and Race: The Religious and Political Leadership of AMEZ Bishop James Hood.* Columbia, SC: University of South Carolina Press, 1999. Out of print.

Morris, Calvin. *Reverdy C. Ransom: Black Advocate of the Social Gospel.* Lanham, MD: University Press of America, 1990.

Payne, Daniel A. and Charles Spencer Smith. *A History of the African Methodist Episcopal Church.* 2 vols. New York: AME Sunday School Union, and Book Concern of the AME Church, 1891 and 1922. Reprinted by Arno Press, Inc., and The New York Times, 1969.

Seraile, William. *Fire in His Heart: Bishop Benjamin Tucker Tanner and the A.M.E. Church.* Knoxville, TN: University of Tennessee Press, 1998.

Singleton, George A. *The Romance of African Methodism: A Study of the African Methodist Episcopal Church.* New York: Exposition Press, 1952. Out of print.

Walker, Clarence Earl. *A Rock in a Weary Land: The African American Episcopal Church During the Civil War and Reconstruction.* Baton Rouge: Louisiana State University Press, 1982. Out of print.

Walls, William J. *The African Methodist Episcopal Zion Church: Reality of the Black Church.* Charlotte, NC: A.M.E. Zion Publishing House, 1974. Out of print.

Weems, Renita J. *Listening for God: A Minister's Journey Through Silence and Doubt.* New York: Simon and Schuster, 1999.

VII. History and Sacred Music of African Americans

Bell, Derrick. *Gospel Choirs: Psalms of Survival in an Alien Land Called Home.* NY: HarperCollins, 1997.

Harding, Vincent. *There Is a River: The Black Struggle for Freedom in America.* FL: Harcourt, 1993.

Horton, James Oliver and Lois E. Horton. *Hard Road to Freedom: The Story of African America.* NJ: Rutgers University Press, 2002.

Myers, Jim. *Afraid of the Dark: What Whites and Blacks Need to Know About Each Other.* IL: Chicago Review Press, 2000.

Remembering Jim Crow: African Americans Tell About Life in the Segregated South. Ed. by William H. Chafe, Raymond Gavins, and Robert Korstad. NY: The New Press, 2001.

Walker, Wyatt Tee. *Somebody's Calling My Name: Black Sacred Music and Social Change.* PA: Judson Press, 1995.

VIII. The Journey of African American Methodists

Billings, Peggy. *Speaking Out in the Public Space: An Account of the Section of Christian Social Relations.* New York: General Board of Global Ministries, 1995.

Book of Discipline of The United Methodist Church 2000. "Historical Statement." Nashville: The United Methodist Publishing House, 2000.

Cary, Francine Curro, Ed. *Urban Odyssey: A Multicultural History of Washington, D.C.* Washington: Smithsonian Institution Press, 1996.

Clark-Lewis, Elizabeth. "'For a Real Better Life': Voices of African American Women Migrants, 1900-1930." In Francine Curro Cary, Ed. *Urban Odyssey.*

Ebony Pictorial History of Black America. Vol. 1, African Past to the Civil War. Chicago: Johnson Publishing Co., Inc., 1971.

Felder, Cain Hope. *Troubling Biblical Waters: Race, Class, and Family.* Maryknoll, New York: Orbis Books, 1989.

Hoover, Theressa. *With Unveiled Face: Centennial Reflections on Women and Men in the Community of the Church.* New York: Women's Division, General Board of Global Ministries, 1983.

Horton, James Oliver. "The Genesis of Washington's African American Community." In Francine Curro Cary, Ed. *Urban Odyssey.*

Horton, Lois E. "The Days of Jubilee: Black Migration During the Civil War and Reconstruction." In Francine Curro Cary, Ed. *Urban Odyssey.*

Hughes, Bishop Edwin Holt. *I Was Made a Minister.* New York: Abingdon Press, 1943.

King, Martin Luther, Jr. *Strength to Love.* Philadelphia: Fortress Press, 1981; original copyright 1963.

King, Martin Luther, Jr. *Where Do We Go From Here: Chaos or Community?* Boston: Beacon Press, 1967.

Sandburg, Carl. *Abraham Lincoln.* Vol. 2: *The War Years.* New York: Harcourt, Brace and Co., 1936.

IX. Exodus Websites

For extensive links to web resources, go to:
http://gbgm-umc.org/umw/exodus

For a United Methodist history of the Central Jurisdiction and other issues involved in the 1968 union between The Methodist Church and the Evangelical United Brethren Church, visit: http://www.umc.org/churchlibrary/discipline/history/movement_toward_union.htm (underline one space after "movement" and after "toward").

White Privilege website: http://www.whiteprivilege.com

World Council of Churches' Statement on Racism:
http://www2.wcc-coe.org/ccdocuments.nsf/index/plen-4-en.html

Hartford Seminary summary page of Historical African American Denominations: http://fact.hartsem.edu/denom/denom_aa.htm (underline one space after "denom")

Official African Methodist Episcopal history website:
http://www.ame-today.com/history/index.html

Official Christian Methodist Episcopal heritage website:
http://www.c-m-e.org/core/CME_Beginnings.htm
(underline one space after "CME")

Official African Methodist Episcopal Zion website:
www.theamezionchurch.org

Full text of C. H. Phillips' book, *The History of the Colored Methodist Episcopal Church in America: Comprising Its Organization, Subsequent Development, and Present Status.* (Jackson, TN: The CME Publishing House, 1925): http://docsouth.unc.edu/church/phillips/menu.html

Eden Seminary's fact page on the Christian Methodist Episcopal Church:
http://www.eden.edu/cuic/members/denominations/cme.pdf

Slavery in Ancient Rome:
http://departments.vassar.edu/~jolott/republic1998/spartacus/
slavelife.html
http://www.fordham.edu/halsall/ancient/slavery-romrep1.html
http://www.aber.ac.uk/education/PGCE/dbm98/
romanslavehomepage.html

Civil War information and links:
http://www.cwc.lsu.edu/cwc/civlink.htm

Detailed analysis of how the motion picture *The Ten Commandments* shaped U.S. civil religion and concepts of freedom after World War II:
http://moses.creighton.edu/JRS/2001/2001-9a.html

X. Video Resources

Brotherly Love, one tape in a four-part PBS series, *Africans in America,* includes a 20-minute segment on the AME "Mother Bethel" church. The four-part series is $39.95 per tape or $150 per set. Call your conference UMW to borrow a tape or contact PBS toll-free at 877-727-7467 to order.

Crossing Borders, the three-part companion video for the 2003 mission studies includes a 10-minute segment on the all-Black Central Jurisdiction of The Methodist Church, which existed between 1939 and 1968. Produced by the General Board of Global Ministries and the Women's Division. Available from Service Center or your Conference UMW. (#03290) $19.95.

XI. Hymns, Spirituals, and Canticles

"Canticle of Moses and Miriam," "Go Down, Moses," "Many Gifts, One Spirit," "Marching to Zion," "Nobody Knows the Trouble I See," "Standing in the Need of Prayer," "We Shall Overcome," "Were You There?" *The United Methodist Hymnal.* Nashville: The United Methodist Publishing House, 1989.

"Go Down, Moses," "Nobody Knows the Trouble I See," "Oh, Freedom," "Standing in the Need of Prayer," "We Shall Overcome," "Were You There?" *Songs of Zion.* Nashville: Abingdon Press, 1981.

The Authors

Christine Dean Keels is a United Methodist laywoman, writer, orator, community organizer, and advocate for children. Her lifetime of commitment to the ministries of The United Methodist Church includes service as a conference officer of United Methodist Women, appointment to Bishop Yeakle's Youth Diversion Project Committee, and deanship of the Conference School of Christian Mission in the Baltimore-Washington Conference. As a two-term Women's Division Director, Mrs. Keels became Vice President of the division and chaired the Section of Christian Social Responsibility. She has served as a delegate to General, Jurisdictional, and Annual conferences. She also founded and coordinated a Teen Pregnancy Intervention and Prevention Project at A. P. Shaw United Methodist Church entitled "Sisters." Mrs. Keels works as a supervisor, outreach coordinator, manager, and trainer for the Division of Parole and Probation in the State of Maryland. She is a member of Delta Sigma Theta Sorority and a board member of Children's Choice Christian Adoption and Foster Care Agency.

The Rev. Bernard "Skip" Keels serves as Senior Pastor of the Newark United Methodist Church in Newark, Delaware. He has served several churches in the Peninsula-Delaware and Baltimore-Washington conferences and was District Superintendent of the Baltimore West District. He is a native of Birmingham, Alabama, was an honors graduate of Haverford College, and holds a Master of Divinity degree from Yale University. The Rev. Keels is a veteran workshop leader and study leader in Schools of Christian Mission for United Methodist Women. As a media commentator on WBAL Radio's "Black Journey" and WTYY's "Taking It to the Streets," Skip Keels became president of the Baltimore Chapter of the National Black Media Alliance. He now serves on the boards of the General Commission on Communications, United Methodist Publishing House, Yale Divinity School, Goodwill Industries, and the Addict Referral Organization.

A sociologist, educator, and activist, Loretta J. Williams directs the Gustavus Myers Center for the Study of Bigotry and Human Rights. The Center reviews and annually honors outstanding books published in this area. Dr. Williams is also the President of Racial Justice Connection, Inc., a national antiracism consulting organization. She served as the founding Chair of the National Interreligious Commission on Civil Rights and has taught at the University of Missouri, the State University of New York at Buffalo, Brandeis, and the Women's Theological Center.

The Rev. Joseph Agne, pastor of the Memorial United Methodist Church in White Plains, New York, grew up in Oak Park, Illinois, and was among the students who worked as an organizer with Dr. Martin Luther King, Jr., in Chicago. He served as a commissioner of the World Council of Churches' Program to Combat Racism and in 1990 became Director of the Racial Justice Program for the National Council of Churches in New York. He serves on the board of the Center for Democratic Renewal and the Martin Luther King Institute for Nonviolence.

J. Ann Craig is Executive Secretary for Spiritual and Theological Development in the Women's Division and has overseen spiritual growth studies on John Wesley, the Bible, Jesus and Courageous Women, and many other topics over the last 15 years. After graduating from Nebraska Wesleyan University, she began her career as a US-2 home missionary in Virginia. She later received a Master of Divinity degree from Yale University and is currently working on a Ph.D. from Drew University in early church theology.